Pelican Books
Human Ageing

Dr D. B. Bromley is Professor of Psychology at the University of
Liverpool. He is a Fellow of the British Psychological Society and of
the Gerontological Society of America. He is a founder member and
first Chairman of the British Society of Gerontology. He is editor of
Gerontology: Social and Behavioural Perspectives and has published
reports on several aspects of human ageing. He is co-author of *Person
Perception in Childhood and Adolescence*, and sole author of *Personality
Description in Ordinary Language* and *The Case-Study Method in
Psychology and Related Disciplines*.

D. B. Bromley

HUMAN AGEING

An Introduction to Gerontology

Third Edition

Penguin Books

PENGUIN BOOKS

Published by the Penguin Group
27 Wrights Lane, London W8 5TZ, England
Viking Penguin Inc., 40 West 23rd Street, New York, New York 10010, USA
Penguin Books Australia Ltd, Ringwood, Victoria, Australia
Penguin Books Canada Ltd, 2801 John Street, Markham, Ontario, Canada L3R 1B4
Penguin Books (NZ) Ltd, 182–190 Wairau Road, Auckland 10, New Zealand

Penguin Books Ltd, Registered Offices: Harmondsworth, Middlesex, England

First published as *The Psychology of Human Ageing*, 1966
Second edition 1974
Third edition, published as *Human Ageing*, 1988
10 9 8 7 6 5 4 3 2

Made and printed in Great Britain by
Richard Clay Ltd, Bungay, Suffolk
Filmset in Lasercomp Bembo

Contents

Preface to the Third Edition

No one is more surprised than the author that this book should have run to three editions spread over twenty years. It is evidence, perhaps, of the gradual but steady growth of interest in adult life and ageing and of the difficulty of compiling a text that is comprehensible and useful to a wide range of readers. Gerontology – the scientific study of adult life and ageing – is essentially a multidisciplinary subject.

The opening words of the preface to the first edition in 1966 were, 'We spend about one quarter of our lives growing up and three quarters growing old': a forceful way of saying why human ageing is worth studying. I have persisted in my view that adult life and ageing stands in marked contrast to juvenile development, and is a distinct area of scientific research and professional practice, but I acknowledge that others wish to combine these two areas into what is called 'lifespan development'.

The new title given to this revised edition indicates that the psychological contents have been reduced. The intention is to provide a concise and representative account of modern gerontology. However, psychology – the study of human behaviour and experience – still provides an important and convenient way of linking all the areas of interest covered. There are many areas in the psychology of ageing that I would have liked to pursue in more detail, but considerations of space and readership prevented me from so doing. This requires a separate publication, now in preparation.

This edition has been revised in a number of ways. In order to produce a book of reasonable length, the chapter on 'The History of Human Ageing' has been omitted. Readers who are interested in this aspect of gerontology should consult the previous edition (entitled *The Psychology of Human Ageing* and published in 1974). Also omitted is a lengthy chapter on 'Research Methods', replaced by a brief note on 'Scientific Method' (pp. 304–12). I hope this will do something to remedy what I see as a widespread misunderstanding of what it means to adopt a scientific attitude towards the study of ageing. Some other sections from the 1974 edition have been omitted in the interests of economy, or to make way for new material. Specific references to sources in the text have been greatly reduced. The text is intended to provide a secure base from which readers may seek to explore some of the recent literature cited at the end of each chapter. The references and suggested readings have had to be limited in number and represent only a fraction of the recent literature. There is a new chapter on 'Social Policy and the Elderly'. The material on age and achievement has been curtailed and redistributed.

The book is designed to meet the needs of the serious general reader as well as the needs of people in a wide variety of scientific and professional disciplines; in particular, the social and behavioural sciences, biology, medicine and nursing, adult education, and administration. I trust that it will serve as an introductory textbook on human ageing for the growing number of taught courses in higher and further education.

D. B. Bromley
Liverpool, 1987

Acknowledgements

I again gratefully acknowledge the help given to me in writing the first and second editions of this book. In preparing the third edition my thanks go to Mrs Olive L. Keidan for her help with the chapter on 'Social Policy', to the librarians at the University of Liverpool, and to innumerable authors who have kindly sent me offprints of research articles. Mrs Dorothy Foulds and Mrs Anne Halliwell have provided invaluable secretarial support.

The figures and tables based on *Social Trends*, 1971 and 1986, and *Mortality Statistics, England and Wales, 1984*, are published with the kind permission of the Controller of Her Majesty's Stationery Office.

As usual, my deepest gratitude is to my wife Roma who, apart from providing all essential and many luxury services, has, quite unawares, given me an unexpected statistical advantage in mortality risk! (See Foster *et al.*, 1984.) I doubt that the effect is reciprocal.

One
Gerontology and Adult Ageing

1. Introduction

Gerontology is the scientific study of the processes of growing old. The term is derived from the Greek *geron, -ontos*, meaning an old man. This root is used to form related terms such as gerontocracy – government by the elderly – and geropsychology – the psychological and behavioural study of ageing. A closely related term is geriatrics, derived from the Greek *gēras*, meaning old age, and *iātros*, meaning physician; it refers to the medical care of the aged. The 'g' in geriatrics is soft; it is a matter of personal preference whether the 'g' in gerontology is hard or soft. The British usually put an 'e' in 'ageing', the Americans leave it out.

The scientific study of human ageing reaches into the biological and medical sciences, the social and behavioural sciences, and even into technology and the natural sciences. Research in ageing makes calls on the full range of scientific methods. Beliefs and attitudes about later life find expression in the arts, in social welfare and government policy, and in philosophy. The fact that each of us is growing older makes itself felt in all sorts of personal ways in ordinary everyday life.

Ageing is a complex sequence of changes. The organs and functions of the body are impaired. Some people suffer mild or severe psychological disorders brought on by degenerative disease or other causes. There are adverse changes in sensory and motor capacities, in the central processing functions associated with intelligence and the organization of behaviour. There are complex changes too in the autonomic nervous system (ANS), the endocrine system and the central nervous system (CNS). These are almost certainly implicated in changes with age in motivation, emotion and personal adjustment.

People's position in society changes; their beliefs, attitudes and personal qualities alter, as does their behaviour. The accumulating experiences of adult life lead to changes in the content and organization of one's beliefs, values and attitudes, including those that relate to the self.

The effects of ageing are complicated by interactions and feedback loops between many variables – biological, psychological, social – see Figure 1.1. The problems of human ageing cannot be evaded, especially in advanced communities where a substantial proportion of members survive beyond the end of their active productive lives. These problems include occupational redundancy and retraining, social and economic provision for dependency in old age, leisure and retirement, and those associated with the social medicine of later life – physical and mental infirmities.

The ways in which individuals are affected by the passage of time in adult life and old age differ widely. There are also substantial sex differences and, to a lesser extent, differences in socio-economic class. Some of these effects are attributable to intrinsic factors (genetic and other basic constitutional characteristics), others to extrinsic factors (environmental characteristics such as diet, stress, exposure to health hazards). The effects of ageing, perhaps by definition, are gradual, ramified and cumulative. Consequently research into ageing is difficult, expensive and time-consuming.

The scientific study of human ageing faces three main tasks: theoretical, methodological and applied. The theoretical task is to confirm and extend the conceptual systems which integrate and explain the observed facts of ageing; the methodological, to develop suitable research procedures and to examine carefully the logic of arguments about the nature of ageing; the applied or practical, to prevent or reduce the adverse effects of ageing.

A person's chronological age is closely associated with, but by no means a perfect index of, physical and mental capacities, or life expectation. Moreover, the outward and visible signs of ageing, which appear earlier in some individuals than in others, need not presage a decline of physical or mental capacities. These discrepancies have led research workers to think in terms of 'physiological age' and 'functional age', in their attempts to describe and explain time-related changes in adult life.

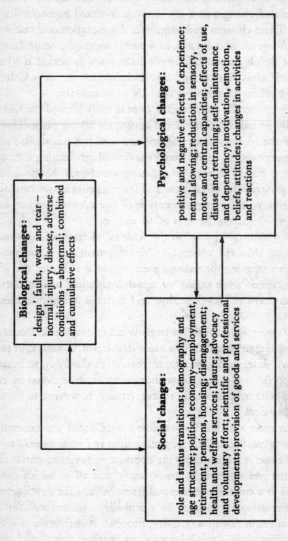

Biological changes:

'design' faults, wear and tear – normal; injury, disease, adverse conditions – abnormal; combined and cumulative effects

Psychological changes:

positive and negative effects of experience; mental slowing; reduction in sensory, motor and central capacities; effects of use, disuse and retraining; self-maintenance and dependency; motivation, emotion, beliefs, attitudes; changes in activities and reactions

Social changes:

role and status transitions; demography and age structure; political economy—employment, retirement, pensions, housing; disengagement; health and welfare services; leisure; advocacy and voluntary effort; scientific and professional developments; provision of goods and services

Figure 1.1 A schematic representation of the inter-dependence of biological, psychological and social factors in human ageing

It is a mistake to think of chronological age itself as anything more than a time-marker. In abstract terms, 'adult ageing' is a series of time-related changes in a set of interconnected psychobiological variables. These changes lead to greater deterioration and culminate in death. Adult life and old age, however, also exhibit some kinds of growth or development. Life beyond the juvenile period is a combination of adult ageing and adult development, in which the cumulative effects of ageing eventually preponderate.

It is not generally realized that, even in early life and throughout the juvenile period, the processes of ageing are taking place. This is a matter for the biology of ageing and we shall not pursue it. For all practical purposes, in social and behavioural gerontology, human adult ageing begins as soon as a person completes the genetically regulated programme of growth, and for convenience we can locate this transition point at the intersection of late adolescence and early adult life, say between the ages of 16 and 20.

The concept of 'ageing' in the sense of 'deterioration' is much less elaborate than the concept of 'development'. It is instructive, therefore, to examine the various meanings of the former and so to form a concept of 'adult ageing' or 'age deterioration' which contrasts with the concept of 'development' and matches its complexities, as follows.

Adult ageing, age deterioration: to grow old, to develop the characteristics of old age; to retreat from a more developed, complex, or more fully grown state; to degenerate, to regress, to diminish, to become depleted, to fall into disuse; to withdraw; to become closed in, constricted; to wither, to languish, to lose vitality, to shrivel; to become degraded, to decay.

This cluster of ideas shows how complicated the concept of 'adult ageing' really is. Clearly, ageing does not refer merely to the passage of time; it is not simply the opposite of development; it takes many forms and operates at many levels, not all of which can be assimilated to a coherent conceptual framework. Like development, it finds expression in changes in morphology (form, structure) as well as changes in function (activity, process). A definition of ageing based on these ideas is given later in this chapter.

2. The Human Life-Path

The term 'life-cycle' is commonly used to refer to the sequence of birth, growth and reproduction (followed quickly by death) in many animals and plants. In human beings, however, the cessation of reproduction normally occurs relatively early in the lifespan and is followed by many years of active life and later by many years of less active life and dependency. Thus middle age, retirement and old age dependency are increasingly recognized as normal stages of post-reproductive life. Hence I prefer the term 'life-path', which refers to an expected sequence of stages in the normal course of life.

People differ widely in the 'paths' their lives follow. One can think of the life-path as an historical sequence of biological, psychological and social events. A detailed life-history would attempt to narrate these events in a way which would bring out the relationships between them and thus tell a story about the person's life. The life-path is the complex sequence of events which takes the individual from conception to death. However, for reasons which are discussed elsewhere in the book, it is convenient to maintain a distinction between the juvenile and adult phases of the life-path, and even to contrast them. Within each of these phases, it is possible to define a number of successive stages, which can be described in biological, psychological and environmental terms – see Tables 1.1 and 1.2.

(a) Juvenile phase

Life starts at conception with the fertilization of an ovum. We go through about seven weeks of embryonic development, and during the foetal stage gradually acquire the morphological properties necessary for life outside the womb, which begins roughly 38 weeks from conception. Children rapidly develop competence in a variety of interrelated areas: perception, thinking and action.

Between the ages of about 11 and 16 years, biological, social and psychological changes known as puberty occur. Primary and secondary sexual characteristics appear, giving rise to reproductive capacity and to widespread changes in behaviour and inner experience, such as outlook and motivation. Early adolescence is a period of rapid development in other areas: secondary education is completed; some legal responsibilities and rights are acquired; stature

Table 1.1 *Juvenile Phase of Development*

Stage	Approximate age	Name	Main characteristics (ignoring wide individual differences)
	From conception		
1	0 →	Zygote	Conception (fertilized ovum)
2	→ 7 weeks	Embryo	Early stages of biological development
3	7 weeks →	Foetus	Later stages of biological development; 'human-like' appearance
4	38 weeks	Birth	Change from intra- to extra-uterine life

Gestation

On average the longevity of offspring is affected by the longevity of parents. Adverse pre-natal and post-natal circumstances – malnutrition, drugs, and so on – may have long-term effects on development

Stage	Approximate age	Name	Main characteristics
	From birth		
5	→ 18 months	Infancy	Acquisition of basic skills in locomotion, perception and manipulation (sensori-motor schemata); non-verbal communication; parental (especially maternal) relationships, socialization
6	→ 5 years	Pre-school child	Development of basic skills in locomotion, perception, manipulation (pre-operational representations); non-verbal and verbal communication; family and other social relationships
7	→ 11 years	Junior-school child	Assimilation of cultural characteristics through education and socialization, symbolism (concrete operations, groupings); morality

Childhood

Development depends upon complex processes of interaction between genetic endowment and environmental circumstances.

Stage	Approximate age	Name	Main characteristics
8	11 to 16 years	Puberty; secondary school child; early adolescence	Development of secondary sexual characteristics and reproductive functions; limited legal responsibility; completion of basic education; trend towards adult appearance and behaviour; changes in social attitudes and interests; approaching end of growth-period, including intelligence (formal operations)
9	16 to 21 years	Late adolescence	Further education; vocational training; end of main biological growth phase (physical maturity); transition from dependence to independence; peak years for anti-social behaviour; legal maturity; voting rights

Adolescence

Some characteristics – e.g., age at menarche–height, intelligence, appear to have been associated with cohort effects (gradual changes from one generation to the next)

Table 1.2 *Adult Phase of Development and Ageing*

	Stage	Approximate age	Name	Main characteristics (ignoring wide individual differences)
Adulthood	10	21 to 25 years	Early adulthood	Acquisition of adult roles; employment welfare; economic responsibilities; marriage; parenthood; continuation of professional training; full engagement in adult activities; peak years for athletic achievement (up to about 35 years)
	11	25 to 40 + years	Middle adulthood	Consolidation of social and occupational roles; peak years for intellectual achievement; slight decline of some physical and mental functions apparent in tests of maximum performance; seniority; accumulation of relatively permanent material possessions and social relationships
		The mid-point of the male working life is about 40 years. The long-term trend has been for more females to enter the workforce		
	12	40 + to 55 + years	Late adulthood	Continuation of established social and occupational roles; departure of children; diminution of sexual and reproductive functions (menopause); re-entry of some women into occupational roles; further decline of physical and mental functions
		The average age at the menopause is 49 years, but there is considerable variation		
	13	55 + to 65 years	Pre-retirement	More obvious decline of physical and mental functions; peak years for some kinds of social achievement and authority or partial disengagement from occupational roles and community affairs; further diminution of sexual functions and interests
Old age	14	65 → years	'Young–old'	Retirement; disengagement from occupational role and community affairs, or continuation of some kinds of social authority; greater prominence of kinship and primary-group relationships; heightened susceptibility to physical and mental disorders; deterioration of physical and mental condition; biological and psychological impairment of ordinary activities in everyday life
		The long-term trend has been to reduce the proportion of older people in paid employment		
		Life expectation at birth, UK, 1984: Men: 69·8 years Women: 76·2 years		
	15	75 → years	'Old–old'	Dependency; full disengagement; physical and mental inadequacy
	16	→ to a maximum of 120 years	Terminal illness and death	Final breakdown of critical biological functions

increases and the child becomes more 'adult' in appearance and behaviour. The main programme of genetically regulated growth is nearing completion.

Late adolescence, say 16 to 20 years, marks the transition from the juvenile to the adult segment of the life-path. The person reaches the end of his or her juvenile growth programme, although some capacity for growth of different sorts is maintained throughout adult life and old age. The education and training typical of late adolescence are designed to fit a person more specifically into an adult occupational role. A transition has to be made from the largely dependent juvenile status to the largely independent adult status. In urban industrial communities, the combination of biological and social changes often engenders unstable, short-lived and sometimes deviant patterns of behaviour; anti-social behaviour reaches a peak, but there is also a surge of adventurism, creative activity and social concern.

This brief description of the juvenile phase reminds us that adult life and old age are parts of an *historical process*. What we become depends in part on what we are now, which in turn depends on what we were in the past. However, the historical narrative is not a causal analysis. Study of the juvenile phase may not be immediately relevant to the study of age-changes in adult life and old age. What is first required is a description and analysis of the *proximate*, i.e. immediate or direct, causes of the effects of ageing and, where possible, an account of the main determinants of ageing.

(b) Adult phase

As in the juvenile phase, the biological, social and psychological determinants of behaviour are closely interwoven. Compared with the juvenile phase, the biological processes in the adult phase are relatively slow – although cumulative in their effects – and do not show rapid transformations, except perhaps at the menopause or with disease or injury. The absence of well-defined shifts in biological and behavioural competence means that division of the adult phase into stages is to some extent arbitrary and largely defined in terms of social characteristics. With the onset of old age the emphasis shifts back as biological and behavioural competence diminish to levels below those required for the normal activities of adult life.

For convenience we can distinguish seven stages in the *adult* phase of the human life-path:

(I) EARLY ADULTHOOD. This stage, from 21 to 25, follows late adolescence; it completes the transition from juvenile to adult status. The average person in urban industrial society acquires a variety of adult social characteristics – legal maturity, voting rights – and socio-economic responsibilities. He or she usually marries and raises a family. They continue to invest time, money and other resources in anticipation of future circumstances. Individuals become more fully 'engaged' in a variety of formal and informal social activities; the ensuing emotional and functional relationships bind people together into a complex system of interlocking social groups. Early adulthood may include further education and occupational training. Physical health and many athletic achievements are at their highest level. Intellectual vigour and experience have begun to produce achievements in science, literature and the arts.

(II) MIDDLE ADULTHOOD. This stage, from 25 to 40, usually consolidates each individual's public and occupational roles, and family and private interests. We accumulate material possessions and establish relatively stable social relationships. Occupational and other sorts of progress continue, depending upon circumstances. Output – in the form of physical work, emotional investment and intellectual creativity – is at a relatively high level, and experience accumulates. The entry of the last child into school creates more opportunities for social and occupational activities for women outside the home. Nevertheless, some deterioration in biological and psychological capacities takes place, for example in vision, and some aspects of intelligence also decline. Such deterioration is slight; it is not usually obvious in ordinary everyday life but can be detected by testing *maximum* performance capabilities. There are obvious changes in physical appearance too.

(III) LATE ADULTHOOD. This stage, from 40 to about 55 or 60, is normally characterized by further consolidation of the individual's public and occupational roles unless socio-economic or political upheaval disrupts the fabric of society. Socio-economic differences and sex differences, however, complicate the description of 'middle age', which corresponds broadly to this period (see Chapter Six, Section 4). There may be problems of marital and family relationships and of children leaving home. The menopause closes the reproductive life of women and provides an obvious biological marker for adult ageing, but seems to engender few social or psychological consequences. Adverse changes in physical and mental health, and overall reductions in biological capacities, continue to accumulate and begin to limit the nature and scope of the individual's life, including pace of work, leisure and sexual activities. Many of these changes are needlessly accelerated by ignorance and unhealthy ways of life. Individuals vary in their willingness and ability to counteract, compensate for, or adapt to, the effects of ageing.

In middle age, individuals may experience an increased awareness of self; they may become more reflective and may undertake serious revaluations and readjustments of life-style.

(IV) PRE-RETIREMENT. The period from 60 to 65 clearly illustrates the interweaving of biological, social and psychological factors. The rate at which adverse changes take place – as judged, for example, by the proportion of people who become physically ill, emotionally disturbed, or functionally less competent – accelerates sharply during late adulthood. The decline in physical and mental capacities, including such obvious characteristics as appearance, sexual vigour, stamina and speed, further limits the nature and scope of activities. The effects are more noticeable in situations which push people close to the limits of their capacity, like heavy paced work or tasks requiring native intelligence rather than acquired experience. Many individuals, however, manage to retain a relatively high level of biological and behavioural competence.

Towards the end of the pre-retirement stage – near the end of active working life – people tend to 'disengage' from the mainstreams of social (mainly commercial and industrial) activity and in anticipation of retirement, to shed work, hand over responsibilities and prepare for retirement by developing leisure interests and curtailing living costs.

Hitherto, the ages of retirement for men and women have been different. The age of 65 years for men is relatively arbitrary, an accident of history, and no longer justifiable except on grounds of normal practice. The retirement age of 60 for women simply reflects the assumption that wives are usually several years younger than their husbands. The future is likely to bring a flexible retirement age, with normal limits of about 60 and 70 years for both men and women.

(v) RETIREMENT. For many people, this stage, from 65 to 70, marks an important and rapid transition from an economically productive status to an economically non-productive and relatively dependent status. This raises many issues (some dealt with in Chapters Four and Five). Retirement means different things, depending upon the individual's sex, socio-economic status and psychological make-up. In general, however, people disengage from their main occupation. This brings about a number of changes in their life – in daily activities, social contacts and standards of living. On the other hand, it may entail radical readjustments outside the occupational sphere. In time the cumulative adverse effects of adult ageing, and the greatly increased chances of disease and disability, lead people to disengage from a variety of social commitments and interests, because they cannot cope with the physical and psychological demands. Personal relationships with family and neighbourhood may become more important. Some individuals, however, may still hold positions in established social organizations, especially if the duties are largely ceremonial.

(vi) OLD AGE. Old age, from 70 until the terminal stage (see below), can be defined by an individual's diminished ability to cope with the ordinary affairs of everyday life – because of a variety of late-life infirmities – without help. The chronological age of 70 is even more arbitrary than the others. Individual differences are considerable, and elderly people living together, such as husband and wife, can provide mutual support. The average expectation of life at birth in advanced urban industrial societies is about 70 for men and 76 for women, with a further expectation of about 10 years for those who have reached these ages.

In old age, people are normally fully disengaged from the mainstreams of economic and community activity, though they may

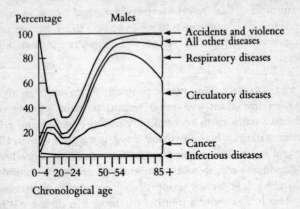

Figure 1.2 Percentage of male deaths from various causes at different age-levels in the United Kingdom, 1983; based on *Social Trends*, no. 16, 1986

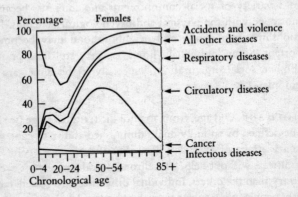

Figure 1.3 Percentage of female deaths from various causes at different age-levels in the United Kingdom, 1983; based on *Social Trends*, no. 16, 1986

lead more (or less) active social lives with kin, friends and peers. Most individuals do not become senile; they die from natural causes without exhibiting this or other distressing psychological disorders. Figures 1.2 and 1.3 show the relationships between chronological age and various causes of death.

(VII) TERMINAL STAGE. The terminal stage is hardly recognized as a functional part of the human life-path. Dying tends to be regarded in a negative way: as part of death rather than as part of life. It expresses the final stage in the breakdown of physiological functions necessary to sustain life. But there are grounds for regarding it as a *functional* stage in the human life-path, which means including psychological and social criteria in any definition of 'dying'.

Each individual dies either through terminal illness, whether manifest or not, defined as a 'natural cause', or through violence or other 'non-natural' cause. The most frequent natural causes of death in later life are malignant neoplasms of various kinds, arteriosclerotic and degenerative heart disease, vascular lesions affecting the central nervous system, pneumonia and bronchitis. The most frequent causes of death by violence are motor vehicle accidents, falls and suicide. At present, the maximum length of human life is thought to be marginally above 120 years.

(c) Life and years

One way to conceptualize the course of human life is to think of it as following a trajectory in which the individual is launched at conception and reaches a maximum level of functional capacity or vitality in early adult life. From then on, because of intrinsic 'design' faults and extrinsic damage (injuries, infections and so on), functional vitality decreases gradually, or at times abruptly, until the individual is no longer capable of coping with the demands of living, and dies.

Gerontology, as the scientific study of ageing, is concerned not merely with longevity and the biological health of the individual throughout the lifespan, but also with 'the quality of life', i.e. with the conditions which maximize the good things of adult life and old age and minimize the bad. This is neatly expressed in the well-known aphorism that we should not only add years to life but also add life to years.

The human body is a system of interrelated organs. The organs are composed of different kinds of cell. The organs and cells age in different ways at different rates and are differently susceptible to disease, damage and renewal. It is therefore difficult to calculate the biological age (or fitness or vitality) of an organ as compared with its chronological age. However, it is possible to measure the average lifespan of some cells and to measure the functional capacity of an organ relative to age norms. Thus a person's respiratory or circulatory capacities could be assessed relative to the norms (based on standardized measures on representative samples of subjects) for his or her chronological age. The term 'functional age' is sometimes used in this way. Whether this notion can be applied to the person as a whole is debatable, since functional effectiveness is determined not by the average effectiveness of all subsystems in the biological make-up, but rather by the least efficient part of the system required to carry out the function.

The effects of ageing can be analysed at many levels: molecular, cellular, organ system (respiratory, reproductive and so on), organismic (the psychological and behavioural functions of the organism as a whole), social (interpersonal relationships) and sociological (demographic, institutional). In some respects the effects seem to run in one direction: random defects of a biochemical nature lead to malfunctioning cells and cell death; these cellular changes lead to impairment of specific organs − liver, brain, heart and so on; the deficiencies in the physical basis of behaviour give rise to losses in functional capacities and actual performance; these psychological and behavioural deficits lead to increased social dependency; the aggregate effects of ageing have sociological consequences − changes in the age-structure of a population, socio-economic changes, changes in the law and social arrangements.

In other respects, however, the effects of ageing may run in both directions. That is to say, changes in social arrangements, such as retirement or segregation, may have adverse psychological and biological effects (stress, malnutrition, poorer health). Failure to maintain a high level of psychological adjustment may lead to disuse of function and to social isolation, and hence to poorer physical condition, which may aggravate the process of ageing.

Unfortunately, it is difficult to find reliable biological markers of chronological age in adult life. This contrasts with juvenile development, since dentition, bone growth and sexual characteristics can be used to estimate chronological age, or to determine whether a child is advanced or retarded biologically for its age. The occurrence of discontinuities in the process of ageing, i.e. abrupt transitions from one level of functioning to another, would constitute such markers. The menopause provides an example. Virtually all other normal changes with age are gradual and exhibit wide differences between individuals (as does the menopause). When discontinuities do occur, they are likely to be regarded as pathological changes (due to injury or disease) rather than as normal changes or markers. Physicians who attribute an adverse change in a patient's physiological functions or psychological capacities to 'old age' will get little support from the geriatric consultant who will look hard and will probably find underlying disease or injury which is age-specific only in the broadest sense.

(d) Lifespan development

Human ageing can be studied as a logical extension of developmental psychology – the study of infancy, childhood and adolescence. There is much to be said in favour of this 'lifespan developmental' approach. It attempts to study the human life-cycle in its entirety, to incorporate the juvenile and adult phases in one all-embracing framework of ideas, and to study the long-range relationships between development and ageing. However, its obvious merits tend to mask its limitations.

Juvenile growth can be thought of as an orderly, genetically regulated and directed programme of biological and behavioural development culminating in the young adult status – this is most obvious in physical characteristics and sexual maturity. Adult ageing, on the other hand, can be described as an increasingly disorderly and undirected process of biological and behavioural disorganization and degeneration, culminating in death; it seems to lack the coherence and logic of juvenile development, even though it converges on and culminates in death. The impression of convergence is given by such facts as the average or maximum expectation of life; the divergences are brought out by considering the variations between people in age at death – see Figure 1.4.

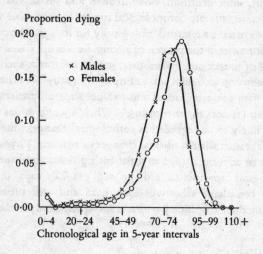

Figure 1.4 Distribution of age at death separately for males and females in England and Wales, 1984; based on Office of Population Censuses and Surveys, *Mortality Statistics, 1984, England and Wales,* 1986

3. Images of Ageing

An historical survey of human concern with the process of ageing shows that the transition to a scientific, i.e. rational and empirical, view has been relatively recent. Nevertheless, a number of present-day scientific concepts relating to ageing had their beginnings in remote historical periods and most of the imagery of ageing – in art, literature and daily life – derives, perhaps naturally, not from modern scientific concepts of ageing but from the more primitive, familiar, mystical views characteristic of medieval times and antiquity. The medieval quest for a cure for ageing, by means of an elixir or fifth essence (*quinta essentia*), is one of several persisting issues in the history of concern with human ageing.

The 'images' of human ageing can be summarized fairly briefly.

The first sees the human body as a container, like a furnace or cask, full of an essential substance or spirit – innate heat, moisture, movement, life, spirit or vigour – which is gradually depleted or destroyed, leading to cooling, drying, diminished energy and greater vulnerability to damage or disease. From this first image derive the symbols of the inevitability of ageing – the candle burning out, the near-empty well, the withered leaf. The recent concept of ageing as a reflection of 'biological time' is thus related to the historical image of a fixed quantity of life which runs its course – hence the symbols of the emptying hour-glass, the lengthening shadows and the sunset, the four seasons, the end of the road.

The second image represents a conflict within the individual: a growing imbalance between the positive forces of goodness, health, growth and repair, and the negative forces of evil, disease, damage and corruption, which eventually prevail. This image gives rise to various symbols – wormy and decaying substances, dilapidated buildings, worn and tattered clothing, rusty and broken equipment.

The third image is a process of renewal symbolized by the seed within the dry decaying shell, or by the insect or reptile shedding its outer skin, hence perhaps the idea of casting off our 'mortal coil' in life after death.

Part of the problem of conceptualizing the process of ageing lies in the confusion between ageing as a cause and ageing as an effect. The easy transition from one to the other makes it difficult to identify the basic and contributory causes of ageing, hence 'ageing' becomes self-explanatory and almost a metaphysical concept, though not entirely closed to rational and empirical examination.

In recent years, scientific explanations for age-related changes in behaviour and its physical basis have been put forward. These include ideas such as normal versus pathological ageing (disease), intrinsic versus extrinsic ageing (stress, damage) – see Chapters Two and Three.

4. A Definition of Adult Ageing

The concept of ageing is much more difficult to define than the concept of juvenile development. An adequate definition has to include some reference to the passage of time, i.e. to chronological age.

It also has to bring out the essential implication that the process is one of deterioration (although some gerontologists object to this). A further feature is that the process is post-developmental: all the latent capacities for development have been actualized, leaving only late-acting potentialities for harm, i.e. those post-reproductive characteristics which have escaped the selective effects of evolution. The process of age deterioration appears to be retrogressive, degenerative, and to lead to a more disorganized, simpler, more primitive state; resources are depleted, capacities are diminished or less available for use. The whole process is one of lessened vitality, vigour, speed and strength, of reduced ability to respond to demand – in short, decline and disorderliness. Thus ageing, in a sense, undoes the work of development. It does so not through a systematic process of dismantling, but rather through unsystematic processes of decay and demolition, working both intrinsically and extrinsically, and both normally and abnormally.

This rather brutal statement is intended to separate the process of ageing from that of maturation and development, or growth.

In brief, *human ageing can be conveniently defined as a complex, cumulative, time-related process of psychobiological deterioration occupying the post-developmental (adult) phase of life.*

At present, the most we can hope for is to delay the onset of such deterioration, to mitigate its effects, and consequently to extend the average expectation of life by a few years.

References and Suggestions for Further Reading

Baltes, P. B. and Brim, O. G. Jr (eds), *Life-Span Development and Behavior*, New York: Academic Press, 1984.

Behnke, J. A., Finch, C. E. and Moment, G. B. (eds), *The Biology of Aging*, New York: Plenum Press, 1978.

Binstock, R. H. and Shanas, E. (eds), *Handbook of Aging and the Social Sciences* (2nd edn), New York: Van Nostrand Reinhold, 1985.

Botwinick, J., *Aging and Behavior, A Comprehensive Integration of Research Findings* (3rd edn), New York: Springer, 1984.

Carver, V. and Liddiard, P. (eds), *An Ageing Population*, Sevenoaks: Hodder & Stoughton, 1978.

Harris, D. K., *The Sociology of Aging. An Annotated Bibliography and Sourcebook*, New York: Garland Publishing, 1985.

Hendricks, J. and Hendricks, C. D., *Aging in Mass Society. Myths and Realities*, Cambridge, MA: Winthrop, 1977.

Kimmel, D. C., *Adulthood and Aging* (2nd edn), New York: Wiley, 1980.

Office of Population Censuses and Surveys, *Mortality Statistics, England and Wales, 1984*, London: HMSO, 1986.

Riley, M. W., Hess, B. B. and Bond, K. (eds), *Aging in Society: Selected Reviews of Recent Research*, Hillsdale, NJ: Lawrence Erlbaum Associates, 1983.

Troll, L. E., *Early and Middle Adulthood* (2nd edn), Monterey, CA: Brooks/Cole Publishing, 1985.

Two
The Physical Basis of Ageing

1. Introduction

There are wide differences between individuals biomedically; each of us is unique. This fact, coupled with the incredible complexity of anatomical and physiological functions, means that simple age-trends and relationships are difficult to establish.

Many of the psychological and social effects of biomedical ageing are self-evident and need little if any commentary. Gradual changes can usually be adapted to quite well but the effects accumulate over time until they force major changes of life-style. Abrupt and substantial changes pose much greater problems of adjustment, especially if they impair our feeling of self-worth.

Although biomedical changes with age may appear to be quite objective, relative to psychological changes, there are nevertheless all sorts of methodological problems, such as sampling, measurement, confounds and the like, which require us to maintain an open mind about most issues even while accepting – for the time being – what the available research concludes.

This chapter will not deal with specific methodological problems in any detail. Its major concern is to promote some knowledge of the underlying changes in human biology, upon which an understanding of some of the social and psychological aspects of adult life and old age depends.

2. Anatomy and Physiology

(a) Skeleton

The skeleton reaches full stature by the late teens or early twenties. There is little or no subsequent change in the length of the individual bones though a slight loss in overall stature, especially after the age of 50, may be brought about by atrophy of the discs between the spinal vertebrae. This may be exaggerated by a stooping posture due to muscular weakness and, in some people, by atrophy in parts of the central nervous system. Some growth in adult life may occur in the soft parts of the body, such as the nose or the ears. As age advances, the chemical composition of bone changes, the bones become less dense, and this increases the risk of breakage late in life. More serious adverse changes occur if there are gross deficiencies of diet, or in the presence of certain diseases. Movements of the joints become stiffer and more restricted, the incidence of diseases affecting these parts of the body increases with age, and the skeleton suffers from the cumulative effects of damage and disease.

The biological effects of ageing on the teeth are difficult to separate from the influence of diet, dental hygiene and repair. Teeth, in adult life, may be a cause of pain and discomfort. The gums recede and the teeth become yellowish because of a thickening of secondary dentine. Loss of teeth or changes in their appearance bring home the fact that one is ageing physically. Tooth decay in later life is aggravated by a reduced flow of saliva (in some cases caused by drugs prescribed for medicinal purposes). Normally, the minerals in saliva help to replace tooth surface material eroded by decay (caries), especially in the areas exposed by receding gums. Dental care, preventive measures and resort to dental repair and prostheses are important in relation to oral health and general appearance; these affect social interaction and self-regard.

(b) Skin and fatty tissues

The skin consists of two layers: an outer or hard layer (cuticle), and an inner layer (dermis) which contains numerous glands and nerve-endings. The glands secrete sweat; its evaporation cools the surface of the skin and helps to regulate the temperature of the body.

Age-changes in the surface of the body, especially in the face (wrinkles, loss of bloom, flabbiness), are obvious to the ageing person and, with other changes such as thinning hair, baldness, greying, and varicose veins, may be upsetting. The skin becomes paler and more blotchy; it takes on a parchment-like texture and loses some of its elasticity. Such changes affect self-regard, confidence and social attitudes; 'apparent age' could be important in the initial stages of social interaction.

In the early and middle years of adult life, people tend to put on surplus fat unless they adjust their intake of food to their physical requirements. They become increasingly bulky until, much later in life, the subcutaneous fat begins to disappear, together with the muscles, leaving the now inelastic skin hanging in folds and wrinkles. The health and general appearance of the skin depend upon many factors. In old age the loss of subcutaneous fat contributes most to its characteristic appearance. The tissues become less capable of holding water, so that under the microscope cellular structures have a thinner, denser appearance.

The regulation of food intake depends upon psychological factors such as habits and attitudes, and its utilization depends upon complex physiological processes. Some older people go short of essential foods such as proteins and vitamins, partly from poverty, partly from ignorance. Overfeeding, leading to excess weight, contributes to degenerative disorders in old age and tends to shorten life. In laboratory rats, such disorders can be inhibited by maintaining an adequate diet but restricting the number of calories; moderate restriction increases their life expectation. Overfeeding results in increased metabolism and the inadequate elimination of waste products. Excess weight has adverse effects on the circulatory system, the kidneys and sugar metabolism, being associated with hypertension, arteriosclerosis and diabetes. Weight reduction can have beneficial results.

(c) Voluntary (striped) muscles

The voluntary, or striped, muscles lie along the arms, legs and other parts of the skeleton, and are attached to the bones either directly or by strong bonds of fibrous tissue called tendons. By contracting they exert a force on the bone, which acts as a lever. As they contract, the muscle fibres shorten because of complex biochemical changes in the protein molecules of the fibres. Maximum muscular strength is normally reached at about the age of 25 or 30. There is then a gradual reduction in the speed and power of muscular contractions, a decreased capacity for sustained muscular effort, less elasticity in the muscle and increases in fibrous material. There are, however, wide differences between individuals in muscular efficiency, and exercise can improve disused muscles by increasing the quantities of protein in the muscle fibres and by increasing innervation. Actually, striped muscles may increase in bulk and density up to about the age of 50 but after that the number of active muscle fibres and the amount of protein steadily decreases, and the typical wasted appearance results. Muscle cells are not renewed.

The cerebellum, underneath and towards the rear of the main cerebral hemispheres, is important in co-ordinating muscular activity. Changes in it appear to play only a small part in the loss of muscle tone in old age; the decline of posture and muscular co-ordination is more often affected by damage to the basal ganglia. There appears to be little change with age in the speed of reflexes or simple repetitive movements, although both speed and amplitude of movement may be affected by disease.

Muscular effort is limited by stiffer and more restricted movements at the joints, the lower working capacity of the heart and the lungs, and other factors. Prolonged muscular activity not approaching the limits of effort may be sustained for long periods by older men. The judicious use of rest pauses improves work performance. Physical exercise greatly improves physiological capacities in general, even late in life.

(d) Involuntary (smooth) muscles

The involuntary, or smooth, muscles are those in the walls of the stomach and the intestines, in the air tubes, and in most of the internal organs and blood vessels. They normally operate automatically, under the direction of the autonomic nervous system. The effects of age on them appear small compared with other structures (except the smooth muscles of the blood vessels) and they seem to function fairly adequately even until late senescence. Although a few individuals suffer from increased frequency of micturition, any normal weakening of smooth muscle action – for example, in the bowels – is small compared with changes in the nervous system which controls such functions.

(e) Connective tissues

Connective tissues are distributed widely throughout the body. They comprise collagen, elastin and reticulin, binding together various parts of the body and providing support. Some are involved in storing food, others in forming blood. Adipose tissue consists of closely packed cells containing large globules of fat.

As age increases, the amount of ground substance decreases and the density of the fibres increases, thus restricting the passage of nutrients and other substances through the tissue. The smooth surfaces of some joints become worn and diseases of the joints are more common. The large molecules of collagen establish more cross-linkages throughout life and so render the connective material less capable of stretching; this effect has had considerable theoretical interest for biologists. Collagen is found in the scar that forms over a wound; the scar tissue that forms late in life appears to be 'lightly bound' collagen, characteristic of the collagen normally found in the connective material of young people; it forms more slowly in older people, so that wounds heal less quickly, although other factors no doubt play a part. Collagen, like some other substances in the body, can become calcified with age, thus contributing to decreased flexibility of the joints.

(f) Digestion

The body requires food to maintain its temperature, to produce energy and to develop and renew its tissues. A well-balanced diet contains the correct proportions of proteins, carbohydrates, fats, mineral salts, vitamins and water, though people's food requirements differ. Food is digested mainly in the stomach and intestines by digestive juices secreted from various glands. The digestive processes are affected by a variety of factors – dietary habits, the kinds and amounts of food eaten, its preparation, concurrent activities – as well as anatomical and physiological factors. Older people, especially the socially isolated, poor and physically or mentally infirm, may lack adequate food intake; serious neglect may lead to a deficiency disease. A decrease in the secretion of saliva, and gastric juice, including the digestive enzymes, results in less efficient digestion. On the whole, the digestive system is relatively robust, and not seriously impaired by ageing, except for the increased risk of pathology common to all physiological systems.

The pancreas secretes sufficient quantities of the enzyme amylase to digest carbohydrates, although the output of ptyalin in the saliva is reduced. The pancreatic endocrine substance steapsin decreases as age advances, and this may help to account for the slower utilization of fat in older people. The liver and the gall bladder appear to be relatively unaffected by the normal processes of ageing, but these organs become more vulnerable to disease.

Digestion of a meal containing fat produces microscopic particles of fat, known as chylomicrons, in the bloodstream. Their numbers increase to a maximum and then return to a baseline level. As we grow older, the rate of absorption is much slower and the concentration of chylomicrons reaches higher levels. There may be some association between ageing and diseases connected with lipid metabolism.

The timing of the digestive processes is important and largely automatic, and some, such as salivation and the secretion of digestive juices, are set in motion before food actually reaches the mouth. There is also a psychological component: an old person's poorer appetite may lead to a poorer digestive response. Old people secrete less saliva and have less acute senses of smell and taste; extra attention to cooking and presentation is important to secure an adequately varied diet. Mastication is less effective because of weaker facial muscles and poorer teeth, so food should not require extensive chewing. This may inadvertently lead to a poorer diet.

Changes in the autonomic nervous system and the endocrine system at times of emotional arousal interfere with the digestive processes. Minor neurotic disorders can lead to stomach upsets, constipation, or loss of appetite in some, and to overeating in others.

It is clear that nutrition is a key factor in adult development and ageing even if the effects are not as obvious and serious as in earlier life. The considerable shift recently in public awareness of how much and what sorts of food are appropriate to healthy living seems to have had little effect on the cost and availability of foods, or on the sorts of food provided in public places – schools, hotels, transport services, institutions.

At present, nutrition in relation to ageing is concerned with five main issues: first, the avoidance of malnutrition among the infirm elderly; second, the inclusion in diets of essential ingredients – for example, certain vitamins – which may not be present in apparently 'normal' diets; third, the avoidance of overeating leading to ill health; fourth, the reduction of ingredients, such as animal fat and refined sugar, now regarded as undesirable; fifth, the shift to a more natural diet, including fibre (especially natural fibre in fruits and vegetables).

People differ widely in their dietary needs, preferences and habits. Generally speaking, a varied diet – all essential ingredients in sufficient amounts – which maintains a relatively lean, strong body, is recommended. Beyond that, it is for experts to decide whether a nutritional deficiency, perhaps in association with a disease, is responsible for a person's ill health. The exact relationships between common sorts of nutritional deficiencies and psychological disorders are difficult to formulate.

There is no evidence either that intestinal bacteria are seriously implicated in the biology of human ageing or that certain kinds of food will delay the onset or rate of normal ageing.

(g) Excretion

Some excretory products formed during cell activity are carried by the blood to the kidneys. A complex chemical process removes these products selectively from the blood and they drip as urine into the bladder. Waste materials from food intake are expelled from the lower end of the alimentary canal.

The kidneys form urine by filtering water and dissolved substances from the blood and then reabsorbing some of these substances; for example, glucose and some body salts. The organ as a whole atrophies gradually with the degeneration of its constituent parts, such as tubules and glomeruli; there is, however, some compensatory growth of cell elements. The functional capacities of the kidneys – urea clearance, glomerular filtration and effective blood plasma flow – are not normally diminished to any great extent until late in life. The kidneys of older people are less efficient at filtering out drugs, so that there is a risk that the drug dosage level and duration will be wrong. There is, with ageing, a fairly steep rise in kidney disorders. These are usually linked with vascular conditions, and sometimes lead to brain disturbances and abnormal behaviour (see Chapter Nine).

Both urination and defecation are subject to a type of voluntary control through social learning, and regular habits have deep emotional significance for some people. Loss of control (incontinence) from various causes can be a source of embarrassment and a serious inconvenience in old age. Constipation at later ages may result from poor bowel function at earlier ages, lack of exercise, unsatisfactory diet (too little fibre or insufficient vitamins), as well as from damage and disease.

Incontinence is mainly a medical and nursing problem, but psychological intervention can help by assessing the behavioural aspects of the disorder and, by means of counselling, advice, habit training and environmental management, rearranging the patient's daily activities so that incontinence is less likely, less inconvenient and less stressful.

(h) Metabolism and thermoregulation

A person's basal metabolic rate – the rate at which oxygen is used while at rest – is measured by analysing a sample of the air breathed out. Metabolic rate increases during exercise or excitement. Basal metabolic rate declines with age. This is partly accounted for by diminished thyroid secretion and other factors, but mainly by a decrease in the total number of cells and diminished activity in the major regions of the body such as the liver and muscles.

The body's core temperature is slightly higher than the oral temperature, which averages about 98.6°F (37°C). Temperature regulation involves receptors in the skin which are very sensitive, within limits, to the rate at which surface temperature changes. The body's normal compensatory reactions to a fall in heat production include the secretion of adrenalin, contraction of the surface blood vessels and shivering. Older people react less quickly and less adequately to cold, their voluntary muscular activity is less and the shivering reflex poorer. As they do not produce as much heat, they run the risk of a serious fall in body temperature. Hypothermia – abnormally low body temperature – is a serious risk for old people.

High body temperature can be reduced by stopping or slowing down muscular effort, by sweating and by dilatation of the surface blood vessels to cool the blood. Older people cannot cope as well with heat and cannot work as effectively in moderately high temperatures. If fat, they generate heat more quickly when active and lose it more slowly. The sweating reaction and the circulatory system become less efficient. Age-changes in temperature regulation have been observed in industrial workers; for instance, older miners sweat less when working and more when resting, because the sweating and circulatory mechanisms are sluggish and no longer capable of the same range of reaction. Temperature discrimination appears not to decline with age, which is surprising, since the general pattern of biological degeneration is towards poorer sensory discrimination. Younger animals (and younger human beings) quickly become acclimatized to changed physical surroundings – to higher or lower temperatures, to drier or more humid atmospheres; acclimatization is less efficient in later life.

Temperature affects longevity, at least in some lower organisms like fruit-flies; cold conditions appear to slow down metabolism and prolong life, while high temperatures have the opposite effects – but not because the 'rate of living' has changed. Living creatures, however, have evolved biological systems adapted to a narrow range of optimum conditions; departure from these in either direction tends to shorten life. Stress conditions, such as heat and cold, and other 'extrinsic' factors, such as diet, exercise or radiation, have a particular relevance to gerontology in that they enable research workers to accelerate or retard ageing – and so to modify the lifespan, or the level of age-related functional capacities. The normal expectation of human life is greater in temperate than in tropical or cold climates, though obviously factors other than temperature are at work.

The effects of age on protein metabolism in rats are that, broadly speaking, the proteins like collagen and elastin tend to increase with age; the central active constituents – like nuclei and mitochondria (intracellular structures) – decrease; the water-soluble proteins increase in brain and muscle but decrease in liver cells.

Carbohydrate metabolism has been studied by the administration of glucose in a test of sugar tolerance – measuring the rate at which excess sugar is cleared from the blood. In older people, the blood sugar level continues to rise longer, to reach higher absolute levels, than in comparable younger people. The effect is more pronounced if a second dose of glucose is administered shortly after the first. The increase in frequency of diabetes through adult life confirms this effect. The impairment of glucose tolerance has been attributed to the reduced sensitivity of specific cells in the pancreas to changes in the level of blood sugar. This example illustrates the fact that some biological mechanisms of ageing are associated with the malfunction of specialized cells under specific conditions, which suggests that some control over the biochemistry of ageing is possible.

As we grow older, some minerals like sodium, calcium and potassium are taken up less readily, although these elements can still be stored. Solid metabolites such as pigments become deposited within and between cells, and cells may be unable to excrete them – rather as a furnace becomes choked with clinkers making it difficult or impossible to maintain a fire. The metabolites have a toxic chemical effect and constitute a mechanical hindrance to the normal activities in the cell.

(i) Cell renewal

The length of life of individual cells varies considerably depending upon the type of cell. For example, adult nerve cells do not multiply; many die only when the person dies, but others die much earlier. Red blood corpuscles are estimated to live about 120 days on average, whereas some leukocytes survive only a few days.

Some tissues of the body are replaced fairly rapidly by continuous cell division (mitosis); others are capable of renewal under certain conditions. In renewed tissues, age-differences in the appearance of cells are usually slight. The rate of renewal of liver cells and skin cells decreases as age increases. Some tissues, however, including those of the nervous system, cannot be renewed. In stained preparations the nucleus of an old cell is darker and its cytoplasm lighter than that of a young cell. This raises the possibility that the nucleic acid metabolism of the nerve cells is reduced as the cells become older. In the liver cells of senile rats the nucleus has been found to become enlarged, invaginated, split, or irregular in shape. Histological studies of nerve cells taken from senile patients at autopsy show various kinds of abnormality. Degenerative changes in ageing cells include: increased fat deposition in the cytoplasm, the conversion of the membrane to fibrous material, increased pigmentation, and – less often – enlargement of the cell together with the appearance of empty spaces within its substance.

Cell colonies descended from a parent cell are called 'clones'. Clones from mammalian cells *in vitro* die out after a limited number of doublings; the reproduction rate falls, the individual cells become less active and physically more deteriorated. Unicellular organisms reproduce themselves as clones; some cell lines — microbal, tumor — show little or no ageing.

(j) Respiration

The normal rate of breathing varies between about 15 and 18 times per minute in adults, but the rate and depth increase sharply during exercise, excitement or stress. Oxygen, absorbed into the bloodstream from the lungs, is carried to the tissues, where chemical processes supply the materials necessary to repair wear and tear and to produce heat and energy. Carbon dioxide, produced by the metabolism, is absorbed into the blood and exhaled by the lungs.

Normal respiration is controlled by an automatic respiratory centre in the brain, which is sensitive to the amount of carbon dioxide in the blood, but voluntary control from higher brain centres is possible too, as, for example, in swimming. The brain is very sensitive to variations in oxygen supply. Moderate lack of oxygen produces varying degrees of inefficiency such as drowsiness, muscular weakness, poorer problem-solving and sensori-motor inco-ordination. Severe lack of oxygen produces confusion, loss of consciousness, damage to nerve cells and eventually death.

Red blood cells and haemoglobin (which carries oxygen) appear to increase somewhat in later life. The general effect of ageing, however, is to reduce respiratory efficiency. Older people, moreover, do not have the same cardiac output (pumping action of the heart) as younger people. Their lungs contain a smaller volume of air; the residual volume after expiration is larger; delivery and diffusion of oxygen may be poorer because the oxygen has to diffuse through fibrous material to reach the cells. Adequate oxygenation is crucial to physical and mental performance. Disturbance of breathing during sleep appears to increase with age and may have ill-effects. Respiratory infections are more frequent among older people. The most common cause of respiratory failure is bronchitis.

(k) Blood circulation

In the normal younger adult the heart beats at an average rate of about 72 beats per minute when at rest; it becomes stronger and faster when people are excited, angry, afraid, or when they engage in physical exercise. It pumps the blood round the body, distributing oxygen and nutrient matter to all the tissues and carrying away waste matter to be excreted. A normal adult has a blood volume of ten or eleven pints (six to six and a half litres). The blood pressure is maintained by the force of the cardiac contractions on the one hand and the resistance of the arterioles on the other, at a fairly constant (resting) level and adjusted to meet demand. Permanently raised blood pressure can damage the arteries. Low blood pressure can cause temporary impairment of the blood supply to the brain, as in fainting. Cerebral haemorrhage can occur if the blood vessels in the brain are damaged by disease or by cumulative normal degeneration. Raised blood pressure is sometimes associated with increased renin in some kidney disorders.

Relative to other organs, the heart changes little in weight with normal ageing. Its weight is related to body weight and to skeletal muscle. Growth in response to increased demand is characteristic not only of cardiac muscle, but also of striped muscle, lungs and sweat glands. A mode of life that promotes a margin of physical capacity over and above normal requirements, for example, by means of dietary regulation or physical exercise, could help to compensate for the normal degenerative effects of ageing by keeping the heart in good form.

After the age of about 55 the rhythm of the heart becomes slower and more irregular, although in extreme old age some individuals show a slight rise in heart rate. Arterial changes with age, if they occur in the brain, have markedly adverse effects. An impaired blood supply to the brain causes permanent structural damage through atrophy of the nerve cells; these effects are greatly increased in conditions of vascular disease. Areas of atrophy can occur without apparent local vascular impairment, but the brain can be selectively impaired by local deficiencies in blood supply (see also Chapter Nine).

The main arteries increase somewhat in diameter in older people, perhaps in response to the normal rise with age in blood pressure (which may itself be a reaction to the restrictions in blood flow imposed by thickening and calcification of the walls of the smaller arteries and by changes in the capillary system).

The tendency for thrombi to form inside the vessels (thrombosis) increases when the vessels are damaged; such damage is serious and becomes more common in old age. Deposits of fat may accumulate around the heart and the valves tend to become harder and less pliable. The working capacity of the heart decreases, diminishing physical performances.

Arteriosclerosis is a form of widespread degeneration in which fat is deposited in and between the cells, and hard calcium salts are built up. Thus, the flexible cellular elements in the blood vessels are replaced by a firm homogeneous glossy substance.

Heart disease is a major cause of illness and death. Not only are the heart and the circulatory system generally less efficient in later life but also adverse changes are increased by such habits as smoking, overindulgence in food and alcohol, and a stressful life-style. There appears to be a natural compensatory reaction to ageing in that oxygen uptake by the body tissues is improved.

Presumably as a consequence of continual stretch reactions, the elastic innermost layers of the arteries gradually become fragmented and infiltrated with lipids, thus restricting blood flow and raising blood pressure. Coronary arteriosclerosis increases in frequency and severity from about 30 years, but many elderly people are not greatly affected by it. The ages from 50 to 70 years show the greatest mortality; selective mortality presumably eliminates a proportion of people predisposed to coronary arteriosclerosis.

Changes involving pigmentation, fibrous degeneration and atherosclerosis also become more common and more pronounced. Atherosclerosis is a form of arteriosclerosis in which materials containing lipids accumulate locally within or beneath the intima (innermost coat) of blood vessels. It is a frequent cause of arterial occlusion and aneurysm and seems to arise as a metabolic defect involving lipids and lipoproteins.

Arteries may become hardened by fibrosis without calcification; and they can lose their elasticity in the absence of arteriosclerosis. The process of arteriosclerosis may start quite early in life with the deposition of small particles within the arterial intima; as age increases, the particles – such as the lipid macromolecules which appear in the blood plasma following a fatty meal – gradually accumulate. Other factors play a part, however, since arteriosclerosis is not a universal characteristic in late life.

Changes in the circulatory system brought about by wear and tear may interact with arteriosclerotic processes to produce localized damage to those segments of the arterial system that are especially vulnerable to the action of heightened blood pressure. Arteriosclerotic changes are prominent factors in 'vicious circles' of impairment – as when narrow arteries lead to raised blood pressure which may in turn aggravate the process of arteriosclerosis.

(l) Homeostasis

The term 'homeostasis' refers to a process whereby physiological mechanisms regulate and stabilize the 'internal environment'. It includes the regulation of the body temperature, acid–base balance of the blood, and electrolyte balance.

Most of the body's sugar is converted in the liver and stored as glycogen. The blood carries glucose for use in the muscles and in other organs of the body, especially the brain. Insulin, secreted by the pancreas, normally checks any undue rise in the level of blood sugar, while adrenalin and other hormones stimulate the release of glucose from the liver into the bloodstream. One of the failures of homeostasis is diabetes, a blood–sugar disorder, which increases in frequency with age.

The blood is slightly alkaline under normal conditions, but in strenuous exercise this alkaline reserve is diminished, and the recovery of the acid–base balance through respiratory and other functions is slower in older people. The homeostatic mechanisms must be flexible enough to adjust to variations in physical effort, changes in temperature and food intake; they must operate appropriately during sleep, and following injury or infection.

Homeostasis is less efficient in older people. Many physiological functions, such as heart rate and metabolic rate, have a range of values permitting the individual to adapt to variations in his or her surroundings and activities. But as these 'tolerance limits' are reduced with age, and as the stabilizing mechanisms become sluggish, adaptability is reduced; for example, in relation to the control of body temperature and recovery from exercise or psychological stress – see also Figure 2.1.

As age increases, throughout adult life our biological capacities tend to diminish. These declines, however, are not uniform or

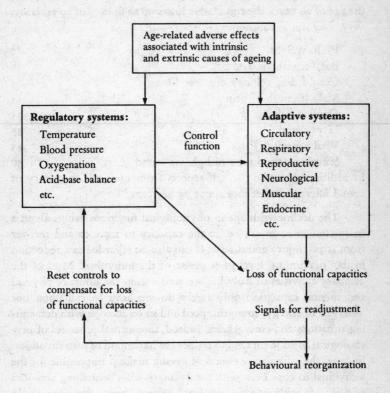

Figure 2.1

A schematic representation
of intrinsic and extrinsic causes
of ageing on the
physiological basis of behaviour

necessarily smooth and gradual. Calculated as a percentage loss of functional capacity from a theoretical maximum of 100 per cent at the age of 20 years, the cumulative losses up to the age of 80 years are, very roughly, as follows:

Brain weight	10
Basal metabolic rate	10
Conduction velocity of nerve fibres	15
Male strength of grip	15
Cardiac output	35
Liver weight	35
Vital capacity	45
Simple reaction time to light or sound	50

In addition, according to self-reports from men, the frequency of sexual intercourse declines about 75 per cent.

The decline with age in physiological functions brings about a 'reduction in reserves', i.e. in the capacity to react to and recover from stress, injury and disease. It can also be regarded as a reduction in the 'maximum' level of response of the individual. Most of the ordinary activities of daily life are well within the limits of physical and mental capacities; only rarely do we have to call upon our 'reserves' of energy, strength, speed and so on to cope with demanding situations and emergencies. Indeed, the normal processes of psychological adjustment tend to reduce the likelihood of such situations. In time, the cumulative effects of ageing make it impossible for the individual to cope even with the ordinary self-maintaining activities of daily life without assistance from others – hence the onset of old age dependency. Eventually, the 'reserves' are incapable of meeting demand and the individual dies from one cause or another.

(m) Physical exercise

Although it might seem obvious that moderate regular physical exercise has beneficial effects on physical and mental well-being, it is surprisingly difficult to demonstrate these effects unequivocally. Methodological problems put severe restrictions on the validity of research findings; one cannot control completely for all the relevant subject variables, such as exercise history, diet, concurrent physical activity, selective drop-out and so on. The indications, however, are that physical exercise does have generalized beneficial effects, although these effects soon disappear if exercise is discontinued. The relationships between physical exercise, health and longevity could be specific rather than general, as, for example, in relation to limited protection against heart disease.

In rats, physical exercise, within limits, appears to delay biological ageing. In human adults, physical exercise leads to improvements in speed, stamina and strength, and in a variety of underlying physiological functions such as circulation and respiration. Substantial improvements following physical training have been reported; this probably means that physiological measures derived from normal subjects of different ages reflect the effects of disuse and adaptation to non-demanding physical circumstances rather than the effects of ageing. The physiological functions of normal healthy adults improve rapidly in response to 'demand', even late in life. It is not clear that the physiological benefit has effects on ordinary behaviour or feelings of well-being, though this seems more likely than not. Physical training does not extend the 'normal' lifespan, except in the sense that it seems to increase individual resistance to and recovery from physical ailments which might otherwise be fatal, like coronary occlusion. It seems likely that central nervous functions play a part in the improvements following regular physical exercises. Many adults underrate their capacity for physical improvement and underestimate the importance of exercise and diet in the maintenance of health and vigour. Exercise, in the present sense, means working against a load and over a period of time, so that the muscular effort required approaches a maximum, as in the use of a bicycle ergometer or treadmill.

The biological effects of ageing on vigorous skills such as tennis, swimming, boxing and football appear earlier than on skills involving less physical effort but equal or greater co-ordination, such as billiards, golf and shooting. The peak years for excellence in the more vigorous skills occur in the late twenties, whereas for the less physically exhausting sports they occur in the early thirties. After the age of 31 there is a sharp fall in athletic and sporting achievement to the age of about 46. This rapid decline should not be interpreted as a sign that physical fitness declines early to a low level. Older men retain considerable capacity for muscular work, although their stamina, effort, co-ordination and speed in physical performance do not match those of younger men. The effects of age on physical prowess are most clearly revealed by testing to the limits.

The average age for peak performance in field sports tended to increase for a time. Lehman (see References, Chapter Eight) put this down to the greater financial motivation in modern commercialized sport and to improvements in physical health in recent years. It would not be surprising, however, to find that this trend has been reversed. In sport, and in the arts and sciences, the secular trends vary considerably from one field of endeavour to another; and it may prove possible, by carefully examining such variations, to reach more positive conclusions about the causes and conditions of age-changes in performance, and to eliminate methodological artefacts.

(n) Sleep

The average duration of sleep, about seven and a half hours, remains fairly constant throughout the larger part of adult life, although wide individual differences exist. Sleep patterns are sometimes disturbed in old age, possibly because older people are less physically active; poor sleeping habits may be hard to break. In later life we find greater difficulty in getting to sleep, more frequent waking, earlier awakening in mornings, less satisfying sleep and greater dependence upon sleeping tablets. The relative amount of time spent in the various 'levels' of sleep varies with age, and REM (rapid eye movement) sleep associated with dreaming appears to be shorter and more fragmented. Other 'biological rhythms' are disturbed in later life.

(o) Nervous system

The nervous system consists of the central nervous system – brain and spinal cord – and two systems of peripheral nerves, the 'somatic' and the 'autonomic'.

The brain is organized anatomically at various levels. The mid and lower brain centres are overlaid by two large cerebral hemispheres; they are connected by a tract of nervous tissue called the corpus callosum. The cerebral hemispheres consist of several regions separated by fissures and cavities. Although there are several areas where functions are localized, such as vision, hearing and motor control, other areas appear to have less specific functions, and the brain acts as a whole. The cerebral cortex provides the association areas necessary for higher mental functions such as intelligence, memory and imagination, and for the organization of experience and voluntary action, for example, learning and emotional control. The individual nerve cells vary in size, shape and function; they are supported, nourished and protected by a massive and intricate system of glial cells which in turn depend upon the other organs and systems of the body such as the circulatory, respiratory and endocrine systems.

The early development of the brain brings about an increase in the size of the nerve cells, in supporting tissues, and in the cerebrovascular system. Nerve cells cannot multiply beyond the age of about one year. They are sensitive to variations in biological conditions such as lack of oxygen or interruption of the blood supply. The long-range effects – on age-changes in adult behaviour and the brain – of undernourishment and other sorts of environmental deficit early in life have yet to be worked out. This is an obvious implication of the lifespan developmental approach to human ageing. The effects of 'behavioural enrichment' on rats during their development seem to be to enlarge the brain and increase cortical thickness. Behavioural enrichment also appears to produce effects, though to a lesser degree, in the adult rat. The implications of such effects for humans are obvious, unless they arise because of experimental artefacts, such as increased cranial capacity. There is some evidence that training and practice in cognitive (mental) skills can result in improved performance. The questions are whether such training can result in worthwhile and lasting effects in older people, and if so what are the underlying mechanisms.

The nerve cells alone are thought to number about 12,000 million. The different types of neuron differ widely in structure, function and location. They are supported and nourished by a much greater number of glial and other cells, with an associated blood supply and fluid surround. Add to this the ramifications of synaptic connections and the neurotransmitter secretions and it is easy to appreciate the problems of neuropsychological research in ageing, especially when many of the important changes seem to originate at the intra-cellular level.

Research emphasizes the pathological aspects of ageing rather than its normal physiological aspects – for example, senile dementia of the Alzheimer type and multi-infacet dementia. Moreover, data on pathological ageing relevant to brain function are frequently obtained from sources which are not typical of normal people. The age-trends thus calculated do not necessarily reflect normal age-trends. In addition, the biological uniqueness of the individual constitutes an obstacle for research into the effects of age on brain functions. The normal and pathological effects of ageing lead to a variety of changes in the anatomy and physiology of the nervous system, and consequently in the organization of behaviour and experience.

Brain weight decreases from about 1,400 grams in males in their twenties (1,250 grams in females) to about 1,250 grams in males in their eighties (1,125 grams in females). The decrease appears to accelerate in late life. Brain weight, however, is a crude measure of the number of intact nerve cells. During adult life, the water content of the brain appears to increase slightly for humans; the amino acid composition of cerebral proteins seems to be unaffected by ageing. Age-changes in the relationships between behaviour and neuro-chemical processes in the brain are likely; for example, a diminution in RNA response to avoidance training in older rats. In rats, cerebral nucleoprotein remains roughly constant in the adult phase up to two years. It is no simple matter, however, to argue from age-effects in animal behaviour to age-effects in human behaviour (or brain function). In humans, brain RNA remains roughly constant during the adult phase but diminishes in very late life, whereas DNA appears to increase. Remember, however, that cross-sectional differences in physiological measures based on pathological and non-representative samples of subjects do not necessarily reflect the normal changes with age of physiological processes within normal individuals. The acid-base balance (pH) of the brain declines slightly with age as it does for other organs. The mineral content of the brain varies with age. Some brain enzymes increase with age. Vitamin levels depend very much on diet, which is often inadequate in late life.

Advances in the study of ageing and brain function have been achieved by the use of special equipment such as the electro-encephalogram (EEG), which magnifies and records the electrical activity of the brain. The dominant EEG alpha frequency (8–12 cps), the delta (1–3 cps) and theta (4–7 cps) frequencies are slowed slightly and may be associated with longer reaction times to complex stimuli, otherwise the EEG records of normal, healthy old people are similar to those of younger people. However, elderly patients with cerebral vascular disorders or disease show various EEG abnormalities. The EEG patterns react less sharply to sensory stimulation than do those of younger people, suggesting a lower level of arousal. On the other hand, older people seem to show more prolonged after-effects from neural (and mental) activity – a kind of 'inertia' which delays or interferes with subsequent activities. Injury, disease and atrophy of the brain can result in a variety of abnormal conditions, depending upon the degree and distribution of the damage.

In recent years, many technological advances have been made in the study of the living brain. Computerized axial tomography (CAT), positron emission tomography (PET), nuclear magnetic resonance (NMR), and other devices are making it possible to examine brain functions in some detail. Although not without their critics, studies making use of such technologies seem bound to advance our understanding of normal and pathological ageing.

There is diffuse cerebral atrophy in which some areas are particularly affected. The fissures in the brain become wider and deeper, the ventricles become larger and deformed; many nerve cells are lost, others suffer degenerative changes. In senile dementia, cerebral vascular disease, and in organic psychoses of old age, the damage may be considerable (see also Chapter Nine). Degenerative changes take place in the cerebellum and the interior parts of the brain. There is an increase in neuroglial fibres (supporting structures) and patchy degeneration of the Schwann cells enclosing the nerve fibres. The spinal cord may show relatively more pronounced atrophy in its upper portion. Age-changes in the brain are not necessarily intrinsic and appear to arise mainly as consequences of adverse biological ageing elsewhere in the body.

Nerve cells die quickly from lack of oxygen. Parts of some fibres may be renewed but the nerve cell itself cannot be replaced. The capacity of a sectioned nerve fibre to regenerate diminishes in adult life. Individual nerve cells shrink and atrophy, the cytoplasm becomes paler, the nucleus shrinks and becomes displaced. Nissl granulation is reduced; the dead cell is replaced by neuroglia. In some instances the cyto-architecture of the cells is abnormal; senile plaques form: neurofibrillar degeneration and lipofuscin pigmentation lead eventually to a fragmentation of the network of neurofibrils and the blocking of cell activity by inert materials. The number of nerve cells is reduced – as shown by counting the number in a given area. For technical reasons, however, such counts are difficult to make and interpret, and there is lack of agreement about the nature and extent of nerve cell loss.

The total number of nerve cells available is probably an important factor. Experiments with animals – at least animals with a relatively unspecialized cortex – have demonstrated the 'mass action' of the cortex. Neuropsychological studies of the human brain, however, need to take account of lesions in both the specific and non-specific areas of the cortex (see also Chapter Nine). The extent of cell loss is not the same for all areas of the cortex; this may help to account for the differential loss of capacities. The brain stem seems to be little affected by ageing.

Arteriosclerosis affects the brain by reducing the blood circulation, thereby reducing oxygenation, the distribution of nutrients and the elimination of waste products including carbon dioxide. Fibrous thickening of the arteries reduces their capacity. A loss of or reduction in blood supply leads to atrophy or death of nerve cells and surrounding tissues, although the relationship appears not to be explicable simply in terms of anatomical localization. A deteriorated blood vessel or a small aneurysm may leak; the bleeding within the brain damages or destroys localized areas, and produces a 'stroke'. The slow onset of cerebral arteriosclerosis permits the establishment of compensatory physiological responses such as the formation of passages between adjacent blood vessels; psychological compensation is also possible; for example, the relearning of skills impaired by the disease.

Cerebral arteriosclerosis can bring about a variety of physical signs and symptoms apart from those which are of psychological interest – changes in posture, movement and reflexes, for example, stroke, and transient ischaemic attacks (temporary loss of sensory, motor or speech functions).

The somatic nervous system comprises parts of the brain, the spinal cord and the peripheral (sensory and motor) fibres. The sensory receptors, such as those in the eye and tongue, and the pain receptors in the skin, are linked to the brain directly or via the spinal cord by sensory fibres, whereas the muscles receive their 'instructions' from the motor fibres. Nerve structures in the thalamus direct some of the incoming sensory information to various parts of the cortex and they have other functions, such as the perception of pain. The hypothalamus influences the pituitary gland, is concerned with temperature regulation and feeding and, as a higher centre for the co-ordination of the autonomic nervous system, plays a part in emotional behaviour. The spinal cord appears to reach a maximum weight of about 25 grams in the thirties, and then to decrease to about 20 grams in late life.

The effects of age on the somatic nervous system appear to be similar to those on other parts of the nervous system. The nerve fibre bundles appear atrophied – thickened in parts and uneven, with splitting and even disintegration. The blood circulation diminishes, connective tissue increases and the essential active constituents of the nerve cells are reduced or lost altogether. Some slowing is apparent in the conduction velocity of the peripheral nerve fibres, and conduction time across the synapse may increase, in which case the extra time accumulated over many synapses (as in central processes during a complex mental reaction) might be considerable. The main portion of the reaction time of a response to even a simple stimulus, moreover, is occupied not by the peripheral sensory or motor nerve impulses but by the central organizing processes of the cortex. This central decision time is proportionally greater in more complex forms of behaviour.

The autonomic nervous system (ANS) is largely outside voluntary control but the visceral responses it controls can be 'conditioned' – as in anticipatory anxiety or anger; they can also be deliberately modified by operant training and relaxation therapy. The ANS consists of a network of nerve clusters (ganglia) and connecting fibres. It carries a few sensory fibres but is mainly a motor system controlling the involuntary muscles and glands and regulating the vital internal functions of the body. There are two subdivisions: (a) the sympathetic division, comprising two chains of ganglia running alongside the spinal cord, connected by means of nerve fibres with the spinal cord and with the visceral organs, whose activity they help to regulate; (b) the parasympathetic division, consisting of two systems of nerve fibres named according to their anatomical positions – an upper (cranial) portion, and a lower (sacral) portion. The hypothalamus is the principal subcortical region for the integration of the ANS.

In conjunction with the endocrine system, the sympathetic division of the ANS facilitates the widespread simultaneous regulation of visceral responses, whereas the parasympathetic division is more selective and specific in its action. The two divisions of the autonomic system have, in some organs, a reciprocal relationship. The heart rate, for example, is accelerated by sympathetic innervation and slowed down by parasympathetic innervation. The overall effect is that of a self-regulating system capable of making adaptive responses and returning to a basic steady state.

The degree of preparedness produced by sympathetic excitation can vary between moderate states of tension and alertness to extremely powerful or disturbing emotional reactions. The action of the autonomic system, in maintaining homeostasis and the vegetative functions of the body, and in making the person ready to meet emergencies, fulfils a biological purpose. Its effects, however, may be excessive in relation to the requirements of civilized adult life. The mild states of tension and anxiety generated by slight deprivations, frustrations and conflicts can serve as the driving forces to sustain and direct a person's responses, but prolonged emotional tension or too frequent emotional upsets may not only be ineffective but also impair rational adjustment and lead to psychosomatic symptoms. Such physiological upsets may have more deleterious effects in later life because of impaired homeostasis and reduced 'reserves', inducing confusion or depression, for example.

There are individual differences (and age-changes) in temperamental qualities such as mood, emotional stability and intensity of feelings. As people grow up, they learn when and how to express their feelings. They are not always successful, however, in handling emotional problems, and their reactions may very well include the kinds of compromise we find in minor neurotic disorders and in the more inadequate strategies of normal adjustment. The interaction of predisposition and stress leads to an increased likelihood of psychosomatic ailments and to neurotic or psychotic breakdown in later life (see Chapter Nine).

Few systematic studies relevant to behaviour have been made of the effects of age on the autonomic nervous system. Degenerative changes in late life in the autonomic and sensory ganglia are probably similar to changes elsewhere in the nervous system. Disturbances of the homeostatic mechanisms, for example, vasomotor and endocrine secretion regulation, have serious implications for functional capacity and survival – in relation to blood pressure, sexual function, thermo-regulation, diabetes and so on. Older subjects show weaker GSR reactions (sweat reaction to slight emotional tension). Conditioned reflexes are harder to establish in older animals (including man) and they are extinguished more quickly. Experimental neurosis in lab-oratory animals, induced by stress, leads to changes in physical condition and behaviour which, if well established and maintained without relief, show some resemblance to premature ageing; for example, loss of functional efficiency, generalized weakness, apathy.

Measures of autonomic function are greatly affected by factors such as posture, state of mind and preceding activity; hence care is needed when making comparisons between age-groups. Failures of the ANS are more common in later life. They can give rise to a number of medical ailments such as incontinence, hypothermia, postural hypotension (reduction in cerebral blood flow when changing from a lying to a standing position), digestive and excretory dysfunctions. Synaptic transmission at autonomic ganglia is altered by a decrease in acetylcholine and its precursor choline acetylase, and a decrease in the effects of cholinesterase. However, these changes are compensated for in part by increased sensitivity of the post-synaptic membrane to acetylcholine. The total number of active neurons is reduced.

The normal effects of ageing on emotional responsiveness have been much neglected in behavioural gerontology. It could be argued that ageing has two main effects. First, the reduction in the overall responsiveness of the autonomic nervous system and associated physiological functions such as endocrine secretion, and thus the physical basis of emotion, might well diminish the level of arousal, and make older people temperamentally 'flatter' and more phleg-matic. There is, however, evidence against this hypothesis. Secondly, the gradual, cumulative, diffuse loss of cortex might diminish cog-nitive control and the person's emotional reactions would become more primitive and more closely tied to the here-and-now situation, rather than inhibited and elaborated by intelligence and experience.

Thus, there might be less build-up of anticipatory emotion – hope, anxiety, aggression – and less prolongation of the after-effects of an emotional experience – disappointment, pain, rage. This rather simple theory might account both for the emotional quiescence and apparent 'apathy' of many old people and for their capacity for intense but short-lived emotional reactions when provoked. It needs further elaboration to explain the general drift towards depression as age increases, perhaps by referring to the increasing frequency of frustrating and disappointing situations, including those arising internally as a consequence of reminiscence. (The psychopathology of emotion in adult life and old age is described in Chapter Nine and normal emotional reactions are discussed in Chapters Six and Ten.)

(p) The senses
Ageing has widespread adverse effects on sensory processes.

(1) VISION. After the age of about 10, the best viewing distance lengthens gradually until, by the age of 50, many people need to wear glasses with lenses to correct this long-sightedness (presbyopia). The lens of the eye 'ages' even from infancy and becomes more opaque and less elastic in adult life. It continues to grow without shedding its older cells (which undergo chemical changes), and changes its shape. It thus becomes less able to change focus, and senile changes in the ciliary muscles (controlling the shape of the lens) also help to reduce accommodation. Visual accommodation is measured in diopters (a lens with a focal length of one metre measures one diopter); in early adult life a normal lens has a range of about ten diopters. By the age of 60 years this has fallen to two diopters, and by 70 years to less than one. Convergence of the lines of sight from both eyes is less efficient later on in life, probably because the exterior eye muscles become weaker, or possibly because cortical control is less effective. Age-changes in the nervous system probably play a part in reducing the diameter of the pupil, thus restricting the amount of light entering the eye, and in slowing its reaction time to a decrease in illumination, thus impairing the older person's recovery from glare (though the response to brighter illumination appears unaffected). The iris fades and the cornea thickens, loses its lustre and becomes less transparent. Age-changes in the retina (the complex

network of light-sensitive elements and nerve cells at the back of the eye) bring about atrophy of the nerve cells and poorer blood supply, which contribute to poorer all-round visual performance, in visual acuity, colour matching, dark adaptation, dark vision and contrast discrimination. Static visual acuity falls with age especially after the age of 50 years, and more so late in life, when maybe three out of four people will not have full vision even with glasses. This comes about for several reasons – increased scattering of light by the cornea, lens and vitreous humor, reduced pupil size, loss of rods, cones and other retinal cells, loss of cells in the visual pathways and cortex. Dynamic visual acuity – the perception of movement and moving stimuli – also declines, presumably for the same reasons plus adverse changes in the muscles controlling vision and central (cortical) factors in visual performance, for example, speed. Critical flicker fusion and two-flash threshold decline little if at all until about the age of 50; some deterioration seems to take place at later ages. Colour sensitivity shows a gradual loss of fine discrimination brought about by the yellowing of the lens, retinal changes and possibly other factors. In certain cases there are restrictions in the field of vision and arterio-sclerosis may produce atrophy in the periphery, where the arterial blood supply is poorer.

Changes in visual perception clearly illustrate that ageing is a complex process; for there are not only various sorts of physical changes in the visual apparatus and the nervous system, but also concomitant changes in arousal and attention (which may help to account for age-effects in the perception of illusions, and inter-sensory functions). Levels of illumination and the visual characteristics of a display, for example, size of print, rate of presentation, are obviously important in relation to work, driving and so on. Degenerative changes in the eye accumulate with age and diseases increase in fre-quency. There is a gradual loss of orbital fat, so that eventually the eyes appear shrunken, the blink reflex is slower and the eyelids hang loosely because of poorer muscle tone. A number of diseases cause impairment of or complete loss of sight in old age; for example, cataract, macular degeneration.

The visual capacities of elderly people can be improved not only by wearing glasses with corrective lenses but also by the use of microscope lenses, stand magnifiers, and other optical devices for maximizing the use of residual capacity. Improvements in vision and other senses, such as hearing, can bring obvious psychological benefits, though special training in the use of these devices may be required. Much might be done to compensate for the poorer vision of older people by way of increased contrast illumination, increased size and spacing of visual stimuli (diagrams, notices, warning signs, printed pages), and the layout of documents of particular importance to the elderly (to facilitate search and comprehension). New medical and surgical techniques may help delay or remedy poorer vision in later life.

(ii) HEARING. Loss of hearing during the adult years – presbycusis – is usually gradual, and may not be noticed because most of the sounds which are relevant to our behaviour are well above threshold value. There are no obvious structural changes, except for atrophy of nervous tissue, especially at the basal turn of the inner ear and presumably the auditory nerves and auditory cortex. This helps to explain why hearing loss is greater for higher tones than for lower. The very high tones are eventually lost completely, but moderately high tones can be registered if the sound is loud. There is some loss of hearing for speech (a mixture of high, medium and low tones), but it cannot be accounted for entirely in terms of the hearing loss for pure tones. Other factors such as intelligence, vocabulary and verbal context are involved. Older people do not appear to compensate for their hearing loss by paying closer attention to the lip movements of the speaker. If anything, they are slightly poorer than younger people at lip reading. Cumulative damage can result from structural injury, disease and prolonged exposure to excessive noise, as, for example, in industrial deafness. Hearing loss is greater for men, probably because of their exposure to noisy occupational conditions, and greater for the left than for the right ear. Local arteriosclerosis (hardening and thickening of the small arteries) may produce limited hearing losses.

Correction for loss of hearing is not simply a matter of amplifying sounds. This leads to distortion, since hearing loss is greater for some sound frequencies than for others. What is required is an enhancement of the 'patterns' of sound, as in speech patterns. So shouting does not help much, compared with speaking distinctly and emphatically.

By about the age of 50 years there is sufficient hearing loss on average to bring about impairment in some of the more demanding listening situations – faint sounds, background noise, multiple sources, and so on. Such listening becomes effortful, tiring and subject to error. This may lead to a reduction in social interaction and to mistaken impressions, on the part of others, of lack of interest or intelligence. A decline with age in central processing capacity – the ability to interpret and respond quickly and effectively to complex auditory information – makes matters worse.

Head noises are not uncommon in adult life. The more usual varieties – ringing, buzzing – are referred to as tinnitus. However, more complex, meaningful head noises of a repetitive insistent sort – loud music, for example – also occur. These are not hallucinatory but self-referred and a source of stress. They may be inhibited for a time if the person is fully engaged in other activities. Presumably different sorts of head noise arise as a consequence of damage or atrophy to different parts of the very complex auditory system. Possibly, too, in association with mental disorder, they provide a basis for hallucinations.

(III) OTHER SENSES. Most age-changes in sensory perception are in the direction of lowered efficiency. There are degenerative changes in the olfactory and gustatory receptors: for example, there is a decrease with age in sensitivity to sugar and salt, and in the number of taste-buds in the tongue; the olfactory bulb (responsible for the perception of smell), at the base of the brain, atrophies. Normal age-changes in taste and smell are particularly difficult to investigate, and there appears to be no *prima facie* case for supposing that the effects of such changes compare in importance with those of vision and hearing. However, they might be associated with certain types of accident (failing to react to danger signals) and with unsatisfactory dietary habits (through lack of sensory stimulation). The proprioceptors include stretch receptors in the muscles, tension and stretch receptors in the tendons and ligaments, stretch and pressure receptors in the joints, and movement receptors in the vestibular apparatus (the senses associated with balance and movement, situated in the inner ear). Various effects of ageing such as hand tremor, body sway and poorer motor co-ordination raise the suspicion that proprioception is impaired. However, other factors – such as muscular weakness and de-innervation and poorer integration at higher levels in the nervous system – may be involved. Touch perception and the perception of movement and vibration appear to decline with age. There is little experimental evidence that the perception of pain is weaker. Pain receptors are free-branching nerve-endings in the skin, joints, cornea, arteries and viscera; they react to tissue damage and excessive stimulation of other sense organs. The study of pain is hindered by both ethical and methodological considerations. There is a considerable subjective element in reported pain; psychological techniques for moderating the experience of pain, and physiological techniques for masking and reducing it, are under investigation. It is reasonable to suppose that at least some deleterious effects of ageing occur in pain perception because most sensory thresholds increase with age. The perception of temperature, for example, may be affected by deposits of fat and vascular changes. A threshold for pain from electrical stimulation of the teeth ranging from about 2 to 20 microamps has been observed, with little change over a wide age-range. If the sensory threshold for pain increases slightly with age but the tolerance level decreases, then older subjects may 'perceive' and report pain at lower stimulus intensities than younger subjects. The vestibular system shows a reduction with age in the number of receptor hair cells and degeneration of the otoliths. These, together with atrophy of the vestibular nuclei, cerebellum, mid-brain and cortex, would help to account for poorer balance and poorer sense and control of whole body movements. Note also the adverse effects on balance of postural hypotension, unusual visual situations (steep stairs, for example), and slower, weaker muscular reactions to loss of balance. Dizziness and poorer patterns of sensory input from the muscles and joints contribute to certain types of accident in later life such as falls.

Not surprisingly, widespread changes with age in the anatomy and physiology of the body, including changes in its outward appearance, give rise to changes in what is called the 'body-image', i.e. the framework of ideas by means of which we try to understand and regulate bodily functions. Consider, for example, the way we deal with diminished strength and speed of response, with reductions in the range of movement, with pains, discomfort and specific disabilities. Bodily functions are not prominent in awareness until they go wrong, and even then we may be able to adapt to them. The way in which the body-image changes, then, is likely to vary widely from person to person. The body-image is normally an important part of the self-concept. Our reactions to ageing are partly a function of the value we place on physical competence and outward appearance, partly a function of the nature and extent of the changes that have taken place, and partly a function of how we compare with other people.

(q) Vocalization

Vocal changes with age are brought about in part by the hardening and decreased elasticity of the laryngeal cartilages, though these processes are usually complete by the age of 40. Later in life the laryngeal muscles atrophy, the vocal folds slacken and changes occur in the pigmentation of the mucous membrane.

The voice becomes more highly pitched as the person progresses from middle to old age, although in the thirties and forties vocal pitch appears to be lower than in adolescence and early adult life. In senescence the voice grows less powerful and restricted in range, becoming high and piping in some. Singing and public speaking, which make greater demands upon the vocal apparatus, deteriorate earlier than normal speaking. Speech becomes slower, probably because of degenerative changes in the central nervous system rather than changes in peripheral mechanisms. Pauses are longer and more frequent. Slurring occurs in senile patients, and various kinds of speech disorder can arise from pathological changes in the brain.

'Inner speech' plays a part in thinking, so that the effects of age on verbal reasoning are likely to be the product of some interaction between degenerative changes in the verbal centres and degenerative changes in other parts of the brain concerned with intelligence. Relatively little, however, is known about the normal effects of age on the more subtle functions of language and communicative behaviour; on the whole they seem to be well preserved (see Chapter Eight).

(r) Endocrine system

The endocrine system comprises the ductless glands, which secrete complex chemical substances called 'hormones' directly into the bloodstream. The hormones act as chemical messengers helping to direct the growth and functions of the body. The endocrine glands can be classified into three groups: first, those regulating specific aspects of metabolism, such as the islands of Langerhans, which secrete insulin, the hormone which regulates the utilization of sugar (inadequate insulin is one of the causes of diabetes), and the parathyroids which control the calcium content of the blood-serum; second, those working in conjunction with the autonomic nervous system, such as the adrenal medulla; third, those which appear to have more permanent effects on the development and integration of the body, such as the pituitary, thyroid, adrenal cortex and gonads.

(I) PITUITARY. The pituitary gland is situated at the base of the brain and plays an important role in regulating the activities of other glands. The posterior pituitary helps in maintaining the water balance of the body; the anterior pituitary regulates growth and other endocrine organs. The pituitary appears to maintain its functions fairly well over the years.

(II) THYROID AND PARATHYROIDS. The thyroid gland, situated at the front of the trachea, secretes thyroxin, an iodine compound; it stimulates and regulates metabolism. Insufficient secretion leads to an illness characterized by lethargy, chronic fatigue and lack of vitality, while excessive thyroid secretion leads to loss of weight, restlessness, excitability, insomnia and anxiety. Ageing eventually brings about a reduction in the size of the gland and the replacement of active cells by inactive connective tissue. It becomes less well supplied with blood and secretes less thyroxin. In normal people, however, it appears to remain fairly effective throughout the greater part of adult life.

Thyroid hormone affects metabolism, pulse rate and peripheral blood flow; so age-changes in thyroid function have repercussions on the normal activity of the cardiovascular system in adult life and old age. In old age, metabolic rate diminishes, thus increasing the risk of very low body temperature in some circumstances.

The parathyroids regulate calcium–phosphorus metabolism; ageing appears to add to the large amount of interstitial fat in the parathyroids, and slightly to reduce essential tissue so that fewer cells are active.

(III) ADRENALS. The adrenal glands, situated near the kidneys, consist of a medulla, which secretes adrenalin, and a cortex, which secretes a variety of chemical substances regulating carbohydrate metabolism and the salt balance of the body. These secretions help to mobilize the physical resources of the body during prolonged stresses, such as danger or hunger. Some hormones of the adrenal cortex have a masculinizing effect.

The absolute and relative loss of weight of the adrenals in adult life and old age is relatively slight, and the concentration in the blood of adrenocortical hormones seems more or less constant – although hormone output cannot be assessed directly. Adrenal insufficiency, therefore, has not been regarded as an important cause of physiological deterioration. Any deterioration – degenerative changes in cells, the replacement of active cell constituents with connective tissues, and arteriosclerosis – appears relatively late in life. There may be some compensatory growth in unaffected tissues, but with a risk of subsequent pathology. Abnormal adrenal insufficiency in older people may aggravate normal age-changes, leading to muscular weakness and tiredness, or to complications in the pathologies of late life.

(IV) GONADS. The gonads – the ovaries or testes – produce reproductive cells and secrete hormones which contribute to sexual development and behaviour. Hormone secretion rises sharply at puberty and remains at a high normal level until it gradually falls off in middle and old age.

In women, degenerative changes in the ovaries and other organs in the body bring about a cessation of the menstrual cycle around the age of 47, although there are large individual differences. This phase of life may be accompanied by irregularities in the menstrual cycle and by premenopausal sterility. Sometimes somatic disturbances, such as hot flushes, occur because of hormone imbalance, but in normal women the menopause appears not to have other serious symptoms, although research reports are conflicting. There is some atrophy of the vagina, uterus and breasts.

In men, degenerative changes in the testes and other organs of the body bring about more gradual changes in sexual functions, though there are again wide individual differences. Structural changes take place in the testes and prostate gland, and fewer sperms are produced. The concept of a 'male climacteric' has not been adequately validated.

Normal age-changes in hormone secretion and hormone balance, and especially age-changes in the hormones concerned with sexual functions, seem to be less critical in the biology of human ageing than had been supposed. The endocrine glands have specific but interrelated functions. They atrophy somewhat with age, but at different rates, so that the overall balance of hormones, including male and female sex hormones (both of which occur in men and women), is altered and compensatory reactions take place. At the time of life known variously as the involutionary period, menopause or climacteric, pituitary gonadotropins (hormones which act upon the ovaries and the testes) are excreted in the urine in increased quantities; this can be regarded as evidence of a compensatory reaction to diminished ovarian and testicular function.

(s) Sex

Although sexual relationships between suitable partners can be maintained until quite late in life, there is normally a gradual reduction with age in the frequency of copulation and all types of sexual behaviour. The exact nature of the complex anatomical and physiological changes underlying the reduction in sex and reproduction is not clear. The absence of adequate stimulus (brought about perhaps by over-familiarity, reduced compatibility with the normal sexual partner, or lack of opportunity for sexual relations with more desirable partners) may contribute to the reduction of sexual activity. If a man is several years older than his wife, the reduction in frequency of sexual relations is more likely to be determined by his sexual capacity than hers. Men whose wives are considerably younger than they are, have an advantage in life expectancy over men whose wives are older than they (see Foster et al., 1984). This is not necessarily a function of improved and prolonged wifely care but may also reflect the viability of men who can attract young wives.

References and Suggestions for Further Reading

Corso, J. F., *Aging Sensory Systems and Perception*, New York: Praeger, 1981.

Finch, C. E. and Schneider, E. L. (eds), *Handbook of the Biology of Aging*, New York: Van Nostrand Reinhold, 1985.

Foster, D., Klinger-Vartabedian, L. and Wispé, L., 'Male longevity and age differences between spouses', *Journal of Gerontology*, *39*, 1984, 117–20.

Hinchcliffe, R. (ed.), *Hearing and Balance in the Elderly*, London: Churchill Livingstone, 1983.

Kenney, R. A., *Physiology of Aging: A Synopsis*, Chicago: Year Book Medical Publishers, 1982.

Miles, L. E. and Dement, W. C., *Sleep and Aging*, New York: Raven Press, 1980.

Shephard, R. J., *Physical Activity and Aging*, London: Croom Helm, 1978.

Thornton, E. W., *Exercise and Ageing. An Unproven Relationship*, Liverpool: Institute of Human Ageing, 1984.

van Toller, C., Dodd, G. H. and Billing, A., *Ageing and Sense of Smell*, Springfield, IL: Charles C. Thomas, 1985.

Whitbourne, S. K., *The Aging Body. Physiological Changes and Psychological Consequences*, New York: Springer-Verlag, 1985.

Three
Biomedical Aspects of Ageing

1. Geriatric Medicine and Psychology

It is not possible to discuss the medical problems of old age in any sort of detail. It is, however, interesting to know what the major concerns are in geriatric medicine. Among those that Brocklehurst and Hanley (1976) list are the following:

(a) cerebral syndromes: arising from impairment of the blood supply to the brain, cerebral arteriosclerosis, transient ischaemic attack, stroke, temporal arteritis, drop attack (failure of postural mechanisms);
(b) autonomic disorders: postural hypotension, hypothermia;
(c) falls: caused by impairment of postural mechanisms, muscular weakness, environmental hazards, poor vision, cerebral and autonomic dysfunction;
(d) mental confusion: chronic brain syndrome; 'symptomatic' confusional states;
(e) urinary and faecal incontinence;
(f) pressure sores;
(g) bone disease and fractures.

Brocklehurst and Hanley also list some characteristic features of disease in old age: anaemia, heart disease, disorders of the digestive system, disorders of electrolytes and body fluids, diabetes, infections, sensory deficits, nutrition, diseases of the peripheral vascular system, the muscles, joints and skeleton.

'Old age' is not a medical diagnosis, although the expression is sometimes so used for disorders which are common in late life and for which there is little effective medical intervention. Unfortunately, disorders which can be treated effectively are sometimes not properly diagnosed or not treated in the most appropriate way. This is a consequence partly of the complexities of biomedical conditions in late life, partly of an underemphasis on geriatric medical training, partly of 'socialization to ill health', i.e. the tendency to accept poorer health in late life as natural and inevitable.

It should now be obvious that the physical basis of behaviour and psychological processes is liable to innumerable faults during adult life and old age. Some of these faults produce clear symptoms, some can be cured or alleviated. Others, however, produce no clear symptoms; they may or may not be apparent at autopsy; and no doubt many are at present beyond scientific understanding or professional intervention. It is important to recognize the complexities of ageing, not only in its biological aspects but also in its social and behavioural aspects, for only then can we hope to avoid what has been called 'therapeutic nihilism'.

Our biomedical condition in late life is one in which there is a general dilapidation of the physical fabric of the body and a reduction in functional abilities brought about by the cumulative effects of normal ageing. This condition is aggravated by a variety of pathological disorders, including possibly mental disorder leading to a breakdown in the organization of behaviour and experience. If our environment is disadvantaged and socially unsupportive, the risks of a worsening condition are greatly increased. Our 'reserves', our 'margins of safety', are much reduced and we are more vulnerable than before. Eventually, any one of a variety of causes will bring about death.

Death in late life, usually in hospital, has become the normal expectation. The main causes are well known. Unfortunately, the process of dying is often accompanied by distressing physical and mental disorders – pain, nausea, respiratory difficulties, mental confusion. In recent years there has been a considerable advance in the medical and nursing care of the dying, and special hospitals – hospices – have been set up in many areas, where much can be done, through skilled nursing and the use of analgesics and counselling, to reduce pain and mental anguish.

Physical illnesses in late life naturally produce psychological stresses – because of pain, anxiety, discomfort and frustration generally. Interest in the psychological aspects of health and illness has been growing rapidly in recent years. This new 'health psychology' is an extension of the traditional work in clinical psychology, which had been concerned mainly with mental illness; it is concerned with the prevention of illness and injury, with the promotion of healthy life-styles, with health education and with all health-related aspects of behaviour and experience.

One of the more important areas of geriatric medicine is that of mental confusion. It presents serious problems of management for care-givers whether at home, in residential institutions or in hospital. It is usual to separate out two sorts of mental impairment in late life: dementia, sometimes called chronic brain syndrome or failure; and pseudodementia, or symptomatic mental confusion. Dementia gets progressively worse, although further life expectation is short. Symptomatic mental confusion is a temporary disturbance associated with one or more specific causes, such as heart failure, depression, infection, cerebral lesion, metabolic imbalance, stress, or drug misuse. By definition, it is relieved by effective removal of the underlying cause. However, symptomatic mental confusion is more likely to occur in those elderly whose debilitated physiological condition has predisposed them to cerebral impairment; for example, cerebral arteriosclerosis.

The word 'psychogeriatrics' is normally used to refer to the psychiatry of old age. Depression is another prominent mental disorder in later life, and in some cases may be mistakenly diagnosed as dementia. Psychology has an important role to play in psychogeriatrics, especially in relation to the psychological assessment of elderly patients – their mental state and functional capacities – and their treatment. A small proportion of elderly people suffer from severe mental disorders; a larger proportion have less disabling conditions which can be investigated and alleviated by recourse to drugs and psychological methods. Consider, for example, the psychometric aspects of assessment and treatment effects, the psychological aspects of communication between elderly patients and professional staff, the psychological techniques used in individual and family counselling and health education. The phrase 'geriatric psychology' refers to psychology related to the wider issues of health and welfare in later life; 'social gerontology' includes not only much of the psychology of later life but also sociology, social work and administration, economics, geography, anthropology and history, in so far as they deal with adult ageing.

There is considerable overlap and duplication in the subject-matter of these various disciplines, although the scientific and professional boundaries are clearly drawn. So, for example, workers in these different areas may refer to historical trends and demographic facts, to epidemiology, to health and social services, to family and social structures, to psychological assessment and treatment. Gerontology is essentially multidisciplinary and inter-disciplinary; that is to say, gerontologists should have some knowledge of aspects of ageing outside their specialized field and should be capable of communicating and working with other specialists.

Geriatric medicine needs to be closely integrated with professional social gerontology. A high proportion of elderly people, the vast majority in fact, reside in the community and make use of a wide range of health and social services, which require elaborate administrative arrangements. Of the population aged 65 and over, only about 5 per cent reside in residential homes, hospitals and nursing homes; the vast majority live in private households (a tiny fraction in lodgings). There are, however, 'patients at risk' who need to be listed and checked upon from time to time, domiciliary services – health visiting, meals on wheels, laundry – to be arranged, day hospitals and day centres to be run. Good physical and mental health depends upon a host of social, personal, economic and environmental factors.

The social character of geriatric medicine can be seen particularly well in relation to preventive work, health education, rehabilitation and long-term care, as well as in the support services recommended for care-givers looking after the elderly in the community and in residential homes. Even in hospital, the emphasis is on chronic rather than acute illness.

Community care of the elderly infirm is provided largely by the immediate family – usually spouse or daughter. The nature and scope of the care provided varies widely according to the condition of the elderly dependant and the personal circumstances of the care-givers. Various health and welfare services are available, not so much as a substitute for family care, but rather as back-up and support services that increase the total amount of care provided and ease the strain on hard-pressed family members. Many elderly infirm would be in institutional care but for their families, and those lacking immediate family are more likely to need it. Among the services that may be provided in the community are day hospitals, day centres, care-giver associations, holiday accommodation, meals, health and welfare visits, alarms, cleaning and laundry. The primary care-giver usually negotiates arrangements through medical, social and voluntary services.

Survey findings suggest that there is a considerable amount of unreported or untreated illness among the elderly in the community. This is perhaps a result of a number of factors: a fatalistic attitude towards the infirmities of later life; lack of adequate health education, i.e. ignorance of the way the body works; unrewarding visits to physicians.

Considering the complexities of human anatomy, it is not difficult to appreciate the diversity of ailments in late life that impair functional capacity and well-being and yet, for one reason or another, are not properly treated: high blood pressure, low-level pain or discomfort in movement, problems with feet, and so on.

Many social sciences in addition to psychology contribute to what is called social gerontology and naturally have a bearing on geriatrics as a branch of social medicine; for example, sociology and social work, social administration, politics and economics, human geography, and even anthropology. But the scope of social gerontology is ever wider, for it has to take account of architecture, planning and technology generally, in its concern with housing, transport, communications and equipment.

The type of accommodation an elderly person occupies is obviously a critical factor in determining health and welfare. Safety and security should be paramount; ease of communication or surveillance is important; there should be easy access to health and welfare facilities; and the ordinary facilities of everyday life – transport, shops, social and recreational facilities – add to the overall quality of life.

Some elderly infirm reside in residential homes, referred to as 'old people's homes' or, in relation to 1948 legislation, 'Part III homes'. Others live in 'sheltered housing', i.e. purpose-built, supervised accommodation for the reasonably self-sufficient.

Another important aspect of ageing is the part played by voluntary and charitable organizations. These try to fill the gaps left by the health and welfare services on the one hand and family and neighbourhood support on the other. The government of the day may channel funds through them in the interests of the elderly.

2. Genetic and Environmental Factors

The relative importance and modes of interaction of genetic and environmental influences as they affect the process of human ageing are not clearly established; but the fact that species differ substantially in longevity means that genetic factors are important. The part played by evolutionary selection with regard to longevity, however, is not clear, and may be indirect. For example, many of the ailments which overtake us in middle and old age escape the selective pressure of evolution because they appear after the close of the reproductive phase of life; for instance, Huntington's chorea. Hence, any genetic predisposition to develop disorders like senile psychosis or hypertension tends not to be limited by differential rates of reproduction in a population, unlike haemophilia, for example, which is self-limiting. Furthermore, characteristics which make their appearance in late life – whether advantageous or disadvantageous to the individual – do so as a remote consequence of some 'counterpart' effect in the juvenile or reproductive period. Another aspect of this issue is the as yet unexplained difference in longevity for men and women, a sex difference also found in other species. Genetic influences are rarely simple: generally speaking, for complex functions anyway, genetic and environmental influences interact in ways which are difficult to explain.

Flies and mice have been selectively bred for longevity. A genetic influence on longevity has been confirmed by studies of twins. The difference between male monozygotic (identical) twins in age at death from natural causes is slightly less than that between male dizygotic (fraternal) twins; the effect is more pronounced for females. Long-term genetic effects in late life would be reflected in the close resemblance in physical condition and psychiatric breakdown of monozygotic twins.

In humans, grandparents and parents who live longer have grandchildren and children who also tend to live longer. The mother's longevity appears to be more closely correlated with offspring's longevity than does the father's, although his longevity is also related to offspring's longevity – especially in sons. Expectation of life for an offspring is partly determined by the age of the mother. Within limits earlier-born offspring have a longer expectation of life than later-born offspring. The effect is caused mainly by neo-natal mortality, premature births, stillbirths and malformations, but a small differential advantage in longevity persists for earlier-born as compared with later-born children. It is difficult to disentangle the 'order of birth' variable from the 'maternal age' variable. The effects of maternal age on offspring need not be confined to obvious kinds of catastrophe but include varying degrees of minor influence. Some of the characteristics of later-born as compared with earlier-born children which are presently attributed to sibling relationships and parent–child relationships might arise from the deeper constitutional (but non-genetic) factors associated with the mother's biological age.

Genetic factors, disease processes, normal ageing and environmental conditions are all involved to a greater or lesser extent in the disorders of adult life and old age. Genetic susceptibility to bronchitis, for example, may not lead to bronchitis except in association with certain environmental factors such as smoking or air pollution, and probably others. Smoking and excessive consumption of alcohol predispose to illness and shorten life, more so for some individuals than for others. Emotional stress, social isolation and dietary factors are suspected of playing a contributory role in certain disorders of adult life. When such connections can be demonstrated conclusively, then preventive and ameliorative measures can be developed. However, even if genetic make-up is a necessary and important cause of a mental or physical illness, it does not follow that the condition cannot be alleviated; certain metabolic disorders, such as phenylketonuria, have a genetic origin and yet respond to treatment.

Although many ailments of old age are incurable, modern medicine has revolutionized human society by increasing the average expectation of life by many years. This has been achieved mainly by a reduction in infant mortality and by the successful treatment of diseases such as smallpox and diphtheria, and the control of tuberculosis and diabetes. The effect has been to increase vastly the expectation of life of young people, as shown in Table 3.1 and Figures 3.1 and 3.2. The further expectation of life for older people, however, has changed very little over the period for which adequate records are available; there may have been a decrease, even, because of the survival to later ages nowadays of people who are less robust. It appears that 120 years is about the upper limit of human longevity. In the United Kingdom the average expectation of life at birth is about 70 years for men and 76 years for women; and, short of a further

Table 3.1 The Expectation of Life

Year	Males			Females		
	1901	1961	1981	1901	1961	1981
Further expectation of life:						
at birth	48.0	67.9	69.8	51.6	73.8	76.2
1 year	55.0	68.6	69.6	57.4	74.2	76.1
10 years	51.4	60.0	60.8	53.9	65.6	67.2
20 years	42.7	50.4	51.2	45.2	55.7	57.4
30 years	34.6	40.9	41.6	36.9	46.0	47.6
40 years	26.8	31.5	32.0	29.1	36.5	38.0
50 years	19.7	22.6	23.1	21.6	27.4	29.0
60 years	13.4	15.0	15.6	14.9	19.0	20.6
70 years	8.4	9.3	9.5	9.2	11.7	13.2
80 years	4.9	5.2	5.5	5.4	6.3	7.3

Further expectation of life at various age-levels for males and females separately in the United Kingdom, 1901, 1961 and 1981; based on *Social Trends*, no. 16, 1986

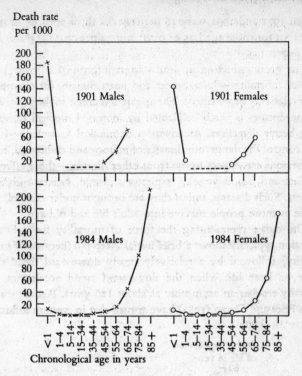

Death rate
per 1000

Figure 3.1 Death rates per 1000 persons at several age-levels for males and females separately in the United Kingdom, 1901 and 1984; based on *Social Trends*, no. 2, 1971 and *Social Trends*, no. 16, 1986

biological and medical revolution, it seems unlikely that this average can be pushed much beyond the early eighties. People aged 80 today can expect to live on only a little longer than people aged 80 did in previous centuries, that is about five and a half years for men and seven for women. Although medical advances have not extended the natural maximum span, they have, through new surgical techniques and drugs, enabled more people to approach closer to this limit. In round figures, the projected increases in the population of the UK between 1971 and 1991 were 16 per cent for those aged 65 or over, 37 per cent for those aged 75 or over, and 42 per cent for those aged 85 or over.

The great reduction in deaths from infection has made other causes of mortality – lung cancer and heart disease, for example – appear relatively more salient. The apparent increase in the prevalence of some diseases is partly explained by increased medical resources giving better detection. As advances in medical knowledge bring under control the dangerous diseases of infancy and childhood, more adult persons can expect to die from other diseases – those affecting the heart and blood vessels, respiratory disease, cancer and brain disorders. Such diseases, unless they are brought under control, will increase as more people survive into adult life and old age.

The curve representing the force of mortality for a human population typically shows a brief initial sharp fall (because of infant mortality) followed by a relatively steady downward trend until middle or later life when the downward trend accelerates and eventually reaches an asymptote at about 120 years. Recent studies such as Fries and Crapo (1981) have argued that in western industrial

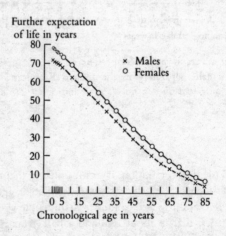

Figure 3.2 Further expectation of life in years for males and females separately in England and Wales, 1982–4; based on Office of Population Censuses and Surveys, *Mortality Statistics, 1984, England and Wales*, 1986

societies we are moving towards a 'rectangular' survival curve, in which the rate of mortality will be low until late in life when the rate will increase sharply as the fixed upper limit is approached. Such a rectangularization depends upon advances in biology and medicine which will delay the onset of existing disorders and thus reduce the average duration of chronic illness in late life, and on the existence of a fixed upper limit to longevity and of a limited number of causes of mortality. The prospect is fairly promising; the effect would be to distribute age at death narrowly around our species specific lifespan, perhaps 80 years; see Figure 3.3.

3. Normal and Pathological Ageing

The biological changes associated with adult life are fairly gradual, although actual 'rates' of ageing are difficult to validate. Degenerative effects accumulate and the individual normally dies as the proximate result of the breakdown of a vital organic process. Different parts of the body begin to degenerate at different ages and deteriorate at different rates. Death can be medically defined by the cessation of circulation, respiration or brain function, but 'recoveries' are not unknown and the functions of the body do not all end abruptly at the same moment. In senescence, they become gradually more unstable and uncoordinated. Senescence arises from the cumulative ill effects of damage and disease, or from degenerative processes inherent in ageing cells and tissues, or from an accumulation of, or deficiency in, biochemical substances. A combination of these and other causes is possible.

Senescence is a general biological impairment which increases the likelihood of death or 'force of mortality' in later life as seen, for example, in the greater liability of older people to secondary infections and complications following an accident. Curves of mortality (graphs showing the increasing number of deaths at successively higher ages) can be described by mathematical expressions such as Gompertz or Makeham functions. Mathematical and statistical techniques are used extensively in biological research in ageing, as in social and behavioural gerontology (see Chapter Eleven); the aim is not merely to describe observed phenomena but to test theories which purport to explain the effects of ageing. Figures 3.4 and 3.5 illustrate mortality rates and survival curves respectively.

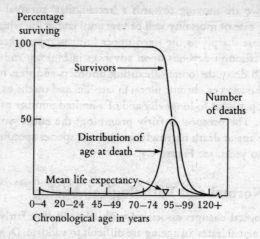

Figure 3.3 An idealized 'rectangular' survival curve with a corresponding distribution of age at death; see the text for further details

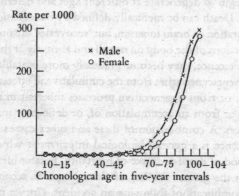

Figure 3.4 The force of mortality: death rates per 1000 population for males and females separately at several age-levels in England and Wales, 1984; based on Office of Population Censuses and Surveys, *Mortality Statistics, 1984, England and Wales*, 1986

By one definition, physical and mental diseases in old age are pathological conditions relatively distinct from, although superimposed upon and interacting with, the normal patterns of biological

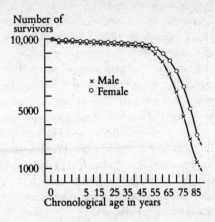

Figure 3.5 Survival curves for males and females separately in England and Wales, 1982–4; based on Office of Population Censuses and Surveys, *Mortality Statistics, 1984, England and Wales,* 1986

ageing and psychological change. Alternatively, ageing can be regarded simply as an accumulation of pathological processes, which eventually kill off the individual by interfering with a vital function of the body. Certain kinds of disease tend to afflict the young; others, such as heart disease, some respiratory disorders, cancer and organic psychoses, tend to afflict older people. To die a 'natural death' in old age is to die from one or other of the non-violent causes entered on death certificates. Subjective estimates of our health are rather like estimates of our driving skill; we tend to judge ourselves as above average.

The distinction between normal and pathological ageing is convenient, but it may be misleading. Adult ageing in the sense of deterioration of function can be observed, and partly accounted for, in terms of pathological processes; but longevity in the absence of senescence is a hypothetical entity, like the philosopher's stone, and may remain so. Stripping away man's diseases to get at the 'intrinsic' causes of ageing may be rather like peeling an onion to get at its core.

Korenchevsky, in *Physiological and Pathological Ageing*, made much of the fact that some elderly human subjects (and animals) possess physiological capacity equal to or better than those of young subjects; he argued that this is evidence for the existence of primary (non-pathological) ageing. Similarly, some elderly subjects possess physiological capacities well below those of young subjects; he argued that this is evidence for the existence of secondary (pathological) ageing. The argument, however, is circular; pathological ageing is defined in terms of a substantial loss or negative deviation in functional capacity compared with a young/normal standard; normal ageing by the absence of such deviation. However, there are wide individual differences in functional capacity, and dangers in making inferences from cross-sectional studies (comparing different people at different ages). Thus, overlap between statistical distributions of psychological or physiological measures for young and old subjects is not sufficient to support the hypothesis that there are two kinds of ageing. Irregularities and discontinuities in statistical distributions are the usual indication that something is 'abnormal' – like the effects of a late-acting genetic factor, a threshold effect in some cumulative process, or a disease. Similarly a distribution of difference measures, i.e. a distribution of the differences between subjects at young and older ages, has to be discontinuous or at least markedly different from normal in order to support the hypothesis that some age-effects are 'pathological' rather than 'normal'.

A wide range of differences between elderly individuals is not incompatible with the hypothesis that adult ageing is a summation of pathological conditions. Individuals differ widely at all ages, not only in the types and degrees of pathology that they exhibit, but also in all kinds of 'normal' physiological and psychological functions. Only hypothetical subjects are free from pathology and damage. Either they cannot exist or they cannot become senescent. In the latter case, they cannot die from disease or injury, so they endure indefinitely unless switched off or run down like some sort of biological clock. The issue of normal versus pathological ageing cannot be resolved unless these terms are defined independently of each other.

Severe sensory and motor impairments – blindness and other visual defects, deafness, paralyses, disablements – become more frequent as age advances. Much depends upon standards of comparison: an old man's blood pressure may be normal relative to that of his age-group, but abnormal relative to that of a young healthy group;

the discrepancy between an old woman's vocabulary and abstract reasoning may be normal for her age and yet show that marked intellectual impairment has taken place since she was a young adult. A physical or mental condition that is common among old people may be regarded as normal, not pathological, whereas if it seriously disables a few older people it may be regarded as pathological. One might say, paradoxically, that there are lots of normal old people but no healthy ones. One serious consequence is that many disabilities are passively accepted as a necessary part of growing old, when in fact effective prevention, treatment and prosthetic aid are available. The older person's self-assessment of his or her health differs from the assessment made by the physician; and the objective health needs of the elderly as a whole greatly exceed the resources allocated to meet demand.

Biomedical advances can be expected to lead eventually to: first, the prevention or alleviation of some physical and mental disorders of adult life and old age; second, the prolongation of normal adult vigour and an increase in average life expectancy; and possibly, third, an extension of the present upper limit of longevity. Improvements in the treatment of physical and mental ill health, however, are not always followed up by corresponding improvements in rehabilitation and social welfare. Poverty, loneliness, squalor, undernourishment and unhappiness contribute to the general burden of ill health in old age and reduce the likelihood that medical and psychiatric treatment will produce lasting effects.

More people are surviving to experience the environmental hazards of adult life and to develop physical and mental disorders of late onset. The pattern of physical and mental disease in old age could be altered by changes in medical and psychiatric care, and by social and economic changes in, for example, social attitudes and living standards. The costs involved in putting into effect preventive, ameliorative and remedial measures must be measured against the benefits derived from increased productivity, longer working lives, decreased rates of illness, less dependence and happier individuals. Old age is not entirely a consequence of biological degeneration; it is partly the product of political, economic and historical conditions. One of the stages in our conception of the human life-path, it is culturally defined by our beliefs about ourselves and nature, and subject to prevailing attitudes and values. Human ageing is thus a biosocial phenomenon and susceptible to some control.

4. Biomedical Theories of Ageing

The main aim in formulating theories of ageing is to conceptualize the causal paths taken by degenerative processes. Some investigations are concerned only with certain segments of certain classes of degenerative pathways; for example, the onset and course of a stroke, psychophysiological changes during the menopause, or adjustment to retirement. The main biological theories of ageing, naturally, attempt to portray the major pathways and constraints in the physical basis of ageing.

Even in a protected environment, there are bound to be adverse cumulative effects from disease and injury, which kill off individual members of a species. Where the environment contains dangers – in civilized communities these include traffic hazards, pollution and infectious organisms – even the luckiest person is bound, sooner or later, to sustain injuries and die. Individual members of a species, including human beings, die perhaps as part of the process of biological evolution – without individual variation there could be no selection, without population limitation there could be no reproduction and survival of individuals; genetic variation is built into living systems. The range of defects and hazards that living systems must contend with is considerable, but the fact that living things grow old and die is less impressive than the fact that they live at all.

Biological theories of ageing are too diverse and too technical to be dealt with at any length in an introductory book on gerontology. The fundamental mechanisms of biological ageing are not known for certain; and some of the conceptual issues, such as the distinction between normal and pathological ageing, or between functional and chronological age, have not yet been settled.

One theory is that cells, like tiny computers, are programmed by a genetic code which is effective up to about the age at which evolutionary forces cease to have any selective effects, i.e. towards the end of the normal period of reproduction. After this, the programme carries on for a time, but it has not been evolved to cope with the further effects of ageing, which, as we have seen in relation to the non-renewal of nerve cells (Chapter Two), may be severe. Nor will it cope indefinitely with the long-term consequences and accumulations of injuries and infections. This long-term inadequacy of the genetic programme may mean that we grow old by 'default' rather than by 'design' of nature.

The idea that ageing is genetically 'programmed' is difficult to accept, because of the diversity of causes of, and ages at, death, particularly in long-lived organisms. The idea of a 'species specific lifespan' means only that under given environmental conditions there is a 'characteristic' or 'average' lifespan for that species. This could well be the outcome of a variety of independent factors, each of which contributes some measure of morbidity, which eventually produces mortality. If we ignore infant mortality and premature deaths in early adult life, the distribution of ages at death is relatively 'normal', i.e. bell-shaped, the sort of distribution produced by the cumulative effects of random events. Human embryonic lung fibroblasts can be grown in culture, but cease to grow after about 50 doublings — the 'Hayflick limit', — either because of an intrinsic counter or because of design default.

Another theory is based on the fact that the production of antibodies by the 'immune system' declines during adult life and old age. Living organisms defend themselves from infection by forming antibodies which are capable of identifying and reacting against foreign or abnormal cells and proteins. The theory is that either (a) the immune system becomes less sensitive to differences between the body's own cells and substances and those that are foreign, or (b) the cells of the body undergo genetic variation (somatic mutation) and become liable to attack by the immune system, which identifies them as foreign and destroys them with specific antibodies. The antibodies produced by an aged immune system may be faulty; hence two sorts of error may occur — foreign elements are not identified, normal elements are identified as foreign and destroyed. These errors lead to pathological changes as well as to an aggravation of the normal degenerative processes. Some medical research in immunology is directed towards the prevention and treatment of autoallergic diseases.

There could be a cumulative loss of chromosome fragments arising from errors in mitosis (cell division). Some types of error may be more likely than others, or more likely to occur under special conditions. Not all lymphocytes contain the normal number of chromosomes (23 pairs) and aneuploid cells (with a deviant number of chromosomes) appear to increase in frequency with age and to be associated with adverse effects. The nerve cells depend upon other cells in the body, such as glial cells; so they could be affected indirectly by changes in the chromosomes of these cells, although nerve cells are fixed post-mitotic cells.

Failure of the organism to synthesize proteins correctly in the required amounts leads eventually to functional impairment. Cosmic ionizing radiation may produce abnormalities in DNA; free radicals may produce cross-linkages in DNA macromolecules; somatic mutation in the lymphocytes may impair immune reactions. Failure of the capacity to synthesize proteins has been regarded as an important, perhaps a basic, cause of ageing – possibly the result of cumulative errors in the complex process whereby DNA gives rise to the synthesis of amino acid chains. The 'errors' are thought to include those arising from radiation, chemical action, cross-linking and breakage. However, not only are the mechanisms underlying the failure of protein synthesis unclear, but there are almost certainly other basic causes of ageing; for example, intrinsic limitations, 'wear and tear', infection.

Molecular mechanisms within individual cells in the body are capable of repairing damage to DNA and of correcting errors in metabolism such as enzyme function or protein synthesis. These mechanisms, however, cannot meet every contingency, and so cells degenerate and die. The cumulative effect is to reduce the functional efficiency of the various organs and systems of the body and of the organism as a whole. The identification of specific repair mechanisms, however, would create possibilities for therapeutic intervention to retard the process of ageing, and constitute a theoretical advance. Measures designed to prevent or neutralize the adverse effects of free-radicals and toxic substances are being developed; some anti-oxidants, for example, appear to prolong life. But the biochemistry of living and dying is outside the scope of this book.

Some physiological functions are associated with the natural rhythms and periodicities – electrical activities in the brain, sleep, heartbeats, ovulation – reflecting clock-like biological mechanisms measuring 'life time' rather than 'physical time'. Genetic mechanisms may operate as switches, starting or stopping biological processes at various 'logical' points in juvenile development and adult ageing; the ages at which these genetic switches operate, however, may be affected by environmental factors which accelerate or retard development and ageing. Further research should throw light on the part played by 'biological clocks' in human ageing.

Experimental studies with animals show that the effects of ionizing radiation are cumulative and lead to the earlier deaths of exposed organisms for various causes. Radiation increases the incidence of some diseases which occur earlier in life, and this has the statistical effect of reducing the average age at death from diseases which occur later. The adverse effects of radiation are greater for older animals, perhaps because older animals have weaker powers of recovery and restoration. The effects of small doses for human beings, however, are difficult to assess. Irradiation effects are by no means simple and do not provide conclusive evidence for a biological theory of ageing, such as cross-linking of molecules, or auto-immunity.

Experimental studies of longevity in animals and surveys of treatment effects in humans show that environmental factors – such as nutrition and drugs, radiation and toxic substances, temperature and stresses – can affect longevity and functional capacity. The advent of man-made substances and man-made conditions of life means that novel causes of ageing are evolving. The complexities of biochemistry and the uniqueness of the individual make it likely that, in addition to the causes and pathways of ageing which are common to large numbers of people, some may affect only a few or perhaps only one person.

References and Suggestions for Further Reading

Brocklehurst, J. C. and Hanley, T., *Geriatric Medicine for Students*, Edinburgh: Churchill Livingstone, 1976.

Fries, J. F. and Crapo, L. M., *Vitality and Aging. Implications of the Rectangular Curve*, San Francisco: W. H. Freeman, 1981.

Health Education Council, *Health in Old Age* (Publications and Training Aids), London: Health Education Council, 1985.

Korenchevsky, V., *Physiological and Pathological Ageing* (ed. G. H. Bourne), New York and Basel: S. Karger, 1961.

Lamb, M. J., *Biology of Ageing*, London: Blackie, 1977.

Manton, K. G., 'Changing concepts of morbidity and mortality in the elderly population', *Milbank Memorial Fund Quarterly / Health and Society*, 60, 1982, 183–244.

Robinson, K., 'Older women – a literature review', *Journal of Advanced Nursing*, 11, 1986, 153–60.

Verbrugge, L. M., 'Longer life but worsening health? Trends in health and mortality of middle-aged and older persons', *Milbank Memorial Fund Quarterly / Health and Society*, 62, 1984, 475–519.

Four
Social Policy and the Elderly

1. Introduction

The boundaries between different policy areas overlap. It is, therefore, preferable to focus on the elderly as a 'client group' and examine social policy in relation to that group. Before the 1908 legislation which introduced pensions for people over 70, the United Kingdom had no official chronological age after which people could be counted as elderly. Since that time, social policy relating to the elderly has been largely concerned with income maintenance – all other needs were subsumed under provisions for the general population. Of course, the inevitable concentration of elderly people in public health hospitals and workhouse infirmaries influenced the provision made. In the United Kingdom, not until the Second World War (1939–45) were the elderly identified as needing special health and welfare provision. The 'Poor Law' mentality persisted for many years in relation to welfare for the elderly.

Social policy is a large and complicated subject. It covers such matters as safeguarding living standards, especially at the lower end of the socio-economic scale, through various forms of social security; coping with relationships between the individual and the State, for example, through personal services at local level; providing, usually through a mixture of public, private and voluntary services, physical and mental health care for the population at large. It deals similarly with education, employment (including unemployment and occupational training), retirement, housing, transport, and other, less obvious features of large-scale, modern industrialized societies.

It does not follow that a country's health and social welfare policies are internally coherent, consistent over time, or free from external constraints, nor that attempts to implement a stated policy necessarily result in the consequences intended.

Social policy and practice for the elderly exist in a context of political and economic considerations. Because this context is subject to change, this introductory account does not describe existing policies in detail, but aims to draw attention to some of the *psychological* aspects of social policy for the elderly and to remind readers of the wider institutional, organizational and cultural factors that influence individual behaviour.

The elderly as a group are less productive (indeed, social retirement policy compels some of them to be so) and they consume more of certain kinds of goods and services; for example, those associated with health and welfare. The notion of the 'burden of ageing' suggests that providing goods and services for the dependent elderly (retired or infirm) is a burden carried by younger productive people. As a client group the elderly have been given relatively low priority. The Beveridge Report of 1942 (para. 236) stated: 'It is dangerous to be in any way lavish to old age until adequate provision has been assured for all other vital needs – such as the prevention of disease and adequate nutrition of the young.' Financing dependency at different stages of life is a complex business. However, the social and economic conditions of the elderly affect and are in turn affected by the social and economic conditions of the society of which they form a part.

Welfare policy is based on social reciprocity over the lifespan. The transfer of goods and services from the more productive to the less productive or non-productive is not static; it changes as the individual passes through childhood, adult life and old age, and as society's political and economic history unfolds. Political debate focuses on organizing the level of funding, collecting and distributing payments; other issues include that of separating out matters of public interest from matters of personal concern.

Considerations of social policy and its implementation inevitably raise ethical issues; for example, how should a country utilize its material and human resources and share them out among competing claimants. Scientific research can generate information relevant to these issues, but cannot usually settle them directly. We need to remain alert to the distinction between positive and normative issues, i.e. between 'what is' and 'what ought to be', between 'what can be done' and 'what should be done'.

Social policies in a democratic society are supposed to promote the conditions which facilitate and reward desirable behaviour, e.g. keeping physically fit and mentally well-adjusted, working productively, co-operating with the police, and so on; and to discourage undesirable behaviour, e.g. cruelty, drunkenness, drug-taking. They may not be well defined or vigorously implemented because of lack of consensus or resistance by vested interests.

The ways in which a social policy is implemented do not necessarily correspond with what the policy intended. Do meals on wheels result in better nutrition, or discourage people from cooking for themselves or lessen contact with family and neighbours? Does sheltered housing provide precisely the accommodation its residents need? Is the administrative cost of providing goods and services through the public sector excessive? Are certain kinds of provision stigmatizing? Cheap travel for the elderly is universally acceptable; supplementary pensions, on the other hand, may be felt as stigmatizing. How are the individual needs of the elderly translated into legitimate claims? And what factors affect the 'gatekeepers' who decide on the legitimacy? Communication and co-operation between the different parties involved in the provision of services is particularly important because the elderly make use of a variety of facilities administered by different organizations, e.g. hospitals, social services departments, voluntary agencies, housing and transport departments.

Deficiencies in one area of provision may have profound effects on others. For example, a lack of sheltered accommodation or community support may delay the discharge of patients from hospital.

Social provision for the elderly varies from one western industrial country to another, although broad common trends can be identified. Readers interested in this area as it affects the United Kingdom may care to consult sources such as Hill (1983, Chapter 2) and Bruce (1968, 4th edn). Present-day social policies are the outgrowths of historical processes, rather than rational solutions to current problems. Just as earlier social policies were, in part, reactions to new social conditions – urbanization, infection, the exploitation of children – so more recent social policies affecting the elderly have been, in part, reactions to the increasing proportion of people rendered physically and mentally infirm or industrially unproductive and thus economically dependent.

Since 1948, in the United Kingdom, there have been a number of changes in social policy affecting the economic status of the elderly – changes in pensions, supplementary benefits, taxation and so on. Fortunately, several organizations, including Age Concern and Help the Aged, have emerged and function in part as pressure groups for mobilizing voluntary resources, with help from local and national government, to assist in a variety of ways, such as meals on wheels, home helps, day centres, mutual aid, which have pioneered the way for statutory provision. The Federation of National Old Age Pensions Associations, as its name implies, has a more specific focus of interest. The National Pre-Retirement Association arose as a form of support and guidance for industrial workers and local authority employees and has since become more consumer-orientated, offering guidance, courses and information to the recently retired and those who are about to retire. Among other voluntary bodies is Cruse, which helps the widowed, and the Alzheimer Disease Society.

2. Policy-Making

Social policy for the elderly derives in part from the broader policies and programmes introduced from time to time by a country's government; for example, those concerned with social order, taxation, management of the economy and health. Various government departments help to formulate policy options and preferences and to implement specific programmes, influencing and being influenced by pressure groups and by other organizations of a statutory, voluntary or intermediate sort, e.g. those concerned with research, co-ordination and the provision of services.

For social policy for the aged to include provision for voluntary euthanasia, or change the statutory age of retirement, or require employers to take on a certain proportion of older workers, the proponents of such policies would have to convince the government in power and the various interested parties that the schemes were workable and would lead to substantial benefits. The policies would then have to be translated into legislation and brought into effect by existing or newly created agencies. Opponents of the proposals and influential groups on both sides would exert pressure, including, of course, popular appeal through the media and local action. Ideological factors (those concerned with basic beliefs and values about human society) would play a major part in the associated debates and developments, perhaps completely obscuring the factual and rational aspects of the proposed policy.

Policy proposals often arise as a consequence of changes in sections of a society. If these sectional interests reflect a general shift in social values, ideologies and morality, they are more likely to find acceptance. Sometimes policies are proposed in order to establish how public opinion has moved or to stimulate interest. As with euthanasia, the proposers may not expect them to be accepted.

Generally speaking, social policy takes the form of legislation which sets out broad principles – aims and methods – but leaves the detailed operation to be worked out at the level of implementation. There is usually considerable room for discretion (the exercise of personal judgement and bias) in applying rules and following procedures.

In a democracy, there is scope for continual evaluation and revision of social policies; for example, through questions in parliament and committees of inquiry. Regional and local considerations may affect social policy for the elderly; for example, differences in social attitudes, urban/rural differences, and ethnic differences. Implementation of policy varies with different methods of local and regional funding and is complicated by different levels of communication, overlapping aims, etc.

The absence of a coherent and explicit national policy for research and teaching in gerontology is one expression of a general lack of concern for science policy, and especially social and behavioural science policy, at national level. There are signs, however, of increased concern, triggered no doubt by the recent reduction in resources and by the growing demand that science, technology and education should be making a more substantial contribution to the nation's economic and social well-being.

A thorough examination of the policy issues in research and teaching in gerontology depends upon knowledge of the resources available, how these resources are allocated, the amount and variety and quality of the results produced, their utilization, and the way gerontology is regarded by the general public and those responsible for allocating resources. These could be regarded as research priorities in their own right. Science policy is not simply a matter of allocating financial and other resources, it is also about justifying and advocating particular policy options to ensure that the interests of individual research workers coincide with the national interest. This is best achieved by consensus – by enabling research workers and educators to play a part in policy-making.

3. The Elderly as a Political Force

Since middle-aged and older people constitute a sizeable fraction of the electorate, they should be able to exert pressure through the ballot box to return candidates pledged to pursue policies favourable to the elderly. There are indeed pressure groups which seek to influence policy and voting, and most parties are sensitive to the potential voting power of older people and of their younger sympathizers. Nor are older people underrepresented in government, in its broadest sense, in large industrial societies. So those representing the elderly will get a hearing. The situation is complicated, of course, by the increased physical and mental infirmity of people in late life, by differential death rates as between men and women and the different socio-economic classes, and by a not uncommon tendency to 'disengage' from the mainstreams of industrial and social activity. This virtually eliminates 'direct action' by the aged as a political grouping or through affiliation to one political party. New social ideas are more often put forward by younger adults (see Chapter Five) although older adults are more likely to hold leading positions in established social organizations. It may be that our ideas and values become ultra-stable, conservative and resistant to change in later life.

No one particular age-group is likely to become a major political force. The wide differences between people – in ability and education, in attitudes, in socio-economic status – limit agreement on policy matters. Chronological age is only one of many characteristics that help to shape a person's political behaviour. Furthermore, individuals usually have social relationships with people of all ages and take the interests of those people into account when voicing their opinions and casting their votes. In a democracy, the health and welfare of any one segment of the population tends to depend on the health and welfare of the community as a whole, so it may be rather short-sighted to pursue narrow sectional interests. Political action by and on behalf of the elderly should be informed by social and economic policies which are in the general interest but directed particularly at those problems which disadvantage the elderly and may be remedied without disadvantaging others. Given scarcity of resources, this is easier said than done.

4. Social Prejudice

To support policies which favour a particular section of the population, a community needs to have a favourable image of that section and to see it as deserving resources relative to other favoured groups. People can have different views on the relative worth of different sorts of people, depending broadly upon their ideological outlook and their position in society. In a democratic society, the distribution of goods and services between different areas of interest and different segments of the population provides a crude and temporary measure of their relative importance, esteem or status.

It is a common belief among social gerontologists that old age and the elderly have a somewhat ambivalent 'image' in modern industrial democracies. There is evidence that old age is not regarded as a desirable stage of life (or as much of an improvement on the alternative!); it is not looked forward to (except perhaps briefly in the pre-retirement period); the elderly are seen not as fulfilling an essential or important role but as having withdrawn or been discarded from the mainstream. At the same time, most elderly are seen as worthy people, deserving support in their retirement and infirmity, and respect for their past contribution. Unfortunately, the prevalent image of late life is built around the notions of physical infirmity, uselessness and maladjustment; stereotyped prejudiced thinking typically identifies some of the more extreme unfavourable features of a group and generalizes these to the group as a whole. Consider how the elderly are portrayed in television and literature. In ordinary conversation, it is the *difficulties* presented by older people that tend to get discussed.

A neglected aspect of social attitudes towards the elderly is the loss of certain attributes by the elderly and the apparent lack of a protective and nurturant instinct on the part of offspring; this contrasts with normal social attitudes towards infants and young children (Bromley, 1978, pp. 22–30).

There is a wide range of differences between individual cases, so perhaps the most important advance to be made in social policy for later adult life and old age is to identify needs and define the relevant groups *without reference to chronological age*; this might eventually break down the stereotype of 'old age' and 'the elderly' and substitute for it a variety of smaller, better-defined client groups. The abolition of a statutory age of retirement (where it applies) and the introduction of flexible retirement schemes; greater provision for part-time and self-employment; greater recognition of and support for self-maintenance and mutual care; greater diversity of facilities and services for the mentally and physically impaired at all ages; a frame of reference using *particular* conditions and groups of people rather than crudely lumping together the 'elderly': such measures would help to destroy our present negative and stereotyped image of ageing. Unfortunately, late life tends to be accompanied by a wide variety of biological, psychological and social disadvantages which are not uncorrelated, although differences between individuals are wide. This makes it difficult to break up the concept of old age in the way suggested.

One alternative would be to redefine old age and to restrict it to a later chronological period. A distinction is sometimes drawn between the 'young-old', aged 60 to 74, and the 'old-old', aged 75 and over. This division is just as arbitrary as the retirement age, and there is no sharp transition in health and well-being at either age, but it is simple and convenient. The old-old are expected to increase as a proportion of the population in the United Kingdom over the next few decades whereas the young-old are not. Also the old-old on average have considerably more physical and mental impairment than the young-old, and so are expected to consume a substantial share of the resources available for health and welfare (see DHSS reports).

Eventually, with the help of medical and biological technology, improved standards of living and education, we can expect to restrict old age to an even later and shorter period of life (see Chapter Three, Section 2). Further improvements in the health and well-being of older people will both result from, and help to create, further changes in social policy.

5. Representing the Interests of the Elderly

How do the interests of the elderly get represented at the policy-making level, given as yet little direct input from the elderly themselves? We can assume, first, that there are some well-informed and reasonable people in national and local government who are aware of social trends and of the needs and resources of older people; second, that scientists, academics and other professionals advise policy-makers about the technicalities of providing resources for later life; third, that people of established ability and character can be relied upon to provide independent and disinterested views on policies; fourth, that the views of voluntary organizations and learned societies concerned with ageing and the aged are represented. Thus social policies for the elderly develop through political ideology and manoeuvre, institutional arrangements, moral and legal constraints, the available scientific or administrative and technical expertise, and advocacy by interested parties.

We should not neglect implicit social policy – that is to say, without being explicitly proposed and implemented as a particular course of action, various consequences follow from neglect or, indirectly, from other, stated policies. No government would propose a policy of increasing unemployment or motor vehicle accidents, but such might be the effects of other policies or of failure to introduce measures such as public works or road safety legislation.

Social policy as a whole is not necessarily coherent, i.e. free from internal contradictions. Policy analysis is concerned to identify such faults as are bound to arise because of the diverse, fragmented and multilevel way in which social policies are formed and implemented, and complex, cross-linked social systems are operated.

6. Programme Evaluation

Information relevant to the assessment of the courses of action that result from social policies can be collected through what is called programme evaluation, which is by no means a straightforward scientific method of investigation, but rather an exercise in the collective appraisal of social action.

Given the necessary resources and time-scale and the co-operation of the people involved it is possible to provide goods and services under a number of specified and reasonably well-controlled conditions. The consequences can be followed up and compared with those of alternative provision. However, the results are unlikely to be clear-cut; and in any event the programme may produce its major effects not through the goods and services it provides but through the increased appreciation of role relationships and co-operation that ensue from greater understanding of how the social system operates, especially in areas where people can exercise discretion in their professional judgements, e.g. approving financial benefits or medical treatment for infirmities, where actual practice may not coincide with stated policy.

Clearly, political considerations must affect people's response to the evaluation of a policy that they themselves develop or implement. Therefore they need to be closely involved in and informed about the exercise from the beginning. Reactions to programme evaluation depend, for example, on such things as professional status, trade union involvement and public opinion. In care for the elderly, voluntary effort and goodwill may be of considerable importance, so that appraisal may require particularly sensitive management.

7. Housing and Relocation

Housing is an interesting example of how welfare policy has its roots in assumptions derived from the old Poor Law concept of the client. In 1948, UK housing policy made little provision for the elderly; only recently has the home ownership ideal formed part of welfare policy for the elderly. This is a difficult area to review because of the apparent lack of easily available reports on the subject – but see Newson and Potter (1985). Clearly the physical structure and location of living accommodation for older people should meet, as far as possible, their disabilities and their changed social and economic circumstances. Thus warmth, absence of physical hazards, convenience, access to services, personal security, easy communication and the like come immediately to mind. Moreover, diverse types of accommodation are needed, together with the means to transfer between them as circumstances change.

The above desiderata are difficult and costly to meet, with the result that we find older people occupying a disproportionate share of poor-quality, unsuitable accommodation, especially in areas which are economically run down and have lost a high proportion of the working population and their children. In such areas, unless efforts have been made by the local authority to renovate old property and develop new industries and housing, elderly people may find themselves in poor and unsuitable homes. They compete for resources with other needy sections of the population.

The extent and variety of housing accommodation in the United Kingdom has changed a great deal in recent years and can be expected to continue to do so, in line with political and economic circumstances. Rented accommodation in the private sector is much less available, but there has recently been a boom in privately run residential homes for the elderly. Some local authority housing has been transferred to owner-occupiers, some sold off to private developers. There has been little deliberate development of retirement villages or areas, but some internal migration of retired people to holiday areas in coastal and country regions has led to marked imbalances in the age-structure of the local population with obvious consequences as regards demands for health and social services and public transport. The elderly internal migrants usually have a relatively high socio-economic status. The poorer elderly tend to stay on in the same locality, and may encounter difficulty finding more suitable accommodation, because of complications and delays in local authorities' rehousing schemes and the almost unavoidable differences in standards between privately owned and local authority housing.

Voluntary relocation in later life results from dissatisfaction with current accommodation (the house is now too large, too difficult to maintain, too far from relatives; the neighbourhood is no longer congenial) and from expectations about alternative accommodation (nearer to relatives and recreational and leisure facilities, better suited to one's needs, interests and abilities).

Relocation may be largely involuntary if deterioration in physical and mental health compels a move to residential or hospital care, either in one's own interests or for the health, welfare and safety of others. Housing developments – slum clearance, home improvements – may mean moves, temporary or permanent, from familiar surroundings. Relocation of the elderly infirm can be stressful and have undesirable consequences on health and personal adjustment. Like other sorts of stress – bereavement, financial loss – it can be alleviated or aggravated by the reactions of other people. Anticipation, preparation, visits, and a sense of retaining control over events, are important in helping the elderly infirm to cope with relocation.

In this sense, then, housing policy for the elderly is not just a matter of designing and building houses or apartments which are functionally effective (having regard to the ergonomics of daily living in later life) and aesthetically satisfying. It is also a matter of making them available in the right places at the right times, and of easing any transition.

A very small proportion of people in mid and later life are vagrants (mostly men) or homeless for various reasons, dealt with through local authority provision or through the voluntary charitable organizations.

Housing provides one example of the problem of developing social policies which take into account the needs and resources of the elderly. The average family needs different accommodation in different localities at different times. When the youngest child leaves home, a married couple may need smaller accommodation, or accommodation in another area. For the older owner-occupier the house is a valuable capital asset, but rates and maintenance may constitute a drain on resources. Domestic facilities and equipment, once regarded as luxuries, become part of normal everyday expectations as times change.

In the United Kingdom, residential accommodation for the elderly is provided by local authority social service departments under Part III of the 1948 National Assistance Act. These homes vary in terms of the number and sort of residents housed, the physical amenities, staffing and 'organizational' character or style of management. Ideally, a full and flexible range of health and social services should offer continuity, with professional staff, well-equipped buildings, and so on. In practice, resources seem insufficient to meet the needs of the elderly, and the administrative arrangements appear not to facilitate the transfer of resources between different departments except under specific joint funding arrangements, or to tailor resources to meet the needs of individual cases. For example, residential homes may have difficulty transferring mentally and physically frail persons to a hospital geriatric department because of a shortage of beds; the hospital, on the other hand, may have difficulty discharging patients who have benefited from the available treatment because the residential homes are short of staff capable of providing the level and type of care needed. The patients are subject to a wide variety of physical and mental disorders which are not all well understood or effectively treated. It may be possible for local arrangements to be made which, by guaranteeing admission and discharge between hospital and residential home, optimize the use of available facilities. Similarly, it may be possible to tailor domiciliary services (help with shopping, cleaning and visiting) to cater for the individual needs and circumstances of the elderly.

Ideally, again, housing policies would foster the provision of accommodation to facilitate moves from less to more appropriate settings; for example, small apartments in leisure-orientated areas, sheltered housing, retirement villages, residential homes, and so on. The barriers to relocation are partly psychological, involving feelings of security, familiarity and habit, and partly economic and demographic, involving the housing market, costs and population distribution. Moving house is an infrequent and major life-change for most people. In late life it may be stressful, unless positively wished for and properly managed (the elderly person should be fully informed and have a sense of control over events). Accommodation in later life is complicated by a variety of factors, such as changes in family relationships, loss of the marital partner, availability of health and welfare services, and in the wider context, developments in the private and public sectors of the economy.

Although one would expect private sector accommodation for the elderly to be subject to inspection and approval, it may be difficult to establish the criteria necessary to test whether, say, private sector rest homes or public sector residential homes meet an agreed standard, and expensive regularly to inspect and evaluate them, especially the day-to-day behaviour of management and staff.

Housing accommodation for the elderly illustrates the complexities of social policy, since we can appreciate the ways in which different strands of government policy interact, not necessarily by design, and the actual outcome may help to shape or define policies. For example, if private sector residential care for the elderly proved capable of setting and maintaining high standards, the procedures thus developed might be accepted as official 'policy' locally and nationally: an illustration of the way in which policy formulation and implementation may interact, and of the relationship between higher and lower levels of administration.

8. Social Security

In the United Kingdom, the main forms of expenditure on social security provisions are based on an underlying contract: (i) contractual insurance benefits for unemployment, sickness, widowhood and old age pension; (ii) non-contractual benefits based on the assessment of need in the form of supplementary benefit, supplementary pension, invalidity allowance and housing benefits; (iii) compensation for the extra burden of care, as for family allowance, invalid care allowance, attendance allowance. Social security, as its name implies, is intended to protect and support people who have insufficient means to maintain a socially acceptable minimum standard of living. However, prejudice against the 'undeserving poor' continues to restrict welfare provision, although the infirmities of old age provide a strong counter-argument. Social security arrangements are quite complicated; this in itself is a barrier to legitimate claims, especially by the elderly, apart from any failure to deal appropriately with the special needs and circumstances of the elderly and their caregivers.

A key date in social provision for the elderly in the United Kingdom was the introduction in 1908 of the Old Age Pensions Act, which was in part a response to dissatisfaction with the state of the country's economy and the health of its population. The old age pension first introduced was not contributory (paid for out of earnings) as now, but rather an extension of outdoor relief based on an assessment of the individual's means (personal resources). Further changes combining means-testing and insurance benefits culminated in the introduction of a comprehensive welfare system in 1948.

Wide individual differences between the elderly in needs, abilities and circumstances make it difficult to frame rules governing entitlement to social security benefits and more likely that inequities will arise because of discretionary judgements, or because the system does not have the resources to meet the demands made on it.

Entitlement to social security benefits can arise either directly through the principle of insurance – making small regular payments throughout one's working life in anticipation of needs arising later – or indirectly through 'citizen's rights' – with all that that might imply. The elderly person should therefore be in a strong legal and moral position to make claims on society. Unfortunately, circumstances change and expectations and promises cannot always be fulfilled. Furthermore, the elderly are not the only claimants on society's resources, so policies have to be developed and carried out in an attempt to reconcile competing claims.

The elderly's wide range of needs and disabilities are difficult to manage administratively because they tend to cut across convenient boundaries. An elderly person may be mentally and physically disabled and so need residential care, hospital treatment, legal protection and so on, all within a short space of time.

Although the total cost of providing services and facilities is huge, because of the size of the elderly population and the range of their disabilities, the expenditure is distributed unevenly and, for the majority, thinly. There is a continuing sense of frustration and injustice because, at times, even reasonable needs cannot be, or are not being, met, although all sorts of schemes have been explored in attempts to cope with the social problems of old age. For example, in some areas there are 'foster homes' or 'holiday homes' where the elderly can stay short term, providing relief for relatives or other care-givers, and agencies which provide domestic services on a contract basis. In the United Kingdom in recent years, the considerable expansion of residential homes for the elderly in the private sector has been accompanied by growing pressure for proper standards, inspection and licensing. In the public sector, co-operation with voluntary organizations has seen attempts to introduce greater flexibility into domiciliary services and to improve community care through day centres, luncheon clubs and the like.

The underlying assumption is that elderly people wish to lead as 'normal' a life as possible for as long as possible. This means living in the small primary groups of their own community (not segregated with strangers in a large institution), being independent (having the resources and the freedom to choose a particular style of life) and having a voice in the community (particularly through local and national pressure groups). The elderly are diverse in their beliefs and values but have some interests in common at both national and local level – for example, pensions, health care and transport – which they will voice in the community.

For the elderly who can no longer survive adequately in the community, residential and hospital care need not mean relinquishing their independence completely, although it must be admitted that administrative pressures and staff attitudes in institutions sometimes tend to restrict individual freedom of action more than is necessary. The elderly and/or their care-givers need to assert their democratic rights. In enlightened establishments, staff will encourage open discussion, participation in decision-making and accountability. The principle of self-determination can be applied even in the case of a life-or-death decision, but complications arise in connection with legality and ethics and when the person involved is mentally impaired. A sense of control over one's affairs is thought to be a major psychological factor in personal adjustment.

If the majority of the elderly are to lead 'normal' lives in the community, the community must adapt, just as it has adapted to the educational needs of children and the employment and family needs of young adults. It should make provision for the common health needs of the elderly, for their recreation, safety and participation; locate medical and social advisory centres at strategic points; register and visit regularly those elderly at risk; offer education and guidance. The new technologies in telecommunications and computing could contribute a great deal.

Local authorities are empowered to provide a range of services to the elderly – the best-known being residential care, home helps, meals, telephones, or structural alterations to the home. If the elderly person is disabled, an attendance allowance may be provided to pay for care. A care-giver may be entitled to an invalid care allowance. Local policy will determine, within the constraints of national policy, what money is available and how it is spent (bearing in mind the difficulties already described).

It has proved difficult to provide services evenly and adequately across the country, especially given regional variations in the proportion of elderly people and changes in political and economic circumstances. The difficulty is increased by uncertainties about and disagreements between the different sectors of service provision. The public sector provides a range of statutory services and facilities through the DHSS nationally and through the local authorities. The community, in the sense of family, friends and neighbours, provides much of the help needed for the ordinary activities of daily life. The private sector can provide a variety of services on a commercial basis. Finally, the voluntary sector looks after those elderly who are not adequately provided for by the other sectors, and supplies a choice of service not otherwise available. This is not to say that, in the end, everyone is looked after. Social surveys and case-reports show that needs are not being met and that self-reported health and satisfaction are not altogether valid indicators of the effectiveness of service provision; for instance, adaptation to low living standards may reduce one's level of expectation below what is actually available.

Both the formulation and the implementation of social and health policies for the aged depend upon the availability of recent empirical data (about the social and health conditions of the elderly) and upon following up and evaluating the effects of the services and facilities provided ('programme evaluation'). Making sense of this information is difficult because there is little or no control over circumstances and because different aspects of the policy interact with one another. For example, regular visiting of elderly people at risk may prevent or delay admission to hospital, and provision for short stays in residential homes may improve the quality and duration of community care.

Given the virtually unlimited needs of the elderly, the limited resources available and the insoluble ethical problems associated with the production and distribution of goods and services in a large complex technological society, it could be argued that social policy for the elderly has developed fairly rapidly in recent years. The problem is partly one of establishing priorities and exercising discretion (taking account of special circumstances). It seems unlikely that a body of rules, no matter how complicated, can fully represent a social policy. What is required, in addition, is a willingness to examine, test, and where appropriate change, the implicit (unspoken) assumptions upon which any policy rests. Circumstances change, social policy for the elderly changes. There are, in a sense, no solutions, only changes. Changes, in the sense of improvements, can often be made not by trying to rethink a policy completely – from first principles as it were – but rather by identifying the specific ways in which failures and inequities can be avoided. What does a particular case of physical abuse imply for the assessment of elderly people at risk? What does delayed discharge of an elderly patient from hospital imply for liaison between hospital and social services? To what extent does a particular sheltered housing scheme provide services appropriate to the needs of residents?

The needs of the elderly are not necessarily expressed by the elderly in need. Some may adapt to and accept poor health and a low standard of living; others may be confused or otherwise incapable of realizing what their needs are; others, aware of their needs, may not be intelligent enough or sufficiently well educated to claim the resources to which they are entitled. Relatives and friends, charitable organizations, pressure groups and professional people concerned with the health and welfare of the elderly, may act on their behalf, identify problems and recommend solutions.

The elderly's needs cannot be neatly summarized, and there is no simple prescription for meeting them. Personal, i.e. human, services can be provided by all sorts of people from the unskilled manual worker to the highly trained professional. How the work gets divided up is itself a policy issue of sorts, since one could argue that people should concentrate on their specific role (assuming it can be properly defined) and refrain from other sorts of involvement. However, this is not always feasible or desirable; a home help may play the role of sympathetic listener, a health visitor find herself tidying up, a social worker, who expected to deal with an individual case, be drawn into community action.

As long as an elderly person remains in the community, his or her needs will change over time in somewhat unpredictable ways. Physical and mental decline in late life does not follow a standard pattern, except in the general sense that the adverse effects of ageing are, on average, cumulative, so that older groups need more services at a higher level of provision. It seems obvious, therefore, that effective services for the elderly depend upon a policy which enables specialists to co-ordinate their efforts. The notions of teamwork and joint planning are well understood and commonly practised in many areas of life – industry, commerce, education, the Armed Forces – but in complex, multidisciplinary systems role relationships are notoriously difficult to establish and maintain.

At present, services for the elderly in the United Kingdom appear to be relatively lacking in co-ordination. For example, there is no formal family policy, i.e. no overall co-ordination of disparate policy provisions (which affects the elderly also), although the importance of the family is strongly voiced by all political parties. This is a result partly of political and economic changes, partly of confusion and uncertainties regarding priorities, partly of the difficulty in finding solutions for the serious problems associated with ageing – poverty, ill health, neglect, confusion and abuse. There is also some uncertainty about where personal responsibility ends and public responsibility begins.

Mutual help and voluntary work by the elderly themselves play a part in the care of the more infirm elderly, much of it informally between husband and wife, friends, relatives and neighbours. Some attempts have been made to extend mutual support schemes, and national voluntary organizations with local branches recruit volunteers and co-ordinate their work, often supported by social service departments. Participation by the elderly in such support activities is probably most obvious in relation to social and recreational activities.

9. Physical and Mental Health

A major component of social policy concerns health services. In 1948 the National Health Service was launched in the United Kingdom with the aim of providing all medical services to all the people. It soon became apparent that demand would always outstrip supply. The realization that a country cannot afford *all* the health services that are desirable brings about a concern with what proportion of a country's resources should be devoted to health (as compared, for example, with defence or education) and how those resources should be distributed, between regions, between hospitals, between medical specialities, even between patients. For example, what resources should go to geriatric medicine and nursing, or to hospices for the dying? The old-old, aged 75 years and over, will form an increasing proportion of the elderly over the next few decades, and they tend to suffer from a multiplicity of physical and mental ailments which are expensive to deal with. This raises ethical questions about the worth of individual lives and the cost-effectiveness of services.

Some 95 per cent of elderly people in the United Kingdom continue to live in the community, even though many have severe health and social problems. Thus, the elderly in the community become the focus of that aspect of social policy concerned with social welfare and personal social services.

Today, community care is generally regarded as the preferred form of health and welfare provision. The resources needed to implement this aspect of social policy are different from but not necessarily much more economical than the resources needed to provide institutional forms of care. In any event, a proportion of elderly people cannot survive or live tolerable lives except in an institutional environment – a hospital or residential home, for example. Hence, social policy for the elderly must be concerned with the effectiveness of the different living arrangements available. The definition of effectiveness should be stated or implied in any social policy. Obviously, an important factor in both community and institutional living arrangements is the amount and quality of the human services provided. Hence the need for education and training in care of the elderly, careful selection and continuing appraisal of staff, and monitoring of the elderly at risk in the community. Family members, particularly daughters, play a considerable part in health care. Support for non-professional carers has been slow in developing because of a reluctance to broaden the definition of 'welfare'.

In particular, we should note the likelihood that elderly people – frail, mentally less competent, and possibly out of touch with social and political developments – can be ignorant of their rights or unable to assert them effectively. Hence the need for effective advocacy and practical guidance within the statutory and voluntary organizations concerned with health and well-being. The Health Advisory Service report in 1982, entitled *The Rising Tide*, drew attention to the plight of the elderly mentally infirm and emphasized the need for more resources to meet the needs of this relatively neglected client group.

The effectiveness of physical and mental health services for the elderly depends upon a number of factors: availability of resources, availability of means to the consumers (the elderly) to secure services, organizational and social factors affecting the delivery of services. Health services are obtainable through either the public or private sector, and willingness to pay obviously helps to determine whether or not a person takes advantage of an available service. At the lower end of the socio-economic scale, benefits and free services may be available on application. An elderly person who is unaware of the available benefits or cannot follow the necessary administrative procedures will need advice and guidance.

Many of the disorders of late life, their interactions and complications, are not well understood. Geriatric medicine and nursing are relatively new disciplines. They form a relatively small part of the training of doctors and nurses. Research in these fields has not been attractive. Thus mistakes occur in the diagnosis and treatment of the elderly, even through fairly obvious circumstances such as nutritional deficiency, dehydration, or drug dosage levels. Elderly patients may fail to understand or carry out the physician's instructions; physicians may fail to guard against this possibility. Disorders do not necessarily manifest themselves in the same way in later life or follow the same course. Some ill-health conditions are preventable, being a consequence of damaging habits (smoking, excessive drinking and eating) or of damaging environmental conditions (exposure to radiation, toxic substances, infection). The health of the community, in other words, is not simply a matter of providing medical and nursing services but of living conditions generally.

Health education and health promotion could conceivably play an important part in improving the health of the elderly. Knowing how the human body works, having some idea of the symptoms, treatment and course of common disorders in late life, appreciating the role of nutrition, exercise and healthy life-styles, and particularly knowing how to communicate and learn in matters to do with health, all these aspects are important to practitioner and patient alike, young as well as old.

The financial costs of health services are a major call on a country's resources, hence the moves towards insurance-based systems, and controls to limit expenditure where the costs are met largely out of taxation. We have already remarked on the fact that the elderly take up a disproportionately large share of the health services, particularly the 'old-old', i.e. those aged 75 and over, who are expected to increase in number over the next few decades, and likely to suffer from chronic illnesses and need lengthy periods of hospitalization.

A substantial proportion of ill-health conditions are dealt with by the individual without recourse to professional advice and treatment. Some disorders are dealt with by the body's own mechanism of defence and repair; medical treatment simply eases the discomfort or reduces the risk of complications. Unfortunately, the disorders of late life are not usually of the common or garden variety characteristic of childhood and early adult life. Nevertheless, medical advances have made it possible to diagnose and treat a variety of disorders that have hitherto been fatal or seriously disabling. Indeed, it is sometimes argued that doctors and nurses prolong life beyond the point at which it is socially or psychologically meaningful.

Changes in social attitudes and practices with regard to physical fitness and medical treatment illustrate the way in which social policy influences, and is influenced by, factors in the wider environment. The longer-term effects are difficult to forecast. Improved physical fitness and medical care may affect older people's attitude to employment, pensions and the associated contributions, and population distribution may alter the pattern of medical and social services and so on. Changes in attitudes towards suicide and euthanasia in late life could be expected to have far-reaching effects, although the actual pattern and extent is difficult to predict. Care of the dying is another example – most people now die in hospital not at home. Ethical issues underpin these and many other aspects of social policy – pension payments, housing standards, transport, regional variations in services, consumers' access to services, public sector costs and so on.

In theory, the consumers of social and medical services are represented on the bodies that formulate and implement the policies which affect them. At the very least, there should be ways to examine their suggestions and complaints. There are, in fact, highly regulated procedures for dealing with complaints and disputes. The policy-makers and the service workers for their part should be accountable to the consumers and to the community at large, in public and private sectors alike. Although rules and regulations, administrative procedures, sanctions and so on can help to ensure effective and equitable services, in the last resort policy depends on mutual under-standing and goodwill between individuals. Rules, sanctions and evaluations are necessary to minimize the adverse consequences arising from human error, negligence and moral failure.

10. Education

Only recently, with the massive and sustained increase in un-employment and the continuing improvement in the health of the young-old, has continuing education and training throughout adult life emerged as a policy issue. Ideally, education policy would enable older children to make a smooth transition from school to productive employment, adults of working age to obtain further education and retraining, and elderly people to continue in productive work wher-ever possible and desirable. Education in and for later life is a rela-tively new aspect of social policy. In times of socio-economic and technological change, 'continuing education', the term commonly used to refer to vocational training and education generally, especi-ally in older adults, is important throughout life. Health and self-maintenance could be an important component since many of the disabilities of late life are associated with preventable effects.

At the same time, further education and training should enable people of all ages to benefit from their leisure time. A substantial part of adult education is already leisure-orientated, being associated with recreational and cultural activities, such as art, music, literature, science and philosophy. Clearly, a great deal of 'education' takes place in-formally through radio, television, newspapers and periodicals; the proportion of older adults who attend courses of education is rather small.

Some forms of adult education may be pursued by young and old alike – from car maintenance to embroidery, from computing to pottery – but obviously the needs, abilities and circumstances of older people tend to restrict the range of educational opportunities.

Pre-retirement courses provide an obvious example of education in and for later life. There is much to be said for courses of a more general nature, touching on the problems of widowhood, living alone, self-care, financial arrangements and so on. Courses in social history are likely to appeal to older people, many of whom will have first-hand knowledge of some of the historical events dealt with, and a deep interest in how those events are being interpreted by historians.

Unfortunately, many adults and older people do not value education in the formal sense or take advantage of the opportunities available. An educational policy for later life would need to consider how education might be made more palatable, and more readily available through distance learning.

Courses in gerontology, the scientific study of ageing, could be expected to play a part in education for late life but appear not to be particularly popular, perhaps because they tend to be somewhat technical and aimed at those engaged in professional or semi-professional work with the aged. Also, the gerontological information currently available is somewhat depressing; there is a great need for material which gives weight to the more enjoyable aspects of later life and provides ways of making the most of one's residual abilities and opportunities. A more positive, optimistic attitude has developed mainly through the efforts of voluntary, charitable organizations and although the material is scattered, many publications offer information, guidance and advice on living a full life to the end.

Education about late life should not evade important common issues, in particular late-life stresses, chronic disabilities and dying. Concepts and methods of treatment are being developed for dealing with stressful events and conditions, and the hospice movement has developed ways of reducing pain and discomfort and helping patients and their families to come to terms with death.

The aged in cultural minority groups in the United Kingdom have not yet received much attention from researchers or the media – presumably because their numbers are small and they have little or no voice in the wider community, relative to other interest groups. In time, however, we can expect them to raise special problems – in family relationships, housing, medical and nursing care and so on. Education could play an important role in teaching them and their care-givers about the social system of which they form a part, and in teaching the majority about the special needs and circumstances of minority groups.

11. Employment

The proportion of elderly people in the population, and the expected increase in the proportion of those aged 75 years and over, implies a substantial demand for appropriate goods and services. In theory, therefore, social policy should take account of these conditions and trends and set in motion plans to deal with them; for example, by training people, allocating funds, adjusting levels of taxation and benefits, and so on.

Employment policy, one aspect of a more general economic and social policy, has profound effects on older people. First, for many it specifies a statutory retirement age which, in the United Kingdom, effectively excludes women over 60 and men over 65 years of age from certain kinds of employment. Second, many occupations, such as the police and the Armed Forces, have age-limited terms of employment, although it is usual for persons leaving them in middle life to plan for, train for and enter a subsequent career. Third, in many other occupations, employment may be terminated unexpectedly through redundancy, and older people may find it difficult and inconvenient to take up fresh employment. In general, employers tend to employ younger people; they are more adaptable, provide a better investment as regards training, and cost less in salaries or wages. There is considerable discrimination against people seeking fresh employment in the second half of their working lives, i.e. after the age of about 40. Fourth, there may be financial disincentives to working in later life, through taxation, for example, or difficulty in securing funds for a small business venture. Fifth, in periods of unemployment there may be social pressures encouraging premature retirement – a benign form of social prejudice.

Employment policy has a more general effect on the health and welfare of the elderly in so far as it may improve or worsen the economic well-being of the country as a whole, thus affecting the living standards of all, but especially the elderly, many of whom will be on relatively fixed incomes – pensions and interest from savings.

In the event of a labour shortage, it may be altered to encourage older people back to work, as in the 1950s.

Ideally, retirement should be more flexible, permitting earlier or later retirement on appropriate terms and conditions so as to recognize the wide range of differences between older workers in their employment abilities and circumstances, another illustration of the interconnectedness of factors in social policy.

Continuing changes in technology lead to changes in employment throughout the working life. This tends to act against the employment of older workers whose skills are obsolete and who may need longer and different forms of retraining from those of younger people. The problems of retraining older workers are probably greatly overestimated, but it is difficult to generalize about the effectiveness of older workers when their occupations and circumstances are so diverse. Some carry on professional occupations and self-employed businesses until very late in life, especially if the amount and conditions of work can be adjusted to suit their needs and abilities.

Vocational guidance, usually thought of in connection with school-leavers and young adults, needs to be made a life-long affair, merging into preparation for retirement and perhaps into leisure-orientated education.

An employment policy may make special provision for the disabled; for example, setting up sheltered occupational schemes or requiring employers to employ a minimum number of disabled people. Obviously, a change in the age of retirement would interact with this because of the increased extent of disability in later life.

A major advance in employment policy for the elderly would be the identification and expansion of those areas and types of work for which older people are specially suited because of their experience, special skills, personal qualities, circumstances and attitudes. In general, these might be small local or home-based activities not calling for sustained, rapid or paced work. It remains to be seen whether the new technologies and the decentralization of industrial activities will open up new employment prospects for the elderly. The common expectation seems to be that the new technologies will reduce manpower needs substantially. If so, then the elderly are likely to find employment mainly in those areas of the economy which the new technologies cannot reach – perhaps many kinds of personal services and craft industries. Even so, they are likely to be at a disadvantage compared with young people also seeking employment, and can expect longer periods of unemployment and a consequential worsening of their living standards. Long-term unemployment is a serious risk, with adverse psychological and social consequences in a society which places a high value on employment and income.

Many older unemployed people have family responsibilities, for their parents as well as their children, so that the financial support they receive from the State may come from several sources – child benefits, rent rebates, attendance allowances and the like. In some instances, the overall benefits of employment may not outweigh the costs of remaining unemployed.

In the United Kingdom and elsewhere there are currently special factors governing the demand for labour, e.g. changes in the age-structure of the population, new technology, foreign competition. These make the prospect for the employment of older people rather poor, except for those who, through their special abilities, experience and circumstances, can generate goods and services for which there is a demand. Even then the extent of such demand will be a function, in part, of the general level of economic activity.

References and Suggestions for Further Reading

Beveridge, W. H., *Social Insurance and Allied Services, Report*, London: HMSO, 1942.

Bromley, D. B., 'Approaches to the study of personality changes in adult life and old age', in A. D. Isaacs and F. Post (eds), *Studies in Geriatric Psychiatry*, Chichester: John Wiley, 1978, 17–40.

Bruce, W. M., *The Coming of the Welfare State* (4th edn), London: Batsford, 1968.

Central Statistical Office, *Social Trends*, no. 16, London: HMSO, 1986.

Department of Health and Social Security, *Ageing in the United Kingdom*, London: HMSO, 1982.

—— *Elderly People in the Community: Their Service Needs.*

Research Contribution to the Development of Policy and Practice, London: HMSO, 1983.

Fogarty, M. (ed.), Retirement Policy. The Next Fifty Years, London: Heinemann, 1984.

Goldberg, E. M. and Connelly, N., The Effectiveness of Social Care for the Elderly: An Overview of Recent and Current Evaluative Research, London: Heinemann, 1982.

Health Advisory Service, The Rising Tide, London: National Health Service, Health Advisory Service, 1982.

Hill, M., Understanding Social Policy (2nd edn), Oxford: Basil Blackwell & Martin Robertson, 1983.

Lawton, M. P., Environment and Aging, Monterey, CA: Brooks/Cole Publishing, 1980.

Newson, T. and Potter, P., Housing Policy in Britain: An Information Sourcebook, London: Mansell, 1985.

Norman, A., Transport and the Elderly: Problems and Possible Action, London: Centre for Policy on Ageing, 1977.

Smyer, M. A., 'Aging and social policy. Contrasting Western Europe and the United States', Journal of Family Issues, 5, 1984, 239–53.

The Market Research Society, Special Issue: Researching the Elderly, Journal of the Market Research Society, 25 (3), 1983, 214–86.

Tinker, A., The Elderly and Modern Society (2nd edn), London: Longman, 1985.

1. Social Gerontology

Social gerontology is concerned with many of the issues already mentioned: government policy towards the aged and the poor, economic provision for retirement through insurance and pensions, health and welfare services, demography, family and kinship systems. The bulk of this sociological knowledge is concerned with *old people* rather than with adult ageing, although some studies of the family have taken account of adult phases of the life-cycle.

(a) Economic and occupational aspects

Modern social gerontology is concerned, in part, with the social adjustment of elderly individuals, with the social and institutional arrangements governing the relationships between elderly people and their care-givers (family and staff), and with social organizations which are directly concerned with the elderly. Modern social gerontology also studies the responses made by industrial societies to the challenge created by the existence of a substantial number of elderly dependent people who consume but do not produce goods and services within the prevailing social and economic conditions. For example, a modern industrial society can expect well over 10 per cent of its members to survive beyond 65 years of age. In the United Kingdom, the percentage is expected to remain fairly constant at about 15 per cent until the year 2001. Within the age-group 65 and over, however, the proportion aged 65 to 74 (the 'young-old') will actually decrease from 57 to 54 per cent, whereas the proportion aged 75 and over (the 'old-old') will increase from 43 to 46 per cent. Because of poor physical health, social isolation and poverty, some elderly people comprise a seriously disadvantaged section of the community and make legitimate, diverse and relatively large claims on a society's resources. A majority of them are women; they command little wealth or income; they have lost many of the physical, social and psychological attributes valued by the rest of the community; they are at a serious disadvantage in social exchange relationships; they are politically impotent.

Social gerontology is related to a number of general sociological themes such as: social change and industrialization in relation to work roles, age and sex roles, family structure and solidarity. Nowadays people tend to marry at a slightly younger age, they have fewer children, the last child is born earlier in the mother's life, the mother is more likely to re-enter the workforce, and people are more likely to survive to a late age.

Industrialization brings a rapid increase in the proportion of younger dependent persons; this is followed in due course by an increase in the proportion of older dependent persons. These changes create problems: individual adjustment to changes in status during the life-cycle; the care of a small proportion of socially isolated and infirm aged people; the distribution of economic resources to elderly

Table 5.1 The Age-Structure of the UK Population, 1984

Age	Male	Female
85+	0.2	0.5
75–84	1.0	1.9
65–74	2.1	2.7
60–64	1.5	1.7
45–59	4.6	4.7
30–44	5.6	5.6
15–29	6.7	6.5
0–14	5.6	5.4

The age-structure of the United Kingdom population for males and females separately in millions in 1984; based on *Social Trends*, no. 16, 1986

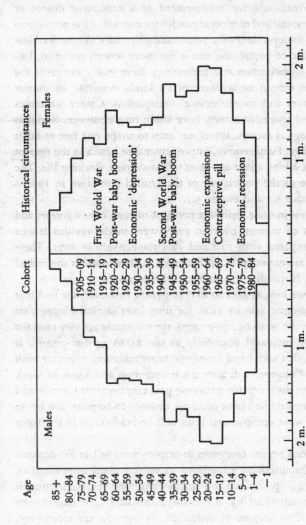

Figure 5.1 Age-structure of the population of England and Wales, separately for males and females, in 1984, in relation to birth cohort and historical circumstances; based on Office of Population Censuses and Surveys, *Mortality Statistics, 1984, England and Wales*, 1986

dependent members. The problem of the age-structure of the population is less important nowadays than formerly. Industrialization, automation and the achievement of a substantial degree of control over social and economic conditions mean that the population is no longer so dependent on a young and physically vigorous labour force. Pressure of population size is the more serious problem. Improvements in education and technology have vastly increased the capacity and output of workers of all kinds, resulting in shorter working hours and more 'service' occupations. Career structures have changed and new careers have come into existence. Social as well as biological factors, therefore, help to shape our fate in adult life and old age. Furthermore, improvements in health in the present century have added about ten years to the average working life. The age-structure of the population of the United Kingdom in 1984 is shown in Table 5.1 and Figure 5.1.

In Britain in 1984, only 8.2 per cent of men over 65 years and 7.6 per cent of women over 60 years were in the civilian labour force, as compared with 19.2 and 12.4 respectively in 1971. These percentages are expected to decline even further towards the end of the century. Naturally, the numbers diminish at later ages.

When we look at ages 20 to 60/65 years, however, we find that whereas economic activity rates for men have declined somewhat (especially in the 60 to 64 age-group), the economic activity rates for women have increased (especially in the 25 to 44 age-group). It seems likely that social and economic reorganization, together with technological change, will alter the distribution and kinds of work available. The prospects for satisfying paid employment for men and women in late middle age or older are thought to be poor. It is by no means clear what occupational skills will be marketable in the 1990s and later.

Whether a person continues in employment in late life depends upon such predisposing conditions as employment opportunities, health, living costs, income and family circumstances. Retirement is eventually precipitated by, for example, an illness, or compulsory retirement. The substantial reduction in income on retirement, combined with lifelong low earnings for many, means that a common reason for wanting to work is to obtain more money. In the 1970s about a quarter of all men retired a year or two before age

65; the rate of retirement at that time of life made it unlikely that raising the age of retirement would make more than a marginal contribution to the economic well-being of the country.

In the changed economic circumstances of the 1980s, however, premature retirement became commonplace, so did prolonged unemployment following redundancy late in the working life. The psychological consequences of unemployment are being investigated; the indications are that it gives rise to depression, other maladjustment, and poorer physical health, although the causal connections are difficult to isolate.

The economic aspects of ageing are difficult to disentangle from the general economic and political circumstances of a community. The basic problem is how to support, out of current and accumulated production, the non-productive members of a community – the children, the sick, the old, the unemployed and others. If the proportion of dependent to productive people is small, the problem is simple. But in Britain the output required to support the dependent members is large in relation to total output, and it is getting larger. This means lower standards of living, less capital for investment, and a slower rate of economic and industrial development. The problem can be dealt with in a variety of ways – by increased productivity (especially by automation and rationalization), extending the working life (which will probably make only a marginal difference), or reducing the amount spent on dependants. Low spending on children's health and education is thought to be short-sighted and self-defeating, but spending on pensions and unemployment benefit and old people has traditionally been kept to a minimum. Present arrangements seem an improvement on the conditions endured by previous generations, although it is possible to argue that state support for the elderly, relative to the income of the working population, is lower now than in the era of the early Victorian Poor Law.

Public funds must be used economically and political considerations cannot be disregarded. Paying benefits to one person to meet his or her needs may reduce the motivation of another, who is still able to work and earn, or bring about gross differences in standards of living between one person who can work and another who cannot. One solution is to make supplementary payments to retired or unemployed people to prevent their standards of living from falling too far. Many individual firms and insurance companies provide supplementary payments, as do the Department of Health and Social Security and various charities, but this does not solve the main economic problem of making provision for old age. Taxation and incomes policies may eventually provide a more effective long-term solution, but part of the difficulty arises from errors in forecasting trends in the country's economy and population.

Improvements will come when it is more widely recognized that security, leisure and reasonable standards of living during old age are rights achieved by an individual in return for his or her contribution, by way of work and services, to the welfare of the community. Living standards depend to some extent on the efforts of earlier generations, and younger working people have a moral obligation to support the elderly.

Industrial changes have created redundancies among workers who are nowhere near the end of their normal active lives. Nowadays unemployment benefits, severance pay, adequate notice, the gradual running down of a work force, earlier retirement benefits and better facilities for retraining and re-employment make it easier for redundant workers to make a satisfactory readjustment. Such measures are more effective if adequate planning and co-ordination take place on a national and regional basis. The problem is to balance the need for industrial change and efficiency against the need to protect the older, more vulnerable worker. A person over the age of 50 is in a difficult position as regards a change of employment. All manner of complications arise – health, disabilities, family commitments, personal outlook, opportunities and constraints, the risks involved, cost/benefit relationships, and so on. Industrial gerontology thus examines not only the larger social problems but also the occupational psychology of adult life with its attendant problems of selection, counselling, retraining, work study and the like.

Whatever the differences between the way societies deal with ageing, certain common features can be discerned. Most people try to survive independently for as long as possible, often in spite of severe hardships. Old people disengage from the more central social activities, either finding themselves unable to cope, or yielding place to younger members who can pursue community interests vigorously and in new ways. People who have played an active part in local affairs often try to retain some measure of involvement, as it is not easy to give up status, rights and authority, but eventually, as physical and mental dilapidation increase, some sort of withdrawal from the mainstream of social interaction becomes necessary, and the individual's social life is largely confined to small primary groups, usually the family and friends. Failing this, the individual becomes isolated or enters into a dependent relationship in a home or an institution. In any event, his or her continued existence is much less important to the larger community. Society is robust and well prepared. No one is indispensable.

In spite of their numbers, the aged are too heterogeneous to form an effective 'pressure group' in the larger society, and their tendency to disengage weakens their involvement in community affairs. In Britain, social movements among the elderly have emerged, concerned with welfare and pensions, and in the United States there are signs that the elderly are becoming politically more significant, although they are not under-represented in the accepted political sense. The underprivileged (minority) position of the elderly is reflected in the small amount of broadcasting time, advertising and newspaper space devoted to their interests. Middle-aged people, by contrast, are in a 'commanding' position.

(b) Health and functional capacity

On reaching the age of 60, a man can expect to live for a further 15 to 16 years, a woman for 20 to 21 years. About 5 per cent of all people over 65 are in institutions of one sort or another – nursing homes, residential homes, or hospitals, for example – because they are incapable of the degree of self-care required for life in the community. The percentage rises with age. Figure 5.2 shows the status of survivors aged 65 years and over. Year by year from age 65 to 74 about 60 per cent of men and women are categorized as suffering from long-standing illness or are living in institutions. At 75 years and over, the percentage rises to about 70. Of these, roughly 15 per cent become bedridden, housebound, or seriously incapacitated, either by general infirmity or by specific disabilities such as blindness, deafness, or vertigo; about 5 per cent exhibit psychiatric abnormalities, but not all are treated. The differences between individuals at all ages are so great that for most measures of functional capacity there is a considerable overlap even between widely spaced age-groups. About one-third of men at retirement age feel that they could continue in employment. In the United Kingdom, however, few can do so.

Old people vary, not only in their capacity for self-maintenance but also in their environmental circumstances – housing, finance, local facilities, social contacts and so on. Such variations contribute to

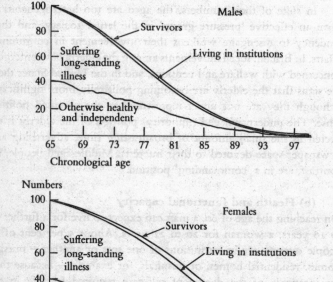

Figure 5.2 Status of survivors aged 65 years and over (assuming an initial population of 100 at age 65) separately for males and females in England and Wales, 1981–3; based on *Social Trends*, no. 16, 1986

differences in social adjustment. They present three interesting facets of social ageing. First, people generally prefer to manage their own affairs and would rather receive financial support and welfare services at home than go into a fully comprehensive residential institution. Second, the daily needs of many old people are met directly by close relatives or friends; the State provides only a small part of the total resources required even for the limited living standards that prevail. This sort of community support for the elderly infirm warrants improved state aid, such as the provision of meals, holidays, day care, domestic help and home nursing, otherwise the 'burden of care' is not fairly distributed. The effect of health and welfare services on the care of the aged person by the family varies from one family to another, depending upon attitudes and circumstances; but there is no substantial evidence that state aid weakens family solidarity – rather the reverse. Third, health is partly subjective: in later life, we become 'adapted' to disability, ill health and poor living conditions; we may not recognize that, by normal standards, we need medical treatment and welfare support.

The average old person in Britain consults a doctor about twice as frequently as a young adult. Screening tests for medical health play a valuable part in the treatment or prevention of some disorders in late life, but they do not reach everyone. Many people are grossly ignorant of medical matters and often fail to understand or follow medical advice. The effects of publicity and health education in relation to disorders in later life would almost certainly bring considerable benefits, as campaigns against smoking and obesity have shown; but the increased demands for medical and welfare services might prove impossible to meet.

The old person's subjective assessment of his or her health does not depend entirely on actual physical condition; and men, particularly, tend to overestimate their health, even relative to other old people. Physicians react to the signs and symptoms of definite diseases, but the old person is more likely to pay attention to sensory and motor impairments and to the disruption of natural functions and activities. Physical incapacity and limited mobility have psychological and social repercussions, so that incapacitated old people tend to feel more lonely, depressed or anxious than those who are more mobile.

Scales for the measurement of functional capacity in late life have been developed. They range from simple questions about negotiating stairs, washing and dressing, and trimming toe-nails, to more elaborate tests, check-lists and rating scales. Dizziness, unsteadiness and restricted limb movements are frequently mentioned as reasons for inadequate self-care. Not all old people in residential care are severely incapacitated, and not all old people in the community are fully self-maintaining. Most of the more seriously incapacitated are single women or widows. Assessment of the needs and functional capacities of old people is essential for the effective administration of health and welfare services and of housing. There appears to be considerable ignorance and disagreement about the extent and kinds of old people's needs, so there is considerable scope for survey work and the compilation of statistical data.

The pattern of care for the elderly continues to move away from full-time institutional care towards sheltered housing and domiciliary care. The long-term social and economic consequences are difficult to work out because of the effects of unanticipated factors. Some of the premises on which policies are based are explicit and open to examination whereas others are less clear – see below.

There are many service occupations in the areas of health and welfare of the aged – occupations which are unlikely to be lost to automation. But their costs have to be met from the 'productive' sector of the economy; so, although we can expect more people to move into service occupations because of automation, resources for the aged and infirm are likely to be the result of moral pressure rather than economic pressure.

(c) Family relationships

The age-structure of the population of the United Kingdom has changed over the last century from one which was pyramidal in shape (large numbers of children and young people, fewer adults and very few old people) to one which is almost rectangular up to about the age of 60 and pyramidal for later ages – see Figure 5.1. Improved life expectancy combined with smaller families has altered the typical pattern of family relationships, extending it over several generations but reducing its collateral connections. In addition, an increased rate of divorce, family break-up, remarriage, single-parent families, unmarried partners, and so on, has complicated family relationships in ways which are still unclear. One family in five in Britain is a four-generation family. A further complication arises with the ageing of ethnic groups in Britain and with the increased assimilation of succeeding generations. Social attitudes and practices are changing; social institutions and the law can be changed to meet changing social conditions.

Positive roles for the aged in family relationships are not well documented for present-day society. Families and households vary, but typical family structures are probably not very different now from former times. Members of the extended family as well as friends and neighbours would provide support if needed, and the ties of duty, mutual obligation and affection, then as now, would persist over long periods of time even in the absence of social interaction.

Social interaction, particularly the exchange of goods and services between people, can be usefully described and analysed in terms of exchange theory – the way costs and benefits come to be distributed. When we consider the 'costs' of supporting the frail elderly in a community, we may forget that a substantial part of those 'costs' are in fact 'benefits' in the form of paid employment for care-givers. If the care-givers are unpaid, the exchange may be balanced by other considerations: enhanced self-esteem, diminished guilt and anxiety, gifts and acknowledgements from the recipient of care, and so on.

One peculiarity of exchange relationships in later life is that an older person may be stigmatized as 'old' and discriminated against – in relation to employment particularly. Consequently, older people tend to be seen as potentially unrewarding relative to younger people. This inhibits further exploration of exchange relationships (Dowd, 1980) and so tends to close off opportunities for older people.

Social interactions analysable in terms of exchange theory – cost/benefit analysis – are not necessarily simple or completely rational. Many factors determine the way a social interaction develops – prior expectations, ignorance, social pressures; not only may the exchange be unbalanced – one gets more out of it than the other – but the relationship may not be in the interests of either party, i.e. both may lose out, perhaps because of unforeseen events, lack of control or faulty reasoning.

An older person may or may not take into account, in a sensible rational way, changes in his or her reward-value or cost-value to others. Nevertheless, patterns of social interaction will tend towards those with selectively effective cost/benefit relationships. The tendencies towards age-segregation in leisure activities and friendships are examples of such 'natural' tendencies, and arise in part because of compatibilities in exchange relationships, and shared understandings and interests.

The ability to initiate, maintain and control social interaction is referred to as power – in the sense that the ability to provide rewards (benefits) enables one to persuade, cajole, negotiate and bargain with others more effectively. Such power is not evenly distributed, partly because of individual differences in personal qualities and circumstances, partly because societies tend to have 'built-in' or 'structural' characteristics which bring about broad age-differences, ethnic differences, sex differences, socio-economic differences, and so on, in social powers and status. Dowd (1980) suggests that as the physical health and occupational performance of the young-old (those aged 55 to 75 years) continue to improve, there may be a conflict between this group and those aged 35 to 55 (sometimes called the 'command generation') because current social attitudes and practices associated with work and retirement act as a barrier to mutually beneficial social interaction between them.

In Britain, more than one-fifth of the elderly live alone, and about one-third live as married couples. Nearly half live with other people, usually a relative. The majority live fairly close to a relative and see their children fairly frequently. Social interaction with friends, neighbours and kin is usually sufficient to maintain stable patterns of communication. To describe in full the social psychology of 'exchange' between older and younger generations in the same family or quasi-family would entail an extensive exercise in behavioural ecology – mapping the kinds of daily activities they engage in. Sample surveys, however, have confirmed and refined common-sense impressions regarding the exchange of advice, gifts, money, emotional support, domestic help and other services, which creates a system of reciprocal obligations and dependencies. The social psychology of human ageing – in the sense of experimental research into the details of social perception and interaction, conformity, attitudes and so on – continues to be neglected.

Half the elderly appear to have almost daily contact with one or more of their children; less than a fifth, apparently, see no relative for a week or more at a time. Class differences and physical distance affect frequency of contact. Investigations into the amount of social contact enjoyed by elderly people show that a small proportion appear to be socially isolated, whereas most elderly – men and women alike – do not feel isolated, even if their frequency of communication is low in comparison with younger people. On the other hand, some people feel lonely when the objective indices of social contact are high. From the point of view of social and psychological welfare, the degree and kind of affective experience associated with particular relationships is probably more important than mere frequency of social contact. Thus, such contacts experienced by the aged can range all the way from brief, routine, superficial, instrumental and merely dutiful to prolonged, spontaneous, deeply felt, rewarding or punishing, and based on personal involvement. The possible effects of ageing on emotional experience and responsiveness are referred to in Chapters Six and Nine.

In urban industrial life social relationships tend to grow out of the work situation and the family and other primary social groupings have to adapt to its demands. The separation of generations within families, and the inadequate social and financial provisions for the elderly, make it difficult for parents and children to reunite after the parents have retired and the grandchildren have grown up. However, the difficulty can be social or psychological rather than economic, since parents and children do not necessarily continue to share the same beliefs and feelings. Technological and social change, occupational differences between parents and children, education, housing, specialization of labour and social pressures are responsible for this 'emotional distance' between one generation and the next.

2. Social Trends

According to *Social Trends* (1986), most people who have reached the normal age of retirement, 60 years for women and 65 for men, are no longer in paid employment and depend for their income on pensions, benefits and savings. In the United Kingdom the proportion of pensioners rose from 13.5 per cent in 1951 to 18 per cent in 1985. It is possible to make three comparisons, one between pre- and post-retirement incomes, one between retirement income and the income of comparable younger people in work, and one between retirement income currently and in former times.

A person's disposable income is the amount of money available after tax and essential contributions have been deducted. When allowance is made for inflation and child dependants, it appears that the disposable income of pensioners has improved substantially relative to that of non-pensioners since 1951, and now stands at about 70 per cent of the disposable income of non-pensioners. This is attributable to improvements in the basic pension, in social security benefits and in occupational pensions. The average figures for 1985 are about £2,800 for pensioners and about £4,100 for non-pensioners. Pensioners' incomes in general are low relative to current expectations for living standards. In comparing the living standards before and after retirement, we must take into account the wealth, i.e. financial assets, that people have acquired – savings, investments, house, and so on. *Social Trends* (1986) reports that in 1982 pensioners had on average a net wealth of £16,900, nearly 25 per cent more than non-pensioners, or 50 per cent if child dependants are taken into account. If recent trends continue, of course, future pensioners should have greater net wealth than today's. Another factor is that older people, people in retirement, may consume relatively more in the way of health and social service provision.

In the United Kingdom the number of people aged 65 years and over increased from 1.8 million in the year 1901 to 4.3 million in 1941 and to 8.4 million in 1984. There are roughly 64 elderly men to every 100 elderly women. Population projections to the end of the century estimate that 8.7 million people will be aged 65 years or more. However, most concern is expressed about the relative proportional increase in those aged 85 and over, from 8 per cent to 11 per cent, i.e. from 656,000 to 1,047,000, because of this group's relatively high consumption of health and social services, together with the cost of pensions and other age-related benefits. It is difficult to draw firm conclusions about future trends because political, economic and technological changes have somewhat unpredictable consequences on living standards, demography, health and social services, leisure, and so on. Changes in health and retirement practices may have quite substantial effects on life-styles in later years. A further, apparently neglected issue, is the extent to which ageing among the country's ethnic minorities will present special problems, especially in association with ethnic mobility and assimilation.

The United Kingdom has a relatively high proportion of elderly people, about 20 per cent aged 60 or over, as compared with other western industrial nations. The present expectation of life at birth is 69.8 years for males and 76.2 years for females. The death rates for adults of different ages are shown in Figures 3.2 and 3.5.

From 1971 to 1984 there was a considerable fall in the percentages of older men in paid employment – from 83 per cent to 57 per cent for 60–64 year olds, and from 19 per cent to 8 per cent for men aged 65 and over. Older women, by contrast, those aged 55–59, maintained their work participation rate, although women aged 60 years and over show a decline in work participation over the same period similar to that of men.

Similar trends can be found in other western industrial societies. In developing countries, increases in life expectancy not matched by the provision of appropriate health and social services create difficulties.

Women are becoming economically more active in the sense of engaging in paid employment more fully in spite of the demands of children and other family members. There is evidence that, at least in some socio-economic groups, the departure from home of the last child is not experienced as a loss but as a relief! Of course, many women return to work soon after the birth of a child, relying on others to provide the necessary care but also continuing to contribute much of their own time to domestic and family affairs. It appears that the provision of labour-saving domestic equipment, paid for in part by income from a woman's employment, does not result in a very substantial shift in the way domestic work is shared between husband and wife. At present (1987), women are relatively under-represented in management, professional work, skilled manual work, and as employers, and are relatively over-represented in subordinate, non-manual and unskilled manual work; technological change, political uncertainties and economic recession make it impossible to be confident about future social trends. For example, between 1971 and 1982 the proportion of pensioners in the lowest family income category decreased from 52 per cent to 27 per cent, whereas that of other low-income groups increased. It remains to be seen whether this relative improvement for pensioners will continue and whether the absolute and relative levels of this lowest income group will improve, and to what extent this income will be derived from social security benefits.

Changes in the further expectation of life at different ages from the beginning of the century until 1981 are shown in Table 3.3. For example, a 65-year-old man in 1901 could expect a further 10.8 years of life, whereas in 1981 he could expect 12.4 years. The advantage that women have over men in both expectation of life from birth and further expectation at any age has been increasing. This is a matter about which there has been some debate. Although longer life expectancy does not necessarily imply better health and well-being, because of the chances of chronic ill health and dependency in later life, it has been argued that the human survival curve is becoming increasingly rectangular. More people survive to a late age even though the maximum expectation of life, about 120 years, may not have changed. Advances in biology, medicine and social welfare have postponed the onset, and therefore shortened the duration, of chronic disorders in middle and later life. There is continuing debate about this, partly because the tail of the human survival curve appears to stretch out towards an indeterminate limit, partly because of uncertainties about the extent to which medical advances are actually improving functional capacities in later life and shortening the period of disability.

We need to distinguish between subjective (self-reported) health and well-being on the one hand and objective (criterion-assessed) health on the other. Except for hypochondriacs, most people probably overestimate their health relative to their objective health status. This helps to account for a great deal of unreported ill health among community residents. At each year from the age of 65 to 90 years, about 40 per cent of men and women regard themselves as healthy and independent. The longer expectation of life for women and the ability of married women to look after their husbands means that many more women than men eventually move into institutional life.

The main causes of death in later life are circulatory diseases (including heart attacks and strokes), cancer and respiratory diseases. Older people are more likely to be suffering from multiple ailments, some of them subclinical, i.e. free of signs and symptoms; one or other or some combination of these ailments will eventually lead to death. The aim is to 'compress' these lethal ailments into a narrow span of years immediately prior to the maximum expectation of life. Certain kinds of condition are characteristic of particular age-groups. Accidents and violence, for example, are particularly marked in young adults, alcohol disorders are particularly obvious in middle life, whereas long-standing illnesses increase steadily to a maximum in those aged 75 years and over.

The increased ill health found in later life has obvious implications for the provision of health and welfare services. However, political and economic changes affect the way health care is distributed between the public and private sectors. Health care costs increase steadily throughout adult life; *Social Trends* (1986) reports an increase in National Health Service costs per person per year in 1983 from about £150 to about £1,000 over the adult years, excluding the costs of administration, capital and maternity care. The cost of geriatric in-patient hospital care was roughly £35 per patient per day in 1983–4.

There are several aspects of modern life which affect and are affected by the health and well-being of older people. Housing is an obvious example, as described in Chapter Four. Transport provides another example. Loss of income in later life makes personal transport relatively more expensive; concessionary fares are an indirect form of saving, although many experience physical difficulty in using public transport.

3. Disengagement

(a) Retirement

Old age creates social as well as medical problems, but only recently has much attention been paid to the cultural aspects of late maturity and old age. It is widely believed that many of the problems of adolescence are brought about by life-history events and inadequacies in surrounding circumstances; so some of the maladjustments and difficulties of old people may arise from analogous causes. Inadequate pensions, poor living conditions, occupational insecurity, harmful social attitudes, and the shortage of psychiatric counselling services are but a few of them.

One of the more obvious features of maturity and old age is social disengagement – a systematic reduction in certain kinds of social interaction. This has received considerable attention from psychologists and sociologists in gerontology. It is a kind of withdrawal from the mainstreams of occupational and other forms of productive activity, normal in late maturity, and encouraged by common social practices such as superannuation, age-limits, and many social norms and expectations affecting behaviour. The most obvious examples are people in retirement or semi-retirement. Most people retire either because of ill health or because they reach a fixed retirement age; some continue to work, part-time, after their official 'retirement', usually for financial reasons, although a proportion enjoy working, particularly if the hours are short and the conditions congenial.

Once retired, individuals no longer interact so much with colleagues or workmates, and take part less frequently in the numerous social activities previously connected with work. The elimination or reduction of occupational relationships tends to weaken ties of friendship. The retired person's relatives and children are likely to be widely scattered and may therefore provide fewer opportunities for visiting. Disengagement looks like a sensible attempt to distribute reduced energies and resources over fewer but more personally relevant activities, to conserve effort and to escape from demands which one cannot or does not wish to meet.

The old-fashioned 'institution' for psychiatric patients and the elderly infirm unwittingly pushed the inmates' disengagement to its limit of absurdity by taking them out of society altogether, providing only custodial care, and failing to help them to reorganize their lives. This kind of treatment is less conspicuous nowadays because of the emphasis on rehabilitation and community care.

Individual differences in disengagement are common. Some elderly people stubbornly resist pressures put on them to reduce their commitments. They refuse to give up activities which have been central to their lives – a job, a small business, a cultural or scientific activity, a social or civic responsibility. Even more likely is resistance to the idea of giving up an independent life and a private home for residence in a nursing home. Some refuse to retire until forced to do so by ill health. Others die as they lived – active and involved with the world.

Although some individuals fight the process all the way, dis-engagement of some sort is bound to come, simply because old people have neither the physical nor the mental resources they had when they were young. Disengagement signifies a practical re-appraisal of one's position. In ideal circumstances, the process is graded to suit the declining biological and psychological capacities of the individual on the one hand, and the needs of society on the other. Normal disengagement seems to lessen the fear of death.

Disengagement is not an entirely negative process; it may in-volve the commencement or renewal of other participant activities (engagements), especially those involving family, friends and neighbourhood. The net effect is a shrinkage in the range of activities, and a diminution in the amount of contact with other people. Gradu-ally older people tend to become less functionally associated with others, less emotionally involved, and more absorbed in their own problems and circumstances.

With disengagement, the range and intensity of the social pres-sures brought to bear upon a person to secure conformity to social norms are decreased. In extreme cases this can lead to isolation and personal eccentricity. Elderly individuals who have a history of diffi-cult social relationships probably disengage more quickly and become more isolated than normal people, and if socially isolated for a con-siderable time may find it difficult to settle into the communal arrange-ments of a nursing home or hospital.

The elderly person's most salient concern is often his or her physical health and, after that, security and standards of living. A reduction in living standards and income consequent upon retirement, coupled perhaps with natural regrets, may bring about temporary depression or anxiety, but often this is caused by the prospect of retirement rather than retirement itself. Studies show that, given reasonable physical health and financial resources, the average retired man or woman soon adapts to the changed circumstances and shows an improvement in physical health and outlook. It is the transition that creates problems of adjustment.

Disengagement is fostered by decreased physical mobility. Whether or not this is experienced as a frustration depends very much upon the person's needs, habits and circumstances. An overall reduction in needs allows limited resources to be deployed more effectively for the attainment of fewer but more personally important goals. This brings about a constriction in the range of activities and outlook and probably makes it more difficult to appreciate the needs and actions of younger people. Many issues and events have much less relevance for us as we disengage from the mainstreams of social concern.

Recent psychological and social research means that retirement can no longer be thought of simply as a sudden enforced dislocation of a working life, almost inevitably resulting in feelings of rejection and physical or mental ill health. A substantial proportion of men choose to retire a few years before the usual age of 65 years. After that age, an even larger proportion do not actively seek paid employment, although the generally low levels of income in late life constitute a strong inducement to work. There have been gradual improvements in the health and welfare of retired people and in their standards of living over many decades. Nevertheless, a high level of morale can be achieved only when their economic status compares favourably with that of working adults.

More women have been entering the workforce. They live longer than men on average yet retire earlier, normally at 60. Hitherto, it has not been usual to think of women 'in retirement' since their social condition was defined in terms of their marital status and their continuing domestic activities. However, a large number of older women are in retirement from paid employment and so have to face not only that problem but also their husband's retirement and, for many, widowhood. The relative neglect of the study of retirement in women can be attributed to a number of factors: they constitute about two-fifths of the workforce (about 50 per cent of adult women are in paid employment); much of the work is part-time; traditionally, even for working women, home and family occupy a major portion of their time, so that retirement is seen as less of a change in life-style than for working men.

For many working men, the release from exacting physical labour over long hours in unsatisfactory conditions is followed not by frustration and idleness but by more enjoyable leisure-time activity, closer family relationships and better physical health. When a man retires there are some forty or more hours in the week to be accounted for. It is surprising and at first puzzling, therefore, to learn that following retirement men do not feel very different from before, except for the obvious fact that they are not working. A great deal of the time spent at work, by definition, excludes 'personal time', and to that extent is not greatly missed. By contrast, much of the time spent in retirement is – or, perhaps, should be – 'personal time'; that is, time spent doing the important things one wants to do rather than the things one has to do. Hence, the extra hours are easily absorbed by extra rest and sleep, a slower pace of work, family and domestic activities, more numerous and more prolonged leisure-time activities, and so on.

A large percentage of men in retirement say that there is nothing they miss. Work itself and money, especially in the United States, are missed by some; the people one worked with and the feeling of being useful are also missed, but to a lesser extent. Attitudes and patterns of adjustment change fairly rapidly during retirement, as one might expect. However, it is not age – the mere passage of time – that explains differences between individuals but rather the biological and psychological changes that take place over time. Men over the age of 65 who are working seem generally less lonely and better adjusted than retired men; but not necessarily because they are working. Physical health and personality factors underlie both morale and work capacity in later life. Retirement is rapidly becoming a normal and expected phase of the life-path, to be looked forward to, prepared for and enjoyed. The measurement of 'life-satisfaction' is a current issue in social and behavioural gerontology.

Paid employment plays a major part in a man's life and, increasingly, in a woman's. It acquires considerable emotional importance, tends to define the main social role, and confers status, prestige and, in the home, authority. The retiring person's problem is to find satisfactory ways of disengaging from employment without suffering economic hardships or emotional deprivations such as loneliness and boredom. The problems can be met only by long-term planning. Preparation for retirement is now catered for by many firms, voluntary organizations and centres for adult education, but many people enter retirement inadequately prepared. Preparation means, among other things, putting money aside, buying and disposing of personal property and assets, attending to health needs, getting information and advice about leisure-time interests, and gradually changing the balance between disengagement and activity. Intelligence, education and social attitudes play a part in such preparations. People need to acquire new skills, new attitudes and interests, and new social relationships if they are to make the most of their retirement.

It is not unusual to find reasonably good morale among very old people living in the larger community, where survival to a ripe old age can be something to be proud of. Moreover, the very old are a highly selected sample, not at all representative of the cohort into which they were born. Their disengagement reaches a stable level, disrupted eventually by terminal illness and death.

It is usual for retired persons to cope with their problems reasonably well, once the initial anxiety and unfamiliarity have worn off, but even a modest living requires certain basic things – food, shelter, clothes, medical care, transport, emotional security, physical comfort, entertainment and recreation. Hence the ability to budget sensibly is important. The fact that so much is heard about actual hardship in old age suggests that many retired people are not adequately adjusted. This problem could be eased if extra money and resources were available.

(b) Social class and sex differences

Disengagement works best for people who have maintained some continuity of activity throughout their lives – people with 'vocations' rather than people with 'jobs'. The professional person can often pursue some aspect of his or her life's work and maintain professional contacts right up to the end. There is likely to be time, money and opportunity to prepare for retirement and to cultivate interests and activities which carry over into the later years. This continuity of activities, relationships and attitudes provides a stable pattern of adjustment which carries the person smoothly from a busy adult working life to a more leisurely but satisfying retirement. People in less favourable circumstances, however, spend a large part of their adult years in fairly routine jobs which earn them a living and a retirement pension but have little or no personal significance in the sense of providing activities and opportunities which extend beyond the job itself and beyond the normal working life. For some men in this situation retirement presents problems of adjustment, since it often occurs abruptly at 65, and they have neither the continuity, which is important for good adjustment, nor the time, money and opportunity to prepare for a satisfactory retirement.

Greater provision for retirement benefits and courses in preparation for retirement would enable many more men to use and enjoy their declining years, when disengagement from work relationships may well be followed by a renewal of kinship ties and involvement in domestic chores (shopping, baby-sitting). In years to come, perhaps, a shorter working week, longer holidays and a gradual retirement from paid work will give every individual ample opportunity to cultivate stable long-term interests and personal activities during the working life, which will carry over into retirement.

Long-term unemployment and premature retirement, however, brought about by economic recession and technological changes, have complicated the situation. Lack of opportunities for constructive and satisfying activities, low income and few assets, social stigma, and so on, create problems of adjustment rather different from those of traditional retirement, especially since the person is usually not adequately prepared for premature retirement.

The problems of adjustment in later life for women can be met by a similar pattern of disengagement. Working women are more closely bound than men to the kinship system; and women in general, on account of their continued domestic activities and established patterns of social interaction, especially with relatives and neighbours, may experience less of a break.

The departure of children from the home changes the environment of the middle-aged mother. Her husband's retirement calls for a further readjustment; and most married women become widows, which in turn creates problems of adjustment. Most women look for support from their children, their own and their husband's relatives. In some instances the late-life problems of adjustment might be met more effectively – by education, preparation and counselling.

Disengagement proceeds differently for most women as compared with men, and some of the stages – loss of children, disability, bereavement – may occur relatively early. Apart from possible sex differences in temperament and attitudes, a man's absorption in work and outside interests can weaken his emotional involvement with members of the family and provide him with powerful external supports, so that he may not react to family events with the same intensity as a woman. Women whose children have grown up, or women who have lost husbands, can often find other women of their age in similar circumstances, but a retired man or a widower is less likely to have a large pool of possible acquaintances and may feel socially isolated unless he has family members to turn to. In extreme old age the range of activities for men and women alike becomes very restricted, so that their social roles are similar.

(c) Criticisms of disengagement theory

In its simplest and crudest form, the theory of disengagement states that the diminishing psychological and biological capacities of people in later life necessitate a severance of the relationships that they have with younger people in the central activities of society, and the replacement of these older individuals by younger people. In this way society renews itself and the elderly are free to die.

Criticisms of the theory can be conveniently sorted into three kinds: practical, theoretical and empirical. The practical criticism is that the theory inclines its believers to adopt a policy of segregation of or even indifference to the elderly, and the nihilistic attitude that old age has no value. The theoretical criticism is that disengagement 'theory' is not an axiomatic system in the scientific sense, but at best a 'proto-theory' – a collection of loosely related sets of arguments depending upon unspoken assumptions and doubtful premises. The empirical criticism, perhaps the most serious, is that the evidence called in support of the theory is inadequate or even untrue. For example, the time made available by retirement from full-time employment may be easily absorbed by alternative activities and social relationships. Although there are losses in social relationships following retirement, the departure of children or the death of the spouse, yet relationships with friends, neighbours or other kin go some way to make good those losses. Furthermore, the activities and relationships of late life may be more important and absorbing because they are fewer in number and more 'personal' in nature.

Disengagement theory has been further criticized because the disposition to disengage is a personality dimension as well as a characteristic of ageing. Moreover, contrary to expectation, engagement and activity are more likely to be sought after by older people, and accompanied by happiness and life-satisfaction. The theory underemphasizes historical and cultural influences and overemphasizes the universality and inevitability of the process of disengagement.

Thus, although patterns of promotion and retirement seem to confirm that industrial society has evolved mechanisms for replacing its obsolescent members, it does not follow that individuals lose their personal will to live. On the contrary, resistance to euthanasia has been strong and old people, the most interested party, appear not to favour it as a social policy. Apart from a small proportion of infirm, deranged or socially isolated persons, the elderly continue to associate with others and to be useful and active in so far as their circumstances permit – not so much through central functional roles in the mainstreams of social organization and economic production, but rather in supportive roles and through affective relationships with kin and friends. A number of factors which might be regarded as indicative of disengagement, such as the proportion of people living alone, or infrequency of social contact, do not in fact increase sharply at the age of retirement, though they do increase steadily from middle age.

On the whole, it is more accurate to speak of 'industrial disengagement and increased socio-economic dependence' than of 'social disengagement'; in this way, the origins and circumstances of retirement are kept in focus, and the theory ties in more closely with empirical evidence and common-sense impressions.

The 'activity' or 're-engagement' theory of adult ageing asserts that the natural inclination of most elderly people to associate with others and to participate in group and community affairs is often blocked and disrupted by present-day retirement practices. Hence arrangements should be made for retired people to find worthwhile activities suited to their age, personal qualities and health. Disengagement and re-engagement are counterbalancing tendencies. The former enables or obliges older people to relinquish certain social roles, namely those which they cannot adequately fulfil; the latter prevents the consequences of disengagement from going too far in the direction of isolation, apathy and inaction.

An older person who is inactive and isolated is likely at first to be bored and irritated, but this state of mind may pass as he or she becomes more passive, apathetic and inert. Stagnation leads to further falls in alertness and interest, and to a loss of mental and physical skills through disuse. Prodding older people into action may be an unwarranted intrusion into their privacy, but stimulation and guidance will often help them to maintain an interest in life and derive enjoyment from the company of others.

4. Isolation and Desolation

An interesting and useful distinction has been made between 'isolation' and 'desolation' in old age. Old people may be isolated from their contemporaries by physical incapacity and disengagement and from younger adults by cultural change and social mobility. Infrequency of social contact can be referred to as 'isolation'. Far more serious, however, is 'desolation': the grief and apathy following the sudden loss of a long-standing close relationship. To be 'desolated' is to be left alone, neglected, forsaken by the person one deeply wants to be with; it is a kind of emotional deprivation; it is having no one in whom to confide or upon whom to rely absolutely. The loss is severe because the emotional investment or attachment was strong and deeply ingrained and because there is unlikely to be any chance of forming a satisfactory substitute.

Bereavement, however, usually triggers strong supportive reactions from other people. Reactions to bereavement, or other deeply felt emotional loss, vary because of differences in psychological make-up and in surrounding circumstances. The ability to re-establish normal patterns of behaviour also varies, for the same general reasons. For example, the presence of an extensive network of sympathetic friends and family members obviously reduces the severity of the loss and hastens recovery, whereas physical incapacity and lack of mobility probably hinder it. Partly on account of their greater life expectancy, more old women than old men are socially isolated – and desolated – and more of them are infirm.

Subjective feelings of loneliness are more closely associated with the severance of strong emotional ties than with solitariness. Both psychological desolation and loneliness may be remediable. Hitherto such suffering has been regarded as 'natural' and therefore acceptable. It is worth emphasizing, therefore, that psychological distress in the later years can and should be alleviated to a far greater extent than at present. Too little is yet known about psychosomatic disorders in late life to be able to specify in detail the physiological and psychological mechanisms underlying such conditions. However, depression and suicide appear to be correlated with physical illness; and psychological stress, such as that following bereavement, is associated with physical and mental ill health, and with an increased risk of death.

Suicide rates are higher for men than for women; the rate for women levels off in middle age but the rate for men continues to rise. There is a fall at very late ages, when survivors are successively selected samples of their original cohort; by definition they are healthier and lacking suicidal tendencies. Some elderly people are incapable of conceiving, planning or carrying out such a deliberate act, and many others lack the means; most probably never seriously consider suicide as a possible course of action. The empirical data leave much to be desired, so that firm conclusions are hard to arrive at.

One of the objectives of applied research into social isolation among the elderly is to identify and satisfy the needs of people who are not in a position to help themselves. Such research also helps to identify people who are 'at risk' in the community and who require regular visits from health and welfare workers. Some old people are isolated partly by choice – they have a history of seclusion, shyness, independence or aggressiveness; others, of course, are socially isolated because of circumstances outside their control.

5. Social Achievements

In addition to studying the relation between chronological age and intellectual creativity in the arts and the sciences, Lehman (1953) studied many other kinds of human achievement in the earlier years of the twentieth century. For example, he found that female film stars rose to fame at earlier ages and reached the peak of their fortunes earlier than did male stars – 25 to 29 years as compared with 30 to 34. The subsequent decline in the money-making achievements of female film stars was more rapid than for male stars. As with intellectual achievement, the decline with age after the peak years was more rapid for the higher levels of achievement. Film directors reached their peak between the ages of 35 and 39 and, with few exceptions, had ceased productive work by 55, a very rapid decline. It would be too simple, however, to argue that these results reflect a decline in the ability to act or to make films. The factors that bring about the rise and fall of actual achievement in any field are numerous and complex; biographies and autobiographies provide suitable life-histories to illustrate this point. In areas of achievement such as film acting, and to some extent in industrial and commercial leadership, the actual peak years for ability (whatever that means) are not known; so the age-effects relate partly to status and reputation. The current relationships between age and social achievement may be different from those found by Lehman – but see below.

Age-changes in the amount of money earned by people achieving very large incomes were quite different from those in intellectual achievement. In the USA, again in the earlier years of this century, the peak years for large earnings occurred in the age-period 53–58; but, taking into account the numbers of people alive in each age-group, the proportion of people earning very large incomes was highest for the age-period 60–64. A study of leadership and power in commerce and industry based on names and ages given in the 1938 US edition of *Who's Who in Commerce and Industry* showed that the largest age-group was 55–59; but when account was taken of the number of people left alive at different ages, the highest proportion of leaders was in the age-group 65–69 (although the proportions were high for all ages between 55 and 80). Further studies of the age factor in income, industrial leadership, commercial success and financial power showed that the years of achievement occur relatively late in life, usually after the age of 60.

Lehman studied various kinds of social achievement: in government and politics, in military and judicial affairs, in learning and religion. Leadership and authority in these areas occurred relatively late in life, usually after the age of 40. For some reason, military leaders attained the peak of their profession between the ages of 40 and 44 as compared with naval leaders, who reached theirs between 55 and 59. Where exacting standards are set, as, for example, in plotting the age-distribution of a small number of successful US presidential candidates and comparing it with the age-distribution for a large number of unsuccessful candidates, the age of success started later, between 45 and 49; it had the same peak years, 55 to 59; and it terminated earlier, between 65 and 69. In other words, the effects of age on leadership were more pronounced for leaders of higher esteem than for leaders of lower esteem.

Lehman compared the age-distributions for three kinds of achievement: founding a religious movement, being president of a religious organization and being chief spiritual leader of the Roman Catholic Church. The age-distribution of the religious innovators showed a few aged 20, a vast majority between 30 and 44, and relatively few over 50. The age-distributions for the other two groups showed a steady increase in frequency from 40 up to a peak period after 80. Thus in religion, as in science, the arts, business and government, the years of creativity and innovation occurred relatively early in life, between 30 and 45, or earlier, but the years of consolidation, recognition and establishment occurred later, from about 45 onwards. The influence of surrounding circumstances − opportunity, competition and so on − is perhaps even more obvious in relation to social achievement than in relation to achievement in the arts or sciences.

Leadership skills and opportunities occur fairly late in life, partly because of the balance of intelligence and experience (knowledge) required and partly because of cultural factors. The membership of older people on committees, councils and other bodies puts into their hands the machinery of social control. Their familiarity with this machinery − rules, procedures, rituals, ways and means, sources of information and the like − enables them to use their experience where younger people's greater intelligence might avail them little. The study of smaller and simpler communities shows that even where longevity is not as great as it is in larger and more advanced communities, the elders tend to move into positions of authority, privilege and control.

One result of the decline with age in unspecialized intelligence – see Chapter Eight – and the increase with age in specialization and routinization of experience is that older people in responsible and influential social positions prefer older, familiar attitudes and methods, and resist the introduction of social reforms.

The secular trend in the age at which people achieve social eminence is for later-born generations to attain status at older age-levels as compared with earlier-born generations. This could be the effect of an increase in life expectation, plus the longer period of learning needed for leadership in modern societies.

References and Suggestions for Further Reading

Central Statistical Office, *Social Trends*, no. 16, London: HMSO, 1986.

Cloke, C. (ed.), *Old Age Abuse in the Domestic Setting: a Review*, Mitcham: Age Concern England, 1983.

Dowd, J. J., 'Exchange rates and old people', *Journal of Gerontology*, 35, 1980, 596–602.

Gilleard, C. J., *Living with Dementia. Community Care of the Elderly Mentally Infirm*, London: Croom Helm, 1984.

Giordano, N. H. and Giordano, J. A., 'Elder abuse: a review of the literature', *Social Work*, 29, 1984, 232–6.

Gray, M. and McKenzie, H., *Caring for Older People*, Harmondsworth: Penguin Books, 1986.

Hardie, M., *Understanding Ageing. Facing Common Family Problems*, Sevenoaks: Hodder & Stoughton, 1978.

Health Education Council, *Who Cares? Information and Support for the Carers of Confused People*, London: Health Education Council, 1986.

Hooker, S., *Caring for Elderly People. Understanding and Practical Help*, London: Routledge & Kegan Paul, 1976.

Lawton, M. P., *Environment and Aging*, Monterey, C.A.:

Brooks/Cole, 1980.

Lehman, H. C., *Age and Achievement*, London: Oxford
University Press, 1953.

Office of Population Censuses and Surveys, *Mortality Statistics,
1984, England and Wales*, London: HMSO, 1986.

The Open University, *Caring for Older People, Study Pack 650*,
Milton Keynes: The Open University, 1985.

Six
Personality and Adjustment

1. Approaches to the Study of Personality

Personality is defined by the consistencies and regularities running through a person's behaviour and experience during some specific period of his or her life-history, including any general fact that identifies and distinguishes him or her from other people of a similar sort. There are two contrasting approaches to the study of personality.

The 'individual differences' approach attempts to identify the main dimensions of personality by means of standardized tests and to demonstrate their effects by means of experimental investigations. So, for example, if measures of extraversion and emotional instability could be shown to be reliable and valid over the age-range under investigation, one might try to study age-trends in these dimensions of personality during the later years, or to examine how they affect adjustment to retirement or to bereavement.

The 'individual case' method attempts first of all, through close description and analysis of a person's current circumstances and life-history, to understand that particular person's adjustment to his or her environment. It is essentially a 'clinical' approach. However, investigating well-chosen similar cases and learning from these examples may reveal a common pattern or 'prototype', i.e. the general case, of which the particular cases are examples. The discovery of basic 'types' of case then facilitates classification and management. So, for example, the identification of a 'type' of elderly person who is socially isolated, suffers from sensory impairment and has a characteristically suspicious and hostile personality, might help in the classification and treatment of some elderly patients with mental disorders.

The methodological problems of studying ageing are difficult enough without the further complications that arise in connection with the methods and concepts of personality study. Nevertheless, psychologists use psychometric methods in their attempts to study the effects of ageing on the 'dimensions' of personality and adjustment. A wide variety of methods can be applied, as follows. Rating scales and self-ratings used in conjunction with flexible interviews yield quantitative data about personal qualities, motivation and complex attitudes. Probing questionnaires enable the investigator to examine in detail such activities as: spending habits, leisure-time activities, social contacts and self-care. Non-directive interviews explore the older person's private world of wishes, personal feelings, recollections and social attitudes. Standardized verbal scales measure traits, morale, interests, values, beliefs and opinions.

Projective methods (interpreting ink-blots, completing sentences or building a story around a picture) are thought to reveal, indirectly, motives and attitudes, and ways of dealing with the world. On the basis of data obtained by projective tests, it has been claimed that older people show changes with age in achievement needs and a growing tendency towards inactivity, submission and introspection. Affiliative needs appear to become deeper and more selective. Older subjects express less emotional involvement in the activities they describe, less worry, and less assertiveness; their lives and surroundings become simpler. However, projective tests are open to a number of objections on scientific grounds, and research claims such as these should be regarded with considerable scepticism.

Biographical analysis includes a range of methods, for example the content analysis of diaries and autobiographies, life-history interviews and inventories. The aim is to identify common features in the lives of people who, for example, become maladjusted, or who live exceptionally long. The attempt to 'average out' patterns of behaviour and experience for people in general is obviously not very productive of new insights; what is required is the biographical analysis of specific and well-defined groups, such as unmarried female teachers or army officers. Biographical diversity is to be expected even within these relatively narrow groups, but the age-trends should average out more clearly, and the results would be of general interest in sociology and psychology. Biographical analysis cannot provide a comprehensive life-history account of the average man or woman; at best it can deal in detail with only one segment (a series of episodes) of a person's life. See Runyan (1982) and Bromley (1986) for an account of the life-history and case-study methods. It would be interesting to examine what sorts of event people themselves regard as making up their life-history. What gives them psychological significance and fixes them in memory?

The reasons usually offered for using psychometric methods rather than relying upon ordinary observation are that, first, they are quick and convenient; secondly, they increase the range of inquiry; thirdly, they improve objectivity and quantification, and so help to provide more systematic evidence about ageing. They can be used in all kinds of research: drug trials, attitudes of supervisors to older workers, age-changes in interests, attitudes to retirement, age-changes in confidence, anxiety and other aspects of personality and adjustment, and capacity for self-care – though this topic illustrates that methods which give quick and convenient, but indirect, measures of behaviour and experience in adult life and old age may be invalid; they may lead the investigator to draw the wrong conclusion. Responses to a questionnaire may not correspond with direct observations of subjects in their normal surroundings. Similarly, subjects may overestimate or underestimate their physical health, depending upon the specific questions asked and the standard of comparison used. An elderly man may claim he can wash and dress without difficulty, do his shopping, and take care when crossing roads, though actual observation may reveal that he is much less competent than he claims. Similarly, he may say that he has very few visitors, when he has more than average. A further disadvantage is that such questionnaires and verbal scales need to be 're-calibrated', as it were, to suit the particular cultural conditions of the samples being investigated. It is important, therefore, to test the validity of methods of assessing personal adjustment, especially in relation to life-satisfaction and the activities of daily living, so that benefits go to those who are most in need of them.

The stages and facets of adult life described in Chapter One correspond broadly to those known to common sense and confirmed by biographical analysis. These include, for example, the transition from school to work, from the single state to marriage. Subsequently, there are transitions through occupational and family stages of adult development. The years of investment, expansion and effort give way to the 'harvest' years of middle age, and to its later phases of reassessment and reorganization. Retirement (disengagement) ushers in some changes, but rarely induces serious discontinuities in personality and outlook, even though one's circumstances and daily activities are substantially altered. Old age and terminal behaviour complete the series – biomedical factors dominate the situation and life is reduced to its more basic dimensions. The study of personality in adult life and old age has been conceived as a developmental study of these stages and transitions in the life-cycle.

Personality can be defined by the stable characteristics exhibited by the person during these stages and transitions. This is not to say that the human personality does not change during adult life and old age. Indeed, the stresses of late life and the onset of dementia may, for the unfortunate few, bring about substantial and adverse changes in basic personality characteristics – even loss of emotional control and personal identity. The fact is that adults at any age differ widely in their reactions to situations – to retirement, illness, relocation and so on; we find it convenient to attribute part of this variation to personality variables, on the assumption that people can be usefully characterized as having stable, enduring personal dispositions, i.e. traits, abilities, values, attitudes, motivations, temperamental qualities and so on.

2. Motivation and Frustration

The problem with human motivation is that it is difficult to assess inner experience, capacity or disposition independently of the behaviour to which they give rise. But then the behaviour is also determined by the physical and psychological resources available to the person and by the constraints and opportunities of the person's environment. Both sets of factors change with age; and it is not at all clear that motivation in general (drive) and the intensity of motivational states (arousal) decrease substantially with age. Certain types of behaviour, such as physical aggression, sexuality, congregate social mixing, seem to be less in evidence in older age-groups, but this does not necessarily mean that the underlying motivations have diminished. Recent studies suggest that the decline of sexuality with age is much less than had been supposed and that in any event the nature of 'sexuality' changes with age. It is clear both that older people can become extremely interested in certain kinds of activities and to that extent exhibit strong motivation, and that some have less intense enthusiasms and frequently need strong incentives, support and encouragement before they are prepared to embark on a new course of action.

Methods of studying motivation and affect are broadly the same as those found in the study of personality and adjustment (of which motivation and affect are part) and include physiological procedures.

Human interests are varied and closely associated with historical changes (for example, television-viewing and motoring), which makes cross-sectional comparisons difficult. Moreover, age-changes in leisure-time interests are obscured by situational influences such as local opportunities and cost. The general trends can be predicted from the known effects of age on physical health, speed of performance and intelligence; namely, a trend away from participation to spectatorship, and a trend towards less energetic, less hazardous activities and home-based, self-paced, passive interests, such as gardening, reading and television-viewing.

Improvements in older people's physical health and living standards, together with the emergence of special-interest groups of the elderly, can be expected to lead to an increase in the provision of leisure facilities, provided convenient public transport can be arranged.

Our long-range aims and our established patterns of social interaction provide a framework within which we play our part in life. Thus the stability, coherence and consistency characteristic of the well-adjusted person arise not only from *within*, from stable dispositions of personality and temperament, but also from *without*, from the controlling, stabilizing and directing influences of the physical and social environment – family and domestic circumstances, work, interpersonal relationships, money, material possessions and geographical position. Each of us is, in part, a 'creature of circumstance'. When we retire, some of this external physical and social framework is removed, and we have to change our ways; if we have not prepared for retirement, adjustment is more difficult.

Under conditions of frustration and emotional stress, our motivational state becomes strongly focused on the immediate future, concerned with protecting our immediate interests and mobilizing our inner resources. During early adult life, presumably, as in juvenile development, motivation towards expansion of the self predominates, although the stresses of adult development in a competitive achieving society produce a certain amount of frustration and failure. In middle age, some kind of equilibrium seems to be established for most people. In later life, however, competitive motivation should decrease because our physical and psychological resources cannot sustain the demands being made upon them. A serious sort of frustration is that engendered by any persistent, stressful, no-solution situation which tends to elicit violent reactions such as anger or panic but eventually leads to depression and despair, or apathetic resignation. This may explain the apathy and resignation sometimes found in the institutionalized elderly, who seem to have lost any sense of their ability to influence events that affect them personally, or learned that it is safer and less stressful to accept full dependency. Attempts to get patients to take a greater interest in, and more control over, institutional activities have met with some success. The problem is how to make the procedures part of an institution's continuing policy.

Frustration during late maturity and old age can arise for a number of reasons including: adverse physiological changes and restrictions on activity; occupational redundancy; failure of occupational aspirations, with a consequent limitation of living standards; failure to keep pace with cultural, social and scientific developments, and so feeling out of date; sadness at the loss of youthful vigour and freedom and the uninviting prospect of growing old, aggravated by prevailing social attitudes; grief at the loss of valued or stabilizing emotional relationships through bereavement; lack of preparation for retirement; the departure of children; the 'no-solution' problem of being caught in a web of unsatisfactory circumstances from which escape seems impossible, such as family ties, physical disability or lack of money.

Critical episodes at any time of life can bring about new attitudes and new adjustments. Some events are traumatic; for example, going bankrupt, being divorced, or becoming deaf. Such episodes mark periods of conflict, frustration and unhappiness, and may result in considerable reorganization of the person's motives and actions. While leaving a scar, they need not undermine (and may even strengthen) the person's emotional stability. Other formative experiences can be very gratifying; for example, falling in love, coming into money, or achieving success in cultural or scientific work. In later life being well-adjusted means being emotionally stable and resourceful in adapting to changed circumstances like bereavement, retirement, ill health or loss or employment. Except in conditions of senescent mental disorder the basic structure of the personality appears to be maintained, perhaps simplified and more clearly delineated, throughout late maturity and old age.

Physical changes in the nervous system and endocrine system are bound to have repercussions on motivational states and affective expression – for example, on sexual behaviour, mood states and stress reactions. Age-changes in motivation can be expected to have pervasive effects on other aspects of the process of adjustment: attitudes, decision processes and learning. Such changes are not wholly endogenous; latent desires can be activated if the environment contains incentives, i.e. opportunities for their fulfilment. Similarly, motivation may diminish if opportunities for satisfaction are persistently curtailed. Environmental conditions set up reinforcement contingencies that 'shape' the motivational characteristics of older people; for example, by decreasing opportunities for sex and physical adventure, and by increasing opportunities for domestic leisure activities and sleep.

The combined effects of internal and external factors lead to behaviour which is difficult to interpret in terms of motivation alone. In fact, motivational concepts are philosophically suspect. Hence any description of age-changes in motivation is difficult to substantiate, especially if the behavioural evidence is indirect, in the form of responses to projective tests or questionnaires. Can or should motivational interpretations of age-changes be de-emphasized in favour of more strictly behavioural concepts – stimulus conditions and reinforcement history? For example, the so-called 'crisis points' in adult life could be understood not as intrinsic phases in motivational development but as the fortuitous effects of a particular life-style.

The existence of powerful situational constraints on behaviour, and of powerful conditioning influences, provides a challenge to the view that 'personality' factors are the prime determinants of individual adjustment. The failure to identify and accurately measure the basic dimensions of personality, at least to anything like the same extent as other determinants of behaviour, reduces the value of standardized personality tests in the assessment of the effects of ageing. This is apart from the question of whether such tests are valid for older age-groups. This point of view must not be taken as a rejection of the psychometric approach to personality and ageing, but rather as a caution against uncritical acceptance of its claims.

3. The Self-Concept

Although most personality characteristics appear not to be as consistent across situations as some investigators had supposed, characteristics relating to the self-concept are fairly consistent in young adults. But is it reasonable to believe that they are fairly stable in relation to ageing? We are on such close and familiar terms with ourselves that we are not likely to register age-changes in our self-concept, just as we scarcely register changes in our physical appearance. Our appearance, however, is an external fact and can be compared with photographic records, whereas only people who diligently keep personal diaries can observe age-changes in the self.

The view that one's impression of oneself stays very much the same throughout adult life is not unreasonable if we accept that the major formative experiences take place in the early years, with adult development making only marginal modifications. On the other hand, the experiences of adult life are cumulative and for some people a number of them may be critical and formative. Biological changes and personal experiences in adult life are bound to have some effects on personality and adjustment, but any effects have yet to be adequately described and analysed. Any effects on the *self-concept* are also uncertain.

The self-concept is difficult to investigate. The methods employed in research include: adjective check-lists, self-ratings, projective tests and the content-analysis of self-descriptions. The apparent increase with age in anxiety, introversion and neuroticism, and the apparent decrease in risk-taking and confidence, point to some sorts of change in the self-concept. Presumably we form a less favourable impression of ourselves as we grow older. The negative value placed on later ages supports this idea. Aspirations normally exceed achievements, and as long as we feel that we still have time, resources and opportunities, we can ignore this discrepancy. Eventually, however, we realize that the discrepancy is there to stay, and we may blame this 'failure' on ourselves.

Psychometric studies of the self-concept, although numerous, have not proved to be of much theoretical importance or practical value in psychology generally. The methods that have been used are open to a variety of criticisms about their reliability, validity and utility. The further methodological complications associated with the study of ageing make this area of interest exceedingly difficult to investigate. Nevertheless, it is important to pursue this line of inquiry because it is concerned with some basic aspects of human ageing: our sense of personal change and the feelings of satisfaction or dissatisfaction it engenders; our sense of personal identity, constructed on the basis of key events, circumstances and relationships in our life-history (partly accessible through reminiscence and life-review) and undermined by mental ill health; our sense of social identity, continually under revision through the process of self-other comparisons and awareness of changes in our social position brought about by such things as retirement or bereavement.

The psychodynamic approach to normal ageing is essentially a psychology of 'ego-functions', concerned with changes in self-awareness, self-other relationships, strategies of adjustment, and the control and expression of feelings. Some psychological disorders of late onset – depression, for example – seem to respond well to a form of treatment called cognitive behaviour therapy: in brief, the person is helped to understand the psychological factors at work, through counselling and other procedures, and shown how to modify his or her circumstances and actions so as to decrease the likelihood of unrewarding outcomes. This approach abandons the simple popular notion of self-control as a stable personality characteristic and replaces it with a more complicated notion of self-understanding and self-direction achieved through systematic self-observation and learning from experience.

One psychodynamic account of ageing suggests that after several juvenile stages of ego development, the young adult either develops an affective and functional relationship of intimacy (usually with a marital partner) or suffers a sense of personal isolation; in middle age the person either becomes generative, i.e. concerned for others and future-orientated, or suffers a sense of personal stagnation; the elderly person, finally, either achieves a sense of integrity, i.e. realism, or begins to despair – see Erikson (1978).

Throughout normal adult life, people are faced with the problem of adjusting their values and attitudes to their changing circumstances and to their changing physical and psychological capacities. These readjustments affect every facet of behaviour and experience – sexual relationships, parenthood, work, leisure, social attitudes, self-regard and so on. The inner experience of old age has been given some expression in literature, but has so far received little scientific attention.

4. Middle Age

(a) The concept of middle age

The term 'middle age' does not refer to any well-defined stage in the human life-cycle and it means different things to different people – depending upon whether they are younger or older, male or female. Nevertheless, middle age is a convenient fiction in so far as it points to an important aspect of adult psychology which has received little attention from gerontologists until very recently.

We have seen that the so-called 'adult' period extends from the later teens to retirement age or beyond – though this span of 40 or more years does not constitute an entirely unchanging phase of the lifespan. During this period the biological effects of ageing are gradual and cumulative but relatively unobtrusive. There are compensatory changes in physiological and behavioural processes and we generally have adequate time and opportunity to adapt to changing capacities and circumstances.

There are no reliable biological or behavioural markers for middle age, except perhaps the menopause; but this is not a satisfactory marker, because it is quite variable in terms both of chronological age and of its effects. Post-menopausal women, however, appear to lose some of the protection they enjoyed against coronary artery disease as a consequence of changes in hormone balance. Contrary to popular belief, the menopause is not associated with uniform behavioural consequences such as emotional upsets. The existence of the so-called 'male climacteric' is doubtful, although the notion has been invoked as an explanation for marked changes in the mid-life behaviour of some men. The age of 40 is popularly thought of as the transition point into middle age; this corresponds roughly with the age at which the average working man in Britain enters the second half of his working life. Among women, child-bearing is usually complete and the biological changes associated with the menopause are in prospect, the average age of women at the menopause being about 47. The midpoint of the adult phase of the human life-cycle is between 45 and 50 for men and between 50 and 55 for women. At this age the average man or woman can expect to live for about another 25 years. This mid-adult age, however, is merely a statistical fact of no particular biological or behavioural significance.

In the popular imagination middle age is associated with having comfortable, settled, domestic and occupational routines. Middle-aged people are thought of as fairly sedate and conservative, a little past the excitements and discoveries of youth. In professional work, people are usually middle-aged before they become 'established'. Hence middle-aged people are in a stronger position financially and as regards authority and influence than other age-groups.

Thus, middle age does not refer to the earlier stage of life when people in competitive achieving societies are making their way through successive occupational levels and establishing a network of family members and lasting friendships; nor to the later stage when they are preparing to disengage from their main occupational role. So, in some respects, middle age is a high point in the life-cycle. Most people then are in fairly good health; their psychological capacities are relatively unimpaired; they have accumulated considerable experience which they can use to advantage; they are usually as well off, secure and privileged as they are ever likely to be. The physical vigour of youth may have passed or the supposed tranquillity of old age not yet arrived, but overall 'middle' age compares favourably with other ages, and is indeed sometimes referred to as the 'prime' of life.

(b) Physical health

The apparent stability of the middle years is, however, something of an illusion brought about by psychological adaptation. For example, familiarity with our own behaviour and physical appearance, and that of close kin and friends, means that we tend not to register the slow but inexorable effects of ageing. Only when people renew acquaintance after a period of separation do age-changes appear noticeable. All sorts of anatomical and physiological changes which we do not notice particularly, such as increased blood pressure and poorer hearing, reduce our functional effectiveness and predispose us to a variety of late-life infirmities. Although there is a surprising lack of evidence on the issue, it is likely that the adverse biological and behavioural consequences of ageing consist in part of stepwise changes consequent upon illness, accidents and stresses affecting a critical function, and of threshold effects resulting from the building up of many small intrinsic changes. Our reliance on average trends to describe the effects of ageing creates the impression that changes are gradual and smooth rather than stepwise and substantial.

The biomedical hazards of the middle years are different from those at other ages. Ill health arises from a variety of interrelated causes. The death rate is two or three times higher in later middle age, about 45 to 60, than between about 20 and 45. The main causes are cancer, heart disease, stroke and respiratory disease. Coronary heart disease is associated with unhealthy living habits, such as smoking, drinking, lack of physical exercise, and inappropriate diet. The proportion of people who are ill rises gradually to about the age of 45 or 50 and then accelerates fairly sharply. The full extent of psychiatric ill health in middle age has yet to be determined but the most common psychiatric ailment is depression. Neurotic and psychosomatic disorders also increase in frequency. Suicide accounts for a very small proportion of deaths in middle age, but suicide and attempted suicide increase in middle age and are more common among men.

Cross-cultural comparisons reveal substantial differences in death rates and causes of death in middle age, even between advanced societies. The picture is complicated by regional and secular variations within different countries.

Physical and mental ill health in the middle years imposes demands on hospital, medical and welfare services; it leads to absence from work, low productivity and economic loss, as well as to difficulties in personal adjustment and interpersonal relationships. Much of this ill health could be prevented or reduced by earlier treatment, healthier life-styles and medical screening. Various forms of treatment have been developed, including surgery, drugs, prosthetic aids and, more recently, behaviour modification for psychiatric disorders.

For some people, serious physical or mental ill health forces an abrupt and major readjustment in their way of life, and the acceptance of restrictions that they would have previously thought intolerable. For the majority, however, the biological changes of middle age are gradual. The individual adapts to them without radical alteration in self-image or daily activities. Nevertheless, the effects are cumulative, and the individual is eventually obliged to accept the fact that he or she is no longer 'young'. This may be brought home through reductions in work capacity, loss of sexual powers, comparisons with other people regarding physical appearance, career status, and so on. This realization is usually intermittent and partial at first, but conviction and acceptance of the fact come gradually through experience.

The cumulative effects of normal ageing and the increased prevalence of definite physical and mental disorders in the middle-aged create a heightened awareness of their state of health regarding weight, digestion, sleep, aches and pains, and the like. Absence from work because of sickness rises sharply from about the age of 45; frequency of consultation with a physician increases. Many middle-aged people, however, are grossly ignorant of matters relating to human biology, and their attempts to improve their appearance and physical fitness or to alleviate minor medical conditions are often unsuccessful. The maintenance of physical fitness, in the strong sense, requires more dedication and resources than many middle-aged persons can muster.

The gradual realization that one is growing older leads to a number of behavioural changes. Many people avoid activities inappropriate to their 'middle-aged' status, but as this status is not clearly defined by chronological age but rather by self-assessment and social pressures, they can quite easily take part in activities appropriate for either younger or older people. Age-segregation is indeed much less marked than in adolescence or late life, and one of the joys of middle age is *making* the social rules instead of feeling constrained by those already in existence.

(c) Socio-economic factors

In Britain, men in manual work achieve their highest earnings in their forties as compared with the fifties for men in non-manual work. Women in manual work reach their peak in their late twenties as compared with women in non-manual work, who have fairly constant earnings over their working life. These differences point to the possibility that the psychological and behavioural features of middle age depend to some extent upon socio-economic class.

Changes in the types and rates of employment for both men and women have been brought about by technological advances in recent years. The changes are so far-reaching that it is impossible to foresee their consequences on employment generally and on living standards over the adult years.

In the past, income and living standards tended to improve with age. The 'trajectory' of socio-economic status, however, varied between the two broad social classes. The average working-class man passed his peak earning capacity by the age of 40, the middle-class man not until 50. Although non-manual earnings started at a lower level, they soon overtook manual earnings and exceeded them substantially after the age of 30. Partly as a consequence of their higher earnings and initial financial assets, and partly as a result of their education and values, middle-class people in professional and managerial posts or in business are more likely to acquire material and financial assets, and to find time and opportunities for constructive leisure and social advancement. Working-class people in unskilled or semi-skilled work are much less likely to have these advantages, and therefore view middle age differently. Working-class men do not have the time and resources to prepare adequately for retirement – or, perhaps, sense that they have less freedom of choice about what to do in retirement. They face a more serious reduction in their social and economic status and in the activities of daily living when they retire than do men in professional and managerial occupations. Middle-class people do not normally have the same degree of insecurity in the pre-retirement period, and they can maintain a substantial degree of continuity throughout their later years. This probably contributes to the stability of their self-image, social interaction, leisure activities and mental health.

If this line of reasoning is sound, socio-economic factors should contribute to an earlier feeling of being middle-aged in working-class people, as compared with middle-class people. Working-class men and women may feel 'too old at forty': they reconcile themselves to such security and status as they have managed to achieve and settle down to a comfortable routine. Professional men and women, on the other hand, may feel that 'life begins at forty': they have probably achieved a high standard of living and family security and can now relax and enjoy their leisure.

The difficulty with this view is that we do not have the empirical survey data that would enable us to 'disaggregate' the middle-aged, i.e. to examine particular sorts of people in particular sorts of circumstances. Consequently, we tend to rely on common knowledge, and generalize widely but without much insight into the subtleties and variations in middle age.

(d) Sex differences

The adult developmental status of married women is closely tied to the following sequence of events: first employment, marriage, birth of first and subsequent children, entry into school of the last child, re-entry into paid employment, departure from home of the last child, birth of grandchildren, retirement from paid employment, husband's retirement, husband's death. There appears to be little information on the adult development of single women following a career in full-time paid employment. Younger divorced women usually marry again. The middle age of a married woman is largely shaped by her marital circumstances, her family and neighbourhood roles. It starts with her release from responsibility for the daytime care and control of her children, a gradual rather than an abrupt process, affected by the number and ages of the children, their schooling and employment, and so on. It coincides broadly with the onset of middle age for her husband. Much of the married woman's domestic life continues unchanged in middle age because social and family activities easily fill the time formerly occupied in looking after her own children. More married women now return to paid employment after 30, when their last child has entered school. Nowadays the typical age-distribution of life-history events differs considerably from that of former days; in particular, a woman's age at the marriage of her last child has decreased from about 55 to 45 since the end of the nineteenth century.

Marital relationships appear to deteriorate on average from early adult life to middle age, then gradually recover. The currently increasing role of divorce – representing perhaps the tip of the iceberg of marital disharmony – supports this idea. Marriage partners feel less satisfied with the relationship, less happy, less likely to agree. Moreover, sexual activity decreases with age (see Chapter Two, section 2s) and, in the United States at least, people report less sharing of interests and activities in the later years of marriage.

Some women are predisposed to physical and psychological disorders precipitated by age-changes and the emotional stresses of adult life. The incidence of emotional maladjustment is higher for women than for men, although the suicide rate is lower. Substantial differences between men and women in death rates for selected causes suggest that some high-risk disorders in men could be avoided, such as lung cancer and heart disease.

Whereas men become more concerned with their own health and anxious to maintain their functional efficiency (at work and play), women become more concerned with their husband's health. That is to say, men engage in what is called 'body monitoring' whereas women engage more in 'rehearsal for widowhood'; they fantasize about what they would do if their husband fell ill, died or became mentally disturbed, and may press for assurances that they will be provided for in the event of bereavement.

In view of the remarkable improvements recently in the status of women in western industrial societies, it is risky to speculate on sex differences in values and attitudes. This is, incidentally, another example of the way in which changes affecting different cohorts can be misconstrued as changes associated with ageing. In spite of the improvements, it seems likely that substantial sex differences in values and attitudes persist. It has also been argued that the relatively underprivileged status of women has handicapped them in respect of the provision of health and welfare services for the elderly.

There is no firm evidence that ageing affects personality characteristics differently in men and women, except that masculinity/femininity differences are less marked at older age-levels. One could expect cohort effects as a consequence of the emancipation of women and increased equality between the sexes. In women, the physical and psychological attributes of sexual attractiveness are highly valued in the late teens and early twenties. These are soon supplemented and to some extent replaced by the socially valued attributes associated with being a wife and mother. In men, the physical and psychological attributes of masculinity can be sustained almost indefinitely, not because there is no loss in virility, physique and appearance but because masculine virtues – vigour, competence, strength, courage – can find direct expression in sexual and parental activities, and metaphorical or symbolic expression in work and leisure activities.

(e) Some advantages of middle age

People who achieve socio-economic security and maintain good health can find middle age rewarding. About three-quarters of the total intellectual output of scientists and writers is distributed over the age-range 30 to 59. Half the discoveries and developments in medicine and psychology are made after the age of 40. The years between 30 and 59 account for about 70 or 80 per cent of the total time spent in important posts in political, military and industrial institutions. Social positions held in high regard involving ritual and ceremonial functions, for example, in religion, government or law, are rarely occupied before middle age, although many elderly people hold such positions. Personal authority and esteem are likely to reach their maximum in middle age even in more ordinary walks of life.

The accumulated experience and stabilized attitudes of middle age make it easier to respond effectively to the normal demands of the environment – even physical performance, as in driving or athletics, is modified by experience. But the same principle applies to the management of one's emotions and to the handling of recurrent situations at work, at home, or in ordinary life. Through experience, one develops what are, in effect, strategies of adjustment that will cope with most situations, given the flexibility to make tactical changes as required. By middle age, most of us are established in a 'psychological niche'; that is to say, we have become adapted to a limited environment and our adjustment to the activities of daily living has been reduced to a fairly regular routine. This can improve life considerably, through feelings of security and fulfilment, for example, and the avoidance of stress and anxiety. One disadvantage is that the behavioural niche may become a rut. Experience provides the perspective and patience needed to make sound judgements and to work out the implications of decisions and actions. Thus we are relieved of the burden of having to think afresh each time we are faced with a problem, and we feel more confidence in decisions based on experience. The middle-aged person often has a wide range of social contacts and is thus in a good position to collect information and solve problems, as in business or scientific research.

(f) The inner experience of middle age

Some middle-aged people achieve a high degree of security; their behaviour becomes stable and regular to the point of routine, their thoughts, feelings and desires become conformist and unadventurous. To what extent can flexible and creative states of mind be maintained within such a secure and regular framework of behaviour? For other people, middle age is a time of achievement and gratification. Far from imposing a humdrum existence, their circumstances call for enterprise, self-reliance and determination.

In an analogy between the course of a person's life and the log of a journey, middle age represents a critical choice point at which the individual tries to review progress so far and make decisions about the rest of the journey. In a sense, the individual constructs a private version of his or her own life-history, and tries to integrate its various strands to make a coherent narrative. This 'life-review' is not necessarily attuned to reality, because recollections are likely to be selected and distorted in order to minimize feelings of anxiety, guilt and regret.

The middle-aged person's subjective account of his or her life so far is not just a matter of adding the latest instalment to the series told at earlier ages, but rather of enlarging the story and revising it in the light of recent events and experiences. Self-justification no doubt plays an important part, but the process is also purposive in the sense that the individual is trying to make sense of the past so as to understand the present and plan for the future more effectively. Biographical and autobiographical analysis, already established in social and behavioural gerontology, are among the more promising methods for studying the inner experience of adult life and old age.

Middle age constitutes a kind of vantage point in the geography of personal experience. Retrospectively, we see that we might have traversed the terrain differently. Prospectively, it looks limited and somewhat bleak, especially in the distance. We may decide to simplify the rest of the journey by being much more selective and realistic in our choice of objectives, and by mobilizing and conserving our resources to maximize the likelihood of success. A young person has not yet discovered his or her capacities and limitations and finds it difficult to formulate long-range strategies in view of life's uncertainties, but at 50 our personal future seems to be shrinking rapidly The realization that one has a further expectation of only, say, 25 years – or worse, perhaps only 10 or 15 productive years – has different effects on different people. Some concentrate on unfinished business and set about reappraising their activities and aims in life. Others feel depressed and demoralized. Most, no doubt, fall somewhere between these two extremes – uncertain of their self-assessment, not disposed to schedule their time rigorously, and inclined either not to think about the problem or to compromise and adapt to prevailing circumstances.

Perhaps the most important aspect of the inner experience of middle age is the intermittent realization that the circumstances and events of our life so far have had cumulative and long-term consequences which have created a set of constraints and limited opportunities which form the inescapable matrix out of which our future actions are born. We may feel very satisfied with the outcome so far; if not, then the growing realization that our freedom of action is becoming severely restricted may precipitate adverse reactions ranging from momentary flashes of regret and anger to psychologically disabling feelings of depression and hopelessness. As middle age continues, the chances of breaking out of the web of circumstances rapidly diminish. For some individuals this constitutes a kind of mid-life crisis which results in maladjustment or even suicide (as a response to a no-solution situation), or in radical re-adjustments in behaviour – marital break-up, emigration, change of occupation.

In comparing ourselves with others, we identify with people who have lived through the same historical episodes – military service, political events, socio-technical changes – and who have been conditioned by them in the same way. Hence the tendency to distinguish different 'generations' of people – the post-war generation, 'liberated' women, the 'new' generation, and so on. This identification strengthens the assertion that middle age is a state of mind. If, in our own private view, we define ourselves as middle-aged and act accordingly, then we are, in a real sense, middle-aged. Naturally, there are differences between individuals in the terms of reference used for these social comparisons. Middle-aged people compare themselves with others in respect of health, circumstances, appearance, career grade and so on. In association with the process of life-review, such self-other comparisons may increase or decrease feelings of self-esteem, making them feel happier and more confident or, by contrast, disappointed and guilty. We may grossly overrate ourselves and fail to appreciate the limited freedom we have to control our own fate, for we have to live with the consequences of our actions. We may underrate ourselves and never discover what we could have become.

In middle age, as at other ages, self-assessment and self-other comparisons are usually related to social values. Adults prefer to look younger, to be healthier and more vigorous than average, to achieve acclaim or seniority while still relatively young; thus they maintain a check on their adult developmental status. Although each of us has a unique frame of reference for making such comparisons, our basic criteria are broadly similar to those that other people use, since we share with them a similar cultural background – norms, attitudes and values.

A prominent feature of middle age, then, is the inner experience, the state of mind. The foregoing account, however, may over-intellectualize the process of mid-life adjustment. For many men and women who are not by education or inclination disposed to reflective thought, middle age is not so much an experience as a way of life.

5. Old Age

(a) Making judgements – a warning

One of the major difficulties in the study of personality is that of distinguishing between the characteristics that people 'really' have and the characteristics that they 'seem' to have. The characteristics that people 'seem' to have – their temperamental dispositions, abilities, faults, values, motives, and the like – are to some extent a function of our beliefs and expectations about people in general. How we go about trying to understand and deal with other people (and to understand and manage ourselves) is the outcome of a long and complicated process of social learning, closely tied in with the forms of language we use to describe and explain human behaviour. In cases where we cannot explain a person's behaviour in common-sense terms, we tend to categorize it as crazy or abnormal and leave the expert to account for it in the technical language of the scientist and professional. Unfortunately, we are not always aware of the subjective character of our notions about human behaviour, and so do not realize the extent to which we impose our own subjective 'patterns of meaning' – through selective attention, implicit assumptions, and interpretation – on the actual facts of the case.

It is not surprising, therefore, that our understanding of elderly people is to a large extent based on the beliefs we hold about ageing and the elderly, beliefs which may be quite erroneous or at least inappropriate in relation to particular cases. Generalizations about the 'elderly' are rarely valid and useful because of the wide range of differences between people – in health, abilities, personality and circumstances. Hence the need to get away from broad categories, including wide age-groups, which lend themselves to oversimplified and stereotyped ways of thinking.

One corrective to unwitting subjectivity in our assessment of other people – the elderly especially – is greater reliance on empirical data (hard evidence), meaning direct and reliable first-hand reports of their behaviour and the surrounding circumstances, preferably collected in a systematic and standardized way by competent well-placed observers. Another corrective is to consider, with the help of other investigators, *all* reasonable interpretations of that behaviour, not just the 'obvious' one or the one we personally happen to think is right. A third is to bear in mind the complexities of human action – it depends on the personal qualities of the individual and on the circumstances surrounding an action.

One can demonstrate the effects that knowledge of a person's age or health has on judgement by carrying out an experiment in which subjects are presented with standard descriptions of people, except that the stated age or health condition is systematically varied. Subjects' judgements and inferences can then be shown to be influenced in subtle ways by this kind of information. Judgements about failure, for example, are likely to attribute it to lack of effort in a younger person but to lack of ability in an older person.

(b) Continuities and discontinuities

When considering to what extent there is stability or change in personality during the adult years, consider first genetic endowment: genetic characteristics are thought to play a part in setting the limits, the general direction, and the order of appearance of many psychological characteristics – intellectual, temperamental, sensori-motor, and so on. Of course, what is inherited is not the characteristics themselves, but the genes which initiate and guide physical development. Juvenile development can be characterized as the emergence of genetic characteristics in the context of environmental conditions favourable or unfavourable to the development of certain characteristics – physical stature, emotional stability, artistic talent. The adult personality is stable in the sense that the individual has reached physical maturity. His or her genetic potentialities are expressed phenotypically, i.e. in response to environmental and life-history factors. Changes in the physical basis of personality – especially in the endocrine system and the cerebral cortex brought about by the normal (intrinsic) effects of ageing and by injury and disease – can be expected to change the individual's behaviour, psychological states and traits. These changes, however, are so complex that it is not possible to arrive at firm conclusions. The most we can do at present is to try to establish approximate relationships between conditions like depression, anxiety or well-being on the one hand, and various physiological and environmental conditions on the other: for example, to investigate the relationship between depression and catecholamine secretion in relation to ageing, or to search for connections between stressful life-events, such as bereavement or serious financial loss, and mental or physical illness.

The second basic source of variation in adult personality characteristics is the environment. It provides opportunities for and constraints upon the expression of inherited potentialities, as in athletic performance, artistic accomplishment and scientific productivity. But we distinguish between performance (behaviour) and the abilities or dispositions which lie behind or are revealed by overt action. Personality characteristics are the dispositions underlying behaviour; lack of opportunity may mean that some dispositions (traits, abilities, tendencies, values, assumptions) do not find expression in behaviour, or find expression indirectly, or in fantasy. Adult life normally occupies about 60 years, so it is not surprising that all kinds of environmental factors and life-history events affect the way we behave. But again, behaviour is not personality; behaviour is the way in which personality characteristics are expressed in a given set of circumstances, i.e. in the environmental conditions which provide the context for that behaviour. So, for example, stable personality characteristics, like sociability, selfishness, introversion and assertiveness, can each be expressed in a variety of different ways in different circumstances at different ages. The problem, then, is to discover whether or not the underlying personality characteristics (which are assumed to be relatively enduring dispositions) have changed, and if so how and to what extent. In pursuing this problem we immediately come up against all the difficulties associated with the psychometric assessment of personality plus all the difficulties associated with research methods in ageing.

The modern approach to personality assumes that behaviour is the outcome of some sort of interaction between factors in the person and factors in the situation. Thus we can explain a particular form of behaviour by reference to the person's aggressiveness, or to provoking circumstances, or by a special combination of personal and situational factors, e.g. 'He gets flustered when he has to speak in public.'

It follows that there is no simple answer to the question of whether personality changes or remains stable during adult life, and that one is likely to find both continuities and discontinuities in personal adjustment, depending upon what personality characteristics and forms of behaviour one is looking at, and what methods of investigation one is using.

A further complication is that the most formative experiences for personality are in childhood; so that cohort and generational influences may be as important as those of adult life.

(c) Types of personal adjustment

The traditional approach in the study of the normal adult personality has been to use psychometric tests in an attempt to identify the basic dimensions of personality (or at least to provide operational definitions of certain personality characteristics) and to study age-differences (cross-sectionally) or age-changes (longitudinally). A few very long-term studies have been carried out.

An alternative approach – that of identifying distinct 'types' of personality – has been pursued much less vigorously, except in connection with abnormal personalities. Nevertheless, the related notions of 'life-styles', 'strategies of adjustment to ageing' and 'stages or varieties of adult ageing' have some appeal, at least as a way of identifying and separating out distinctive areas of interest in both basic and applied research.

Let us briefly consider a classic study of ageing and personality by Reichard *et al.* (1962). They examined 87 men aged between 55 and 84, using intensive interviews, ratings and psychological tests. Somewhat surprisingly the older retired men seemed to have adapted well and to be better adjusted than the younger men, who were perhaps anxious about the prospect of retiring and becoming elderly.

It is useful to note that elderly people who are in good physical and mental condition may be fairly fully engaged in a variety of activities. Over-optimistic aspirations and occasional failures could give rise to disappointment and criticism of others. However, a measure of assertiveness, even selfishness, may have adaptive value in later life.

Good adjustment in later life was associated with the following characteristics: married and living with wife; good standard of living; constructive attitude to retirement; useful activities; realism; wide interests; good health; good social relationships; steady employment history; few or no psychiatric symptoms; acceptance of ageing and eventual death; social conformity.

An attempt to classify the 87 subjects into personality 'types' was only partially successful, in that only about two-thirds of the subjects fell clearly into one category or another. Reichard *et al.* identified five fairly distinct types of older person – or rather five ways of coming to terms with the problems of later life: constructive, dependent, defensive, hostile and self-hating – apt and convenient labels for qualitatively different packages of personal characteristics. The constructive type of older person possesses a range of socially desirable attributes including self-sufficiency, tolerance of others and optimism. The dependent type is well adjusted and satisfied with life but relatively passive and lazy. The defensive or armoured type is somewhat over-controlled, obsessively hard-working, self-contained, and disinclined to face up to personal problems, such as ageing. The hostile or angry type is relatively suspicious and aggressive, is fearful about ageing and has a history of poor social adjustment. The self-hating type seems to be rather infrequent; socially inadequate, with low self-esteem and little feeling of control over life. Other researchers claim to have identified other interesting 'types' of adaptation to ageing.

It is not possible at present to explain how people come to possess the distinctive attributes that enable investigators to label them as this or that 'type' of person. To call it the outcome of the interaction of genetic and environmental factors (including life-history events and maturational/ageing factors) is true but not very helpful. Retrospective analysis – for example, by means of assisted autobiographies – is not altogether reliable; prospective studies are difficult to carry out. Some individuals, the so-called 'prototype cases', are very good exemplars of their type; others are less representative – rather like outliers in a statistical distribution.

In spite of these obstacles to research, closer study of personal adjustment in later life, through extensive study either of individual differences or of individual cases and types, should help us to improve services and facilities for those elderly living in the community. It might also give us greater insight into the early stages of physical and mental disorders in later life.

As a footnote, it is worth pointing out that some investigators argue that the traditional (psychometric) approach to personality is misconceived and misdirected. Among the alternative approaches that have been advocated are three that may be worth mentioning here: to study particular consistencies in behaviour in terms of social learning; to identify prototype cases (see above) through intensive case-studies; to make a comparative analysis of theories of personality and try to establish some kind of agreed conceptual and method-ological framework for this confused area of psychology.

(d) A note on the psychometric approach to personality and ageing

The administration of psychometric measures of personality like Cattell's 16 PF (personality factor) test has not produced results which give a clear-cut answer to the question of how ageing affects per-sonality characteristics. It is possible that variations in the sorts of age-sample used are responsible for the lack of consistency, or that items in self-report personality measures are not equally reliable and valid in different age-groups. On the other hand, there may indeed be little or no change with age in the kinds of personality character-istics typically assessed by self-report measures. In so far as we are able to reflect on our own behaviour and states of mind, it seems that we retain a fairly stable conception of our own personality unless events have drastically altered the course of our life.

Even where statistically significant relationships have been found between chronological age and measures of personality – as, for example, introversion, depression and cautiousness – the relationships are typically small and could be expected to be sensitive to moder-ating influences such as health, education and social class. Some long-lasting personal characteristics, such as anxiety, depression or anger, could arise as a consequence of influential life-events, especially stressful ones – bereavement, professional failure, rape, disablement – particularly if the associated behaviour has the effect of reducing these unpleasant states of mind. The question is, how long must such mood states or behavioural dispositions endure in order to qualify as personality characteristics? The answer it seems depends upon how one chooses to define personality conceptually and operationally.

A further aspect of the way in which life-events can shape personality is in their timing. Those which occur at an appropriate and anticipated time are coped with reasonably well, because they are anticipated and prepared for, whereas those which occur too early or too late may be disruptive. Consider, for example, a late pregnancy, an early bereavement, premature retirement, prolonged care-giving.

6. Successful and Unsuccessful Ageing

People who manage to survive to old age are likely to have evolved strategies of personal adjustment which enable them to avoid emotionally disturbing situations. But, of course, survival is possible with psychologically unsatisfactory forms of adjustment. Anxiety increases steadily with age especially among women but anxiety arising from what social psychologists call 'cross-pressures', typical of adolescence, probably diminishes with age, because the older we get the more likely we are to have ironed out difficulties and contradictions in our circumstances and relationships with others, and because we 'disengage' from those sectors of society that we find difficult.

Older people differ widely, but many appear to become more cautious and less confident although measured age-changes in confidence and cautiousness are slight. Cautiousness becomes more prominent with age, in that older people are less discriminating with regard to the particular hazards of different situations. By contrast, young people are confident in some situations but not in others. Rigidity, the inability to modify an habitual response, is not a simple or single personality trait and unlike 'confidence' does not show a definite relationship with age. People tend to avoid uncongenial situations and relationships and to seek out more rewarding alternatives. So, naturally, habitual ways of thinking and behaving increase with age partly because long familiarity with a stable environment has 'shaped' behaviour in these ways. The slower pace of behaviour brings about, directly or indirectly, changes in personal adjustment, achievement and occupational performance as does the decline in fluid intelligence. There are further age-changes in basic processes such as motivation, feelings and emotions, health and energy which could also bring about changes in measured personality traits. It is difficult to tease out cause from effect, and proximate cause from remote cause, in this welter of interacting influences.

Personal adjustment is rated high if the individual is effective in overcoming frustrations, resolving conflicts and developing socially acceptable satisfactions and achievements. Good adjustment expresses itself in happiness, confidence, sociability, self-esteem and productive activity. Personal adjustment is rated low if the individual cannot overcome frustrations, resolve conflicts, or achieve satisfying results by means of socially acceptable forms of behaviour. Poor adjustment is expressed in hostility, unhappiness, fear of people, morbid anxiety, dependence, guilt, depression, feelings of inferiority, apathy, with-drawal or incompetence. But good personal adjustment for individ-uals depends upon good personal adjustment among the people with whom they interact, since maladjustment in some creates conditions which foster maladjustment in others. Vicious circles of obstruc-tion, resentment, retaliation, anger and guilt may be set up by family discord, difficulties at work, and so on. Neurosis increases in fre-quency as age advances, especially among women (see Chapter Nine). Symptoms of mental and physical disorder, however, are obscured by the complexities of the ageing process and may go unnoticed.

In retirement, allowances are made for elderly people's physical and mental inadequacies, and they are less often relied upon by others to do things which might tax their resources. They are free to do the things which are important to them (and useful in their own right) but not critical in the sense of being essential or urgent tasks involving the real interests of other people.

Personal adequacy is reflected in social adjustment – the affective relationships a person has with those people with whom he or she is in close and frequent contact. Elderly people achieve successful adjustment in different ways. One person is happy to retire to a small house and garden away from everything and everyone (except perhaps a spouse, close friend or relative), whereas another finds happiness in a three-generation house in a crowded neighbourhood. This is another reason why social relationships and inner satisfaction, rather than work capacity or material circumstances, are the ap-propriate indices of personal adjustment in old age.

In spite of their individual differences, people who grow up and grow old in the same community frequently acquire roughly comparable modes of adjustment and can be assessed against accepted values and common standards. Successful adjustment depends upon adequate standards of living, financial and emotional security, good physical health, regular and fairly frequent social interaction, useful activity and the pursuit of personal interests. Successfully adjusted elderly people show enthusiasm for doing things, resolution in pursuing aims (which are realistic), fortitude in the face of adversity, personal insight and a prevailing mood of happiness or contentment. Optimum adjustment calls for continual changes in behaviour and circumstances throughout life.

An elderly person can be sick and yet make an adequate adjustment. Illness affects people in different ways depending upon their personal qualities and surrounding circumstances. Optimism, for example, helps one elderly person to make a good recovery from a heart attack, whereas another, predisposed to depression or passivity, becomes dependent and hypochondriacal. Experiences which make us feel that we are growing in wisdom or competence induce happiness and optimism. Conversely, experiences which make us feel that we are making no progress or even slipping back induce anxiety, guilt and depression. In fact, in so far as it can be measured at all, overall happiness decreases steadily, on average, throughout life from the late twenties.

In late maturity and old age, the 'coming to terms' aspect of personal adjustment becomes more prominent, because time and opportunities are running out. People come to terms with life in old age in various ways: there is no standard or best mode of adjustment. The later years need not be static and unchanging, but personal adjustment should evolve smoothly and logically out of earlier patterns of behaviour. If a sense of continuity and identity can be maintained, in spite of the physiological, social and psychological changes, the process of re-engagement in retirement can proceed successfully; this is important for adjustment since it secures a more effective deployment of the elderly person's reduced resources. Normal ageing is gradual, by psychological standards at least; and with foresight, planning and social support, much can be done to ease the problems of adjustment and to improve the general level of achievement and happiness.

People can 'come to terms' with their environment, although their behaviour may not square with community ideals, statistical norms, or particular psychological notions about what is good or bad for old people. The socially accepted criteria of adequate adjustment in old age include the following: congruency between inner mental states and external circumstances; a degree of continuity between past and present patterns of adjustment; acceptance of old age and death; a degree of euphoria arising out of security and relief from responsibilities; and most important, personal security and adequate financial circumstances. The bulk of well-adjusted old people lead lives which are fairly tranquil and concerned mainly with routine personal activities. In the final stages of life the most that can be reasonably expected is fortitude in the face of illness, reconciliation with people, and some consideration of what consequences one's death will have for others.

Love of life, however, continues strong in many elderly, who are disinclined to surrender even though they realize that they are fighting a losing battle. Dylan Thomas advised them as follows:

Do not go gentle into that good night . . .
Rage, rage against the dying of the light.

References and Suggestions for Further Reading

Bromley, D. B., 'Approaches to the study of personality changes in adult life and old age', in A. D. Isaacs and F. Post (eds), *Studies in Geriatric Psychiatry*, Chichester: John Wiley, 1978.

—— *The Case-Study Method in Psychology and Related Disciplines*, Chichester: John Wiley, 1986.

Butler, R. N. and Lewis, M. I., *Aging and Mental Health. Positive Psychosocial Approaches* (2nd edn), St Louis, K Y: C. V. Mosby, 1977.

Costa, P. T., McCrae, R. R. and Norris, A. H., 'Personal adjustment to aging: longitudinal prediction from neuroticism and extraversion', *Journal of Gerontology*, 36, 1981, 78–85.

The Counseling Psychologist, special issue: *Counseling Psychology and Aging*, 12, 1984, 13–99.

Erikson, E. H., 'Reflections on Dr Borg's life cycle', in E. H. Erikson (ed.), *Adulthood*, New York: Norton, 1978.

Fitzpatrick, J. J. and Friedman, L. J., 'Adult development theories and Erik Erikson's life-cycle model. A critical assessment', *Bulletin of the Menninger Clinic*, 47, 1983, 401–16.

Lawton, M. P. and Maddox, G. L. (eds), *Annual Review of Gerontology and Geriatrics*, New York: Springer, 1985.

Malatesta, C. Z. and Izard, C. E. (eds), *Emotion in Adult Development*, Beverly Hills, CA: Sage Publications, 1984.

McLanahan, S. and Sorensen, A., 'Life events and psychological well-being: a re-examination of theoretical and methodological issues', *Social Science Research*, 13, 1984, 111–28.

Neugarten, B. L. and Associates, *Personality in Middle and Late Life*, New York: Arno Press, 1980.

Reichard, S., Livson, F. and Peterson, P. G., *Aging and Personality: A Study of Eighty-Seven Older Men*, New York: John Wiley, 1962.

Runyan, W. McK., *Life Histories and Psychobiography. Explorations in Theory and Method*, New York: Oxford University Press, 1982.

Savage, R. D., Gaber, L. B., Britton, P. G., Bolton, N. and Cooper, A., *Personality and Adjustment in the Aged*, London: Academic Press, 1977.

Schulz, R., 'Emotionality and aging: a theoretical and empirical analysis', *Journal of Gerontology*, 37, 1982, 42–51.

Seven
Work and Human Performance

1. Introduction

In the context of economic recession and widespread unemployment, under-employment and early retirement, it might seem inappropriate to be much concerned about the occupational aspects of ageing. However, it is quite possible that, in the long run, age discrimination in employment will be made illegal, like other discriminatory practices. We can also expect to see flexible retirement schemes and opportunities for both men and women to go on working beyond the present statutory ages of retirement. Technological, social and economic changes are likely to bring in a multitude of secondary and tertiary industries, particularly service industries and small-scale enterprises, where experience and social skills might give older workers some advantage. It does seem unlikely that any industrial democratic society could survive indefinitely with a substantial proportion of its adults unemployed and relatively deprived. Somehow work and the rewards of work have to be shared out in a way which is acceptable to the majority.

2. Job Design and Training

The changing age-structure of modern communities, the improving physical health of people over 40, and the increasing tendency for women to find employment, bring benefits but also create economic and social problems. These problems include adult vocational guidance, selection, redesigning work to suit older people and retraining older people for new jobs – not only unskilled and semi-skilled industrial workers, but also people in all sorts of occupations, including the professions.

Work study and adult training can be used to help expanding industries and to devise remedial measures for disabled and incapacitated workers. Adult education and preparation for retirement could secure better adjustment and higher morale among older workers. The rate of technological and social change makes it likely that changes of job, education throughout life, and adult retraining will eventually become accepted as normal. An alternative outcome might be an increase in periods of leisure and an extended retirement; but this has little attraction in the absence of economic security and well-being.

Working conditions and output can be improved by the application of work study (or 'ergonomics'). The scientific study of occupational performance in the second half of the working life – after the age of 40 – highlights deficiencies in the way a job is organized; improvements in terms of posture, perception, movement and manipulation, tool design, muscular effort, time and motion, mechanical power, lighting, layout of displays and controls, fatigue and accident prevention, benefit workers of all ages. The new technologies – telecommunications and computing for example – have introduced further complications for operators. Consider the skill needed for word-processing as compared with typing. There is, however, relatively little information on age-changes in the time and motion characteristics of occupational performance among older workers. As older people have less flexible postures and movements, their jobs should be arranged so that stooping, prolonged standing, difficult reaching and holding heavy objects are reduced to a minimum.

Older workers should be protected against hazards arising from slowness of perception and response, poor balance and working too near maximum capacity. Older machines and methods tend to be used by older workers; younger men and women are recruited for new machines and methods, and when the older techniques are abandoned, the workers may be redundant, unless they can be transferred or retrained. Successful retraining has been achieved on a small scale in a range of occupations. However, the age factor in occupational performance and retraining is often less important than intelligence, motivation, attitude and education. Training older workers means more than simply teaching a skill; it means changing attitudes, dealing with anxieties and eliminating established habits.

Job redesign and retraining methods must be examined carefully, because small differences in layout or procedure may create difficulties for older workers.

Certain factors make the training of older workers in sensori-motor activities more successful: if it is gradual; if trainees can approach the task in their own way and at their own speed; if written instructions are available (but not essential); if trainees can practise elements in the skill as they go along; if they are active participants rather than passive listeners; if (unobtrusively) they are prevented from making mistakes, especially in the early stages; if they are guided on simple but important matters such as the proper way to hold a tool; if the connection between perception and action is direct; if knowledge of results gives them a sense of achievement and progress; if memorizing is kept to a minimum; if each element of the skill has a firm position in the total performance.

Advances in technology, however, are decreasing the sensori-motor element of occupational skills and increasing the cognitive element; for example, using a computer or a word-processor involves some sensori-motor skill (reading a display and handling a keyboard), but the main skill is in 'knowing' what to do, i.e. a cognitive or mental skill. Unfortunately, the available evidence suggests that this is precisely where the effects of ageing on performance are most pronounced − in the so-called 'central' organizing activities of the mind − understanding, processing complex information, remembering. It remains to be seen whether the demands of work using high-technology can be adequately met by older workers.

In retraining, older workers may have to adjust from solitary to teamwork or vice versa, adapt to unfamiliar problems, methods and surroundings, or overcome the 'mental strain' of learning after a long period of disuse. Teachers have a great deal to learn about the special problems of educating and training older adults. Hence the need for research on programmed instruction and techniques of assessment. Problems include the content and organization of courses, levels of difficulty, pace, the use of visual and other aids, the provision of background information, the management of anxiety and lack of confidence, and techniques of guidance and assessment.

In some firms special workshops for older operatives have been established. Elsewhere the cost is felt to be too high and older workers who are not capable of normal rates of production work are likely to be transferred, in time, to unpaced work, work based on custom or quality (craft skills or inspection), part-time work, and service jobs such as cleaning or time-keeping. Older trainees should be selected carefully because individuals differ widely in their willingness and ability to learn new skills and concepts. On the other hand, social justice implies equality of opportunity for retraining, and adequate financial protection for older workers who are unsuitable for transfer or retraining. Single crash courses are unlikely to suit older people; education and training are needed at intervals throughout a person's working life. Vocational advice and training are appropriate at all age-levels.

3. Human Performance

(a) Experimental studies of psychomotor skills

In experimental studies of the normal effects of ageing, subjects can be tested to the limits of their performance on particular sorts of task. Deficiencies in their capacities are revealed by changes in the kind and numbers of errors, the organization of behaviour, and the amount and distribution of time for the task. Tasks can be varied according to the particular functions experimenters wish to investigate – for example, sensory discrimination, reaction time, motor control, attention, learning, memory, problem-solving, or fluency of ideas.

Physiological degeneration in the central nervous system, the special senses, the muscles, and so on, leads to restrictions on a person's maximum level of performance. This decrease in potential does not become obvious, however, until either degeneration has progressed so far that his or her abilities fail to meet the demands of ordinary tasks, or severe demands are imposed by difficult tasks, so that the limitations brought about by even slight degeneration are clearly revealed as errors, omissions or delays in performance. A normal conversation, for example, imposes little or no strain on an older person; however, if people speak faster, or in a lowered voice, if the topic changes frequently, or involves long technical sentences, if the conversation shifts rapidly from one person to another, then the older person may lose track, misunderstand and contribute much less. In normal everyday situations, older people appear to be in 'full possession of their faculties'; it is only when their capacities are tested to the limit that their impairment becomes apparent.

As age advances, the difference between *optimum* and *maximum* levels of performance decreases; older people therefore have reduced reserves. This can also be measured by examining age-differences in the ability to perform two tasks concurrently such as driving *and* adding numbers.

Five effects of ageing have been reported. (1) Performance fails completely. (2) Performance does not fail completely, but efficiency is reduced. (3) Efficiency of adjustment is maintained *in spite* of the reduction in biological capacities – older people can readjust their behaviour and surroundings, and compensate for deficiencies. (4) Older people show no loss in performance because the task is still well within their psychological and biological capacities; this sort of adjustment leads people to deny that ageing has had any adverse effects. (5) The elderly *overcompensate* for their reduced 'competence' by improving their 'performance'; physical and mental resources tend to decline with age, but older people can be trained to use their resources more effectively, and exercise usually improves performance.

Training and exercise would be said to improve competence (not just performance) only if their effects generalize to performances which indicate competence but are not an essential part of the training programme. Such interventions have become an important feature of basic research in ageing since they also offer a direct approach to practical applications. Consider, for example, what would be needed to demonstrate improvements in memory, intelligence, personal adjustment, or social interaction.

A small change in the efficiency of a process involved in skilled performance has little overall effect, because the system is flexible, and the person's ability is normally well above the demands of the task. As age advances, however, many small deficiencies accumulate to produce poorer performance. These may be compensated for in all kinds of ways: wearing spectacles and hearing aids, improving working conditions, proper exercise and diet, retraining, changing the pace of the task and the distribution of effort, simplifying the performance, memory aids, drills and checks (older people often fail to derive much benefit from written instructions; these distract and divide their attention, thus increasing the risk of error or slowing down). Too little interest is taken in ways of compensating for the adverse effects of ageing, except perhaps as regards the skills required for the activities of daily living in old age, where the voluntary organizations have made considerable progress.

Individuals differ in the way their performance deteriorates with age, partly because they also differ in the age of onset and in the rate of decline for different sorts of physiological function. Environmental circumstances, experiences, attitudes, and compensatory adjustments also vary from person to person. For example, hearing deteriorates with age even under the best possible conditions, but it deteriorates more rapidly under conditions of excessive noise. The cumulatively adverse effects of alcohol, tobacco and sugar, of disease, stress and injury, and so on can be expected not only to bring out differences between people but also to bring about a steady reduction in many kinds of skilled performance in later life, such as driving, sport, work.

The performance capabilities we build up throughout life are not fixed mechanical patterns of adjustment, but flexible, adaptable strategies capable of dealing with a *range* of situations. Older people have acquired an extensive repertoire of behaviour patterns capable of dealing with many familiar situations and of being applied in modified ways to variations on these situations. Ideas and responses acquired in one context and applied in another give rise to what is called 'transfer of training'. When older people can bring their previous experience to bear on a new problem, they feel more confident; they can organize their behaviour in familiar ways and make an effective response. This is known as 'positive transfer'. There are some situations, however, in which their previous experience becomes useless or 'redundant'. This may have serious consequences for occupational adjustment after the age of about 40. Previous training or experience can be worse than useless, a positive hindrance in fact to the solution of a problem or the acquisition of new knowledge. This is known as 'negative transfer'. Many situations can be dealt with partly or wholly in terms of past experience; so the older person's natural reaction to a novel situation is to apply whatever experience, i.e. frame of reference or 'schema', seems relevant.

The term 'schema' has been revived to refer to a cognitive

framework of understanding, e.g. our experience and understanding of a medical condition, a gardening problem, a social predicament. Such schemata can become highly routinized, automatic ways of organizing our behaviour – mental skills in fact. However, increased age, especially in the context of a routine environment, could lead to a certain inflexibility, i.e. a disinclination or an inability to modify one's behaviour when one's standard response is inappropriate, and a tendency to respond too readily in a routine way. It has not been possible to demonstrate a general disposition to 'rigidity'.

A contrasting fault in later life, the product of accumulated experience, might be slowness in responding to a situation as we try to take account of all the things we know are relevant.

The effects of ageing can be demonstrated in different ways, depending upon how performance is scored. Various indices are employed: time, output, effort, errors, wastage and so on. The instructions given to (or understood by) the subject, emphasizing one or the other of these aspects of performance, affect behaviour. Care is needed in interpreting the results and generalizing the findings to apply to natural circumstances outside the laboratory.

In an experiment in a classic series reported by Welford (1958), subjects attempted to match the position of an object with the position of a pointer on an adjacent display. Older subjects were slower, making only about half as many attempts in a given period of time as did younger people, but they made fewer small errors. They were less able to understand the layout of the problem, conformed less well to the test instructions and programmed their performance in smaller units of behaviour. The performance of older people on maze-tracing tasks is similar in these respects; attempts to simplify the task lead them into error and confusion.

In another experiment, people were asked to trace numbers with a metal stylus. Older subjects required more time and made fewer errors. When the numbers were presented 'back to front', older people needed considerably more time than younger ones, and they showed less improvement on a second attempt. The sensory and muscular demands were much the same for the two experimental conditions. Welford found that the time required for small movements increased only slightly with age, whereas choice-reaction time and the time required for changes of movement, such as from forwards to backwards, increased sharply, especially after the age of 50. He concluded that the main locus of slowing with age in sensori-motor performance is not in the speed of movement but in the time taken by central processes initiating, shaping and monitoring movements.

Small ballistic movements and rhythmic movements, such as tapping, involving a minimum of central organization, appear to be affected relatively little by ageing. Welford's evidence on the component times in a simple lever movement seemed to show that the acceleration and deceleration phases were not affected by ageing, whereas the time required for uniform motion increased by about 50 per cent between the ages of 20 and 70. The time required to stop and change direction also increased markedly. The decline with age in muscular response within the normal range is not large, and for brief movements, involving aiming and continuous control, the limitations on performance are brought about by slower central processes rather than by weaker muscular response. Of course, sensori-motor performance in older infirm subjects might very well be impaired by severe sensory impairment and/or muscular weakness or tremor, as well as by poorer central organizing processes.

Performance can be affected by attitude towards the task; here 'easy and familiar', there 'difficult', 'unfamiliar' or 'risky'. Such attitudes are likely to determine the way speed and error are 'traded off' in a particular performance. For various reasons – reduced capacity, lack of practice, slower mental processing – older people often prefer to minimize error at the cost of taking extra time. They are likely to underestimate their performance capabilities, preferring to 'play safe', and perhaps in consequence, to underestimate how much time and practice they need in order to improve their performance.

The decline in speed of performance is one of the most outstanding behavioural characteristics of ageing. This helps to explain age-changes in intellectual efficiency, skilled performance, work output and research achievement. In situations where there are no serious time limits the effects on performance may not be apparent until late in life.

One part of a performance may be preceded in time by a relatively brief decision period and accompanied in time by perceptual and decision processes relevant to the next phase of the performance. If a control lever has to be moved through a central position to other positions according to a signal light on a display, the slowing down with age in choice reaction is determined partly by *verifying* the preceding movement and partly by *choosing* the subsequent one. The effects of introducing a change into one part of the performance (such as a brief delay at the central position or choice point) are spread over the whole performance. The ability to shift and divide one's attention decreases with age in situations demanding fast performance. In some conditions, older subjects are slower but more accurate than younger subjects. In other conditions pacing will, within limits, improve performance, but the effect is less for older than for younger subjects. The adverse effects of ageing appear sooner for paced than for unpaced tasks.

Under certain conditions and within a limited range of choices, age-differences in decision time are constant over all degrees of choice. Older subjects take longer than the younger subjects under all conditions of choice (so that 'information-transmission' decreases with age), but they do not always appear to take *proportionately* longer for, say, an eight-choice as compared with a two-choice decision. However, even an eight-choice decision may be simple; for example, sorting playing cards. When decisions are more difficult, as judged by the failure rate, performance time increases more sharply for older people.

(b) Occupational aspects

Little is known about age-differences for various types of industrial work, although productivity declines overall to some degree. Many industrial operations are carried out at a reasonable pace, well within the working capacity of older operatives, though an absence of age-differences in the overall time taken to complete a job might be accompanied by marked age-differences in the time-distribution of the component parts of that job. Detailed time and motion studies, i.e. micromotion studies of skilled and semi-skilled work, should throw a great deal of light on age-differences in performance, and on its overall organization; for example, older workers make a complex procedure simple by dropping out those parts which seem less essential, a normal process but one which can lead to serious errors and omissions if a critical element is shed, such as failing to make a safety check at the appropriate time. Thus one question is whether modern computer-based systems are sufficiently 'forgiving' and 'user-friendly' to older operators.

The pace of work is determined not only by the speed of industrial equipment, but also by incentives of one kind or another. Ageing is accompanied by a drift from paced to unpaced work, brought about in part by time-stress, in part by the extent to which the job involves 'continuous bodily movement and activity' (Welford). There is a slight tendency for younger men, up to the age of about 40, to be employed on light industrial operations, especially power-assisted work where speed is important. After this age a slightly higher proportion of older men are engaged on heavier work. Injury, illness, or an inability to keep up the pace of heavy work, lead older men to transfer to lighter work, but this usually means less-skilled, lower-paid work. The same general trend applies to women workers.

Some so-called 'heavy' industrial jobs do not approach the limits of human muscular strength and therefore do not impose excessive strains on older workers. But if heavy muscular work is combined with continuous effort and activity, and especially if it is paced, a proportion of older workers find the demands too great and make use of opportunities to find less exhausting work. Employment can be demanding in other than physical ways, but not much is known about the physical, intellectual and emotional demands of occupations such as general medical practice, teaching, nursing and other professions, other than the general causes and effects of stress, so little can be said about the ability of older people to cope with intellectually or emotionally exhausting work.

In recent years, occupational stress has become a major area of investigation, and a number of disabilities such as heart disease and psychological breakdown have been attributed to stress. It is not likely that stress reactions generally will have any simple relationship to chronological age over the adult years. An alternative approach is to study stress in relation to life-events and difficulties, including 'daily hassles', since certain types of stress, e.g. bereavement, illness, loneliness, injury, relocation, financial hardship, are common in later life. Stress produces a variety of physiological reactions, which if excessive or prolonged, tend to have adverse consequences on health and well-being.

Working conditions play their part in the occupational adjustment of older workers. Although some move into more satisfactory surroundings, many move into jobs where the working conditions are less satisfactory. The better workers escape from time-pressure into salaried positions; the poorer workers move to hourly rates. A few are 'carried' by responsible employers. Younger people, for various reasons, demand a higher standard of working environment.

Social changes arising from industrialization are contributing to the problems of gerontology in a number of ways. First, there are the problems of redundancy and redeployment – sensitive issues for men in the second half of their working life or in occupations generally thought of as 'secure'. Second, there is the problem of shift-work; age-changes in physical health and sleep patterns are relevant to this issue. Third, there are the problems of vigilance (the maintenance of attention in a monotonous task) and quality control (the related problem of inspection); the effects of age on such things as arousal, and proneness to fatigue and distraction, can be expected to affect work involving prolonged close attention. Fourth, many women return to work from about the age of 30; the effects of ageing on their work performance and retraining are complicated by the long disuse of relevant skills. Although many sorts of performance decline with age, this decline would arise partly from disuse. Systematic training can produce improvements, although more slowly and to a lesser extent in older people.

At the level of professional and managerial work, the effects of ageing are likely to be found in such things as adjustment to changes in working practices, occupational status and salary differentials. The attitudes of supervisors and managers vary, but they commonly believe that older workers are slower though not necessarily less efficient, since their long experience and special methods of working often make up for reductions in speed and in sensory and motor capacities, and incline to believe that they have poorer health, become tired more easily, that their eyesight and hearing get worse, that they are apt to suffer from chest complaints and stomach troubles, learn more slowly, but are more dependable, especially in semi-skilled work. The best years for adapting to new work methods or training for a new job are said to be between about 15 and 35 years.

Thus a social stereotype – a prejudice – can serve to stigmatize and discriminate against older age-groups, in relation to, say, selection for employment or retraining or promotion. It fails to recognize the wide range of differences between individuals, the considerable overlap in performance between adjacent age-groups, and, most important, the actual performance capacities of older workers, especially under optimum conditions.

Few efforts are made, however, to improve working conditions, production methods or training schemes to suit the needs of older workers. The usual way of dealing with the problem is to take chronological age and working capacity into account when work is being reorganized, when teams are being made up or when replacements and vacancies occur. It is relatively rare for a man to be transferred because he is not up to the demands of a job. Many firms recognize their obligations to older workers with long service, and even if it means some loss of efficiency, attempt to fit them into the system as best they can, at least when economic circumstances are favourable. In unfavourable circumstances, such as economic recession or severe competition, survival may mean reducing the workforce substantially. In accountancy terms this may be best achieved through redundancy and early retirement of older employees. Lack of foresight and planning, or failure to implement appropriate employment policies, can produce widespread social disruption on a national or regional scale as well as at the level of the individual organization (including changes in the age-structure of a workforce). The reasons often given for transferring older workers are that the work is too strenuous (especially if the man is over 50), requires paced performance, or involves long hours, night work, climbing, fine detail, concentrated attention or physical risks. At the professional and managerial level vague notions such as 'new blood' are used to justify changes in employment practices.

Older workers were thought to need less supervision and seen as having a number of desirable occupational characteristics, including a sense of responsibility, settled habits and attitudes, reliability, conscientiousness, interest in the job and willingness to do a fair day's work. They were said not to be argumentative or to lose their temper, though inclined to resist advice and instruction. Supervisors thought older workers were less likely to have accidents, because they were more careful and more experienced.

Such a roseate view must be considered in the context of historical changes – cohort effects – in the attitudes and working practices of older occupational groups today. Deference to authority and tradition are much less in evidence throughout society. Behaviour at work has been strongly conditioned by union and political affiliations. Age-differences in attitudes to work are by no means clear.

Several reasons were put forward to explain the older worker's good reputation. One was that supervisors themselves were older men – half of them promoted at or after the age of 40. Another was that older workers were more vulnerable than younger men, since they could not find new jobs easily and were less mobile. It was thus in their interest to keep their jobs and work efficiently.

As there are considerable differences between one firm and another, and between one job and another, it is difficult to say anything definite about age and industrial productivity. Older workers are probably not comparable with younger men doing the same work: only those who are able and willing stay on and they become adapted to a particular job in a firm. Moreover, productivity is determined by many factors. Straightforward comparisons between older and younger workers show little change in output.

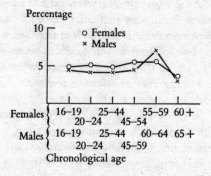

Figure 7.1 Percentage of employees absent from work because of sickness, United Kingdom, 1984; based on *Social Trends*, no. 16, 1986. Note that a graph showing incapacity for work in terms of days per person at risk would show an accelerating increase with age. The relatively low percentages for age 60+ (females) and 65+ (males) presumably reflect the fact that good health is a major factor in continuing employment

Changes in training methods or production methods designed to help older workers would help to raise production at all age-levels; even if the productivity of older workers remains unchanged relative to younger workers, it is important to attend to their occupational difficulties, since the same difficulties may hold down the productivity of workers at all ages.

Sickness absence measured in terms of the number of working days per year lost through incapacity rises gradually up to about age 45 and then more steeply to the age of retirement, when many people are becoming permanently unfit for work. Figure 7.1 shows the percentages of employees absent from work because of sickness.

(c) Accidents

Every accident is the outcome of a number of factors; the results of surveys of accidents need to be treated with considerable care and often with quite elaborate statistical safeguards. It would be incorrect to compare the accident rates for, say, bus drivers of different ages, since the younger and older groups are not comparable (conditions of service tend to eliminate the relatively unsafe driver), and their exposure to hazard might be unequal. It is difficult to make general statements about the association between age and accidents, and most studies limit their findings to particular kinds of work. If younger and older groups are matched for accident rate, differences appear in the sorts of accident suffered. In some circumstances younger people have accidents because they lack experience, whereas older people have accidents because they are slow to respond.

Most accidents happen in the home – the main working environment of the housewife – where falls are an important class. The factors contributing to falls are numerous, from a poor sense of balance to inexperience, from failure to appreciate the danger (usually a younger person's mistake) to failure to react quickly enough. Older people are slower to recover when thrown off balance and slower to dodge.

Comparing the accident rates of older and younger workers in a factory, we sometimes find that the rate is lower for older workers, partly because selective factors eliminate accident-prone individuals from hazardous jobs. Similarly, comparing the abilities of older and younger footballers is really comparing relatively new players, just making their mark, with rather older players, whose continuance in the game is proof of their better-than-average performance (otherwise they would have been dropped).

The number of older people driving is increasing, and drivers over the age of 60 (like those under 25) are more frequently blamed for road accidents, though they drive less and constitute a selected sample. The older driver's impaired skill can be accounted for by a variety of 'ageing' processes including impaired perceptual and motor functions, poorer vision in the dark, slower recovery from glare, poorer hearing, restricted attention and short-term memory (especially in complex shifting circumstances, for example, where both forward and rear vision are important), and slower reaction times. In fast traffic, the 'decision-load' approaches or exceeds their capacity to handle information. Older drivers should drive 'defensively', avoid becoming involved in fast traffic and keep down their speed to match their capacities. Age of itself is an inadequate index of driving skill; nevertheless, the relationship is there and becomes even more pronounced among older drivers who are fatigued, tense, intoxicated or in poor health.

Some minor everyday mishaps – posting a self-addressed envelope, for instance – are commonplace and have provided an interesting source of empirical data for the analysis of accidents. We often distribute our resources over several courses of action in a sort of time-sharing mode. Failure to allocate resources appropriately, or distraction at critical points in the sequence, can bring about unintended consequences. Forgetfulness is also a common experience in later life, but not uncommon earlier in life. Reduced cognitive resources and speed of mental processes in later life imply a need to reduce the number of parallel courses of action one engages in and to arrange one's environment so as to facilitate the monitoring of one's behaviour and its consequences.

(d) Mental skills

Some sorts of performance require very little in the way of sensory and motor capacities, but a great deal in the way of intellectual ability – playing chess is an obvious example. Several of the tasks referred to in Chapter Eight – for example, Wechsler's Digit Symbol Substitution Test or the Block Design Test – are examples of 'mental skills'. Such skills enable the performer to attend selectively to a situation, to construe certain meanings by carrying out symbolic or imaginative transformations on perceptual data, and to apply internalized rules of procedure – schemata – in order to select or organize an appropriate response. Thus chess, driving a car, writing a computer program, making business decisions, or navigating, are mental skills. Occupational skills vary in their intellectual content, some being so complex as to require not only personnel with the appropriate natural endowments but also long training and considerable reliance on external aids such as instruments, check-lists and reference manuals; commercial airline flying is an example, though it requires many physical and psychological qualities in addition to intelligence.

The experimental analysis of mental skills naturally begins with relatively simple laboratory tasks. Welford (1958) described an experiment in which subjects tossed short loops of chain into a box several feet away. There were no age-differences in performance, provided the connection between the perceptual display and the response was reasonably direct, but when the connection between the display and the response was made more indirect, by obscuring the target with a screen and obliging the subjects to view it in a mirror, the older subjects were less accurate and took longer to aim and throw. When people have to 'translate' the situation, any complication in it slows them down and increases the number of mistakes. This holds for young people too, but the effect is more pronounced for older people. If the translation process conflicts with other pre-established rules of procedure, further complications are likely to arise; this is sometimes referred to as 'negative transfer' of training. It is not unusual to observe some 'rigidity' in the adjustment of older persons working under such conditions, in that they find it difficult to abandon a familiar but wrong procedure and adopt a novel but correct one. Common experience suggests that older people are less willing to abandon well-tried but inefficient practices in favour of new and more efficient ones.

In golf and other games, sensations from our organs of balance, and from our muscles and joints, are important in determining the response, but the subsequent evaluation, which psychologists call 'knowledge of results', may be visual or auditory. Knowledge of results sometimes has little effect upon the performance of older subjects, partly because they fail to register the errors visually, partly because they fail to make the proper translation from a visual cue to a kinaesthetic (movement-sense) correction. Some high-grade skills call for extensive co-ordinating translations between several sense modalities; such skills are difficult for older people to master or to maintain.

Welford described an experiment in which a row of lights was operated by a row of keys under three conditions of complexity. Errors probably arose from subjects' natural attempts to simplify the task (so as to bring it within their range of competence), which resulted in inappropriate behaviour. The time required and the number of errors made increased sharply for the older subjects performing under the most difficult conditions. Welford has explained that each translation produces some decrease in performance with age, but several translations taken together produce a disproportionate fall in the performance of older people and, conversely, the removal of one complication may produce a great improvement – an important factor in training.

In another experiment a series of number-matrices were graded in difficulty. Each matrix consisted of numbers which had to be arranged so that the row-totals and column-totals were correct. Normal ageing produced a disproportionate increase in the number of errors on the more difficult matrices. Older subjects were unable to deal with a large amount of information arranged according to numerous criteria, since this involved shifting from one aspect of the task to another, with a consequent interference in the overall organization and continuity of behaviour. They were sometimes prepared to accept an inconsistent solution, illustrating perhaps a breakdown in their capacity for performance evaluation. At other times they abandoned the task as too difficult. Older people may accept an inadequate performance or an approximate result because it represents the best they can do. This sort of attitude is commonly observed in psychological studies of problem-solving behaviour. It is by no means characteristic only of aged people, but it is more characteristic of them. The ability to evaluate a performance is probably a function of the ability underlying the performance itself.

As age advances, the individual shifts from strategies which are intellectually demanding (but accurate and logically efficient) to strategies which are less demanding (but relatively inaccurate and inefficient). Experiments to determine the effects of age on inductive reasoning (abstraction and generalization) show that older persons are more likely than younger ones to become confused about the properties of the objects or events they are trying to classify. They more often fail to discover the distinguishing characteristics of a criterion class (predetermined by the experimenter), especially if the objects in the criterion class have properties shared by objects not in the criterion class.

Older subjects take longer and want more information to achieve the same results. They experience greater difficulty in attaching meanings to cues and they lose track of data because of a reduction in short-term memory and mental speed. The disproportionate increase with age in time and errors on complex cognitive tasks as compared with simple ones may have something to do with the gradual but cumulative loss of brain cells and synaptic junctions. Loss of cells and dysfunction of cells in the nervous system may lead to an increase in random neural activity and worsen the signal-to-noise ratio. Thus the organization of behaviour is reduced in scale, complexity and speed. The earliest indications of difficulty for older people are found in changes of speed and accuracy; simple translation processes also occupy more time in old age, even when accuracy remains unimpaired.

For one experiment, subjects of different ages were presented with sets of statements and asked to work out their logical implications. The younger group confined their attention to the *form* of the argument and kept to the point when answering questions, whereas the older group missed the point and dealt with the *content* of the argument by making comments or bringing their experience to bear. Older subjects adopted a literal instead of a hypothetical approach.

The poorer performance of older people is partly a result of actual interference with intelligence by well-established habits and accumulated experience, and partly a result of their inability to organize complex data in a logical manner. Solving problems by experience is not wrong in itself, but it may be inappropriate in particular instances.

4. Motivation and Attitudes

Adequate motivation and appropriate attitudes are needed if the reduced potentialities of the elderly are to be used to the full. Presenting older people with an initially complex task, particularly an unfamiliar one, can provoke anxiety and a reluctance to put their abilities to the test.

Subjects who are more highly motivated work faster and persist longer at a task. Small improvements in the performance of older people can be achieved by incentives and encouragement, which presumably increase motivation. This improvement, however, is no greater than that which follows increased motivation in younger subjects. Hence the generally poorer performance of older people cannot usually be explained by their insufficient motivation. In fact, elderly subjects who volunteer to take part in psychological investigations are highly motivated to do well and they are working closer to capacity than younger volunteers. In test situations or during training, older subjects tend to be more careful and less confident. They try to minimize the risk of error and overestimate the risk; they guard against failure by combining low aspirations with strong attempts to succeed.

Older people's estimate of their capacities is influenced by the attitudes and norms of the community in which they live. These may not affect what people can do, but they will affect what they are likely to do. The fact that older people try to take greater care, however, does not mean that they succeed in making fewer errors than younger people. On the whole, speed and accuracy go together and, if anything, the association is closer among older people. Older people are more likely to abandon their attempt to solve a problem because they are slower and less able to master difficulties. They are more likely to settle for an approximate solution. This kind of behaviour need not arise from lack of motivation, since it is not difficult to demonstrate that even without time limits the mental output of older people does not reach that of younger people. Moreover, well-motivated and persistent older subjects add relatively little to their overall performance in the extra time they take.

Decreased motivation lowers performance; but if motivation and cognitive capacity are both reduced as age advances, which limits action most? Motivation and ability interact in some way to determine performance. Unfortunately, psychologists cannot measure motivation with anything like the objectivity and accuracy with which they can measure other aspects of human performance, and the problem of ascertaining the part played by age-changes in motivation is likely to persist for some time.

Ideas and techniques in industrial society are changing rapidly, with computerization, automation and improved communications. Such innovations make demands on human adult intelligence which, according to Wechsler's figures, falls by about 24 points (of Efficiency Quotient) during adult life. The complexities of modern life present problems to people whose intelligence is below the average. The reduced intellectual efficiency of old people therefore handicaps them in relation to socio-technical innovations, and this may have something to do with their reputation for conservatism and rigidity. Research into the effects of age on skilled performance has obvious relevance to real-life industrial and professional work, as we have seen, and industrial gerontology is fairly firmly established. As yet, however, little research has been carried out into the effects of age on administrative and social skills which, after all, are supposed to be the fruits of experience.

References and Suggestions for Further Reading

Charness, M. (ed.), *Aging and Human Performance*, Chichester: John Wiley, 1985.

Howe, M. J. A. (ed.), *Adult Learning, Psychological Research and Applications*, Chichester: John Wiley, 1977.

Meier, E. L. and Kerr, E. A., 'Capabilities of middle-aged and older workers: a survey of the literature', *Industrial Gerontology*, 3, 1976, 147–56.

Robinson, P. K., Livingston, J. and Birren, J. E. (eds), *Aging and Technological Advances*, New York: Plenum Press, 1984.

Shaw, L. B. (ed.), *Unplanned Careers: The Working Lives of Middle-Age Women*, Lexington, MA: Lexington Books, 1983.

Welford, A. T., *Ageing and Human Skill*, London: Oxford University Press, 1958.

Eight
Adult Intelligence
and Intellectual Achievements

1. Adult Intelligence

(a) Introduction

The study of adult intelligence is concerned with intellectual abilities from the age of about 20 throughout the remainder of the human lifespan. Its origin can be traced back to the First World War, when thousands of recruits to the US Army were examined by methods based on the Binet test. The results, when published, startled both psychologists and the general public, for they showed that the average American young adult had a mental age of 13.5 years and that test scores decreased slightly with increasing age up to 30 and then more markedly up to 60. The arguments provoked by these findings helped to stimulate research work on intelligence and mental testing and encouraged psychologists to explain and justify their ideas and methods. Not everyone is willing to accept that intelligence decreases in adult life or even that it ceases to develop. Confusion arises because intelligence can be defined and measured in different ways and criticisms can be made of the methods used to investigate the effects of ageing.

Psychologists measure a person's intelligence by administering a standardized test of mental ability and assessing his or her intellectual brightness *relative to other people of the same age*. If a person aged 50 takes the Wechsler Adult Intelligence Scale (WAIS) and obtains a total score equal to the average score for persons aged about 50, his or her intelligence is average. The term 'Intelligence Quotient' (IQ) is familiar now to many people, yet surprisingly few outside the field of professional psychology seem to understand its limitations. Briefly, an I Q test is designed so that, for example, items at mental age 10 can be passed by an average 10-year-old, and those at mental age 11 by an average 11-year-old. The items are said to measure 'Mental Age' (M A), since the ability to pass them depends upon intelligence and not merely upon Chronological Age (C A), although in normal children intelligence grows steadily with age. The I Q is defined as the subject's mental age (e.g. 11 years) divided by the chronological age (10 years) and multiplied by 100 (11/10 × 100 = I Q of 110). A child whose mental age and chronological age are equivalent has an I Q of 100, whereas a child whose mental age is less than its chronological age has an I Q lower than 100. The range of *normal* intelligence is from about 85 to 115 and includes about two-thirds of the juvenile population. Thus the I Q is an index of a person's intelligence relative to other people: an I Q of 100 means 'average' intelligence; an I Q of 130 is in the top 5 per cent of the population; an I Q of 60 is in the bottom 1 per cent.

It is convenient to think of intelligence as a natural biological endowment in respect of which people differ, so that its distribution in an age-group is relatively 'normal' or bell-shaped. Up to the age of about 12 years, intellectual capacity (unspecialized intelligence) grows steadily, but then the rate of growth slows down and eventually ceases altogether. Individual differences in rate of growth and in the age at which maximum intellectual capacity is reached undoubtedly occur, just as they do for dentition, menstruation and height; but for the bulk of the population maximum intellectual capacity in the biological sense is probably reached somewhere between the ages of 16 and 20. People with above-average ability tend to be physically healthier, to live longer and to be higher in socio-economic status.

Intellectual endowment should not be confused with intellectual performance reflected in scientific ability or in the social wisdom needed for dealing with people or for succeeding in business. Such attainments involve factors in addition to biological (or innate) intelligence: general experience, specialist knowledge, technical skill and personal qualities (to say nothing of good fortune, helpful connections and special aptitudes). Clearly, intelligence is only one attribute among many that go into the making of intellectual achievement or good social adjustment, and can be distinguished from the others only with difficulty. For example, success in psychological tests calls for interest, attention, persistence and some familiarity with the sorts of problem presented. It is possible to design tests so that subjects are not penalized unduly because of extraneous factors, such as having been deprived of normal educational opportunities or being deaf or spastic. However, certain kinds of social deprivation – nutritional, educational, health care – may permanently stunt a child's intellectual growth.

Psychologists aim to assess the *natural endowment* expressed in test performance. Time-binding (memory, imagination), relational thinking (abstraction, generalization), symbolism (language, imagery), together with cognitive speed and cognitive power are the main aspects of high-grade adult intelligence. In a sense, intelligence is the ability to organize and expand one's experience.

(b) The Wechsler Adult Intelligence Scale (WAIS)

The American psychologist David Wechsler spent many years attempting to establish the effects of ageing on adult intelligence. In 1939, he published *The Measurement of Adult Intelligence* and in 1958 *The Measurement and Appraisal of Adult Intelligence*. The *Wechsler Adult Intelligence Scale*, the WAIS, a revised version of the Wechsler–Bellevue test of adult intelligence, appeared in 1955. Wechsler's concepts and methods were revised by Matarazzo in 1972. A further revision of the test, the WAIS-R, appeared in 1981.

Wechsler defined and measured adult intelligence in terms of a set of scores derived from a person's performance on eleven tests of intellectual ability. The individual tests are described, and discussed singly or in groups, as follows.

(I) VERBAL ABILITIES

Vocabulary: the ability to define words from a list which becomes increasingly difficult as the words become less familiar (e.g. 'picayune', 'saturnine').

Information: the ability to remember miscellaneous facts, i.e. general knowledge (e.g. that paper is made from wood pulp; that the Wright brothers flew the first heavier-than-air machine).

Comprehension: asking a person to explain familiar facts or state what his or her reactions would be to certain situations ('What are the functions of a court of law?' 'What would you do in this emergency?').

Vocabulary, Information and Comprehension are closely related aspects of intellectual functioning in that persons who do well on one test tend to do well on the others. The three tests are closely associated with educational attainments, largely concerned with reproducing knowledge, and are unspeeded. Even so, in normal young adults they are indicative of general intelligence and correlate substantially with the non-verbal and speeded tests described later.

In spite of their common ground, the individual Wechsler tests call for somewhat distinct performances and make different sorts of demand upon the person's intellectual resources. To facilitate understanding of age-changes in adult intelligence, let us consider each of the eleven sub-tests carefully as a separate measure of intelligence, for although each test takes a sample (or measures a part) of the person's mental abilities, the test performances are very differently affected by ageing.

Vocabulary, Information and Comprehension show little if any decline in performance with increasing age after early maturity and there are many reasons for supposing that performance in them improves at least up to middle age (and possibly later for well-educated people with verbal interests). Several factors help to explain why verbal ability 'holds up' with age.

First, in responding to the tests, we do not have to think creatively; we have only to reproduce what we already know. The three tests are closely associated with mental development during childhood and adolescence (provided the person has had adequate educational opportunities and has not been seriously underprivileged or emotionally disturbed). Up to the time of biological maturity, intellectual capacity and intellectual attainments develop at similar rates, but after maturity capacity tends to decrease in various ways even though attainments are maintained without undue impairment. Adult verbal *attainments* reach a maximum level as intelligence develops; but as age advances, intellectual *capacity* decreases, leaving some attainments as markers, showing the highest level reached. Vocabulary, Information and Comprehension are such markers, since older people's ability to reproduce what they already know reflects not their present level of intelligence but the high-water mark of their intellectual development.

Second, in responding to the verbal tests, we can take our time. Ageing slows the speed of intellectual activity; common sense, as well as innumerable experimental investigations and psychometric studies (using standardized mental tests), provide adequate evidence of this fact. Being able to think quickly is a sign of high intelligence and, contrary to common belief, the more intelligent person performs more quickly *and* more accurately than the less intelligent person on tests which measure the rate of intellectual output, so Vocabulary, Information and Comprehension tests do not measure present intelligence as effectively as do some other tests described below.

Third, with these verbal tests, people have to remember the question but not to 'process' or reformulate it; so the demands upon immediate memory (span of attention) and mental processing are slight. The tests require little 'mental effort', since all that is required is to reproduce what is already known. Within limits, the capacity to hold in mind the information relevant to a problem is an important part of a person's intelligence; so, too, is the ability to shift attention from one aspect to another while retaining the information relevant to the problem as a whole. A decline with age in the capacity for dealing with complex problems – requiring the person to remember many details and to switch attention from one part of the task to another – has been clearly demonstrated in studies of skill (see Chapter Seven).

In conditions of mental disease, brain injury and dementia in late life, even these normally well-preserved intellectual functions may be impaired, leading to such disabilities as failure to recognize familiar objects, and disorientation.

The key to understanding the effects of ageing on adult intelligence is the fact that intellectual attainments are normally preserved (unless they fall into disuse), whereas the capacity to acquire new concepts, or to apply existing concepts quickly and accurately to complex situations, declines steadily throughout the years of maturity and may be accelerated in old age. Verbal ability (as opposed to verbal attainments) can be assessed in many other ways, however, and the study of the normal effects of adult ageing on complex language functions is of very recent origin.

(II) SHORT-TERM LEARNING AND REMEMBERING

Digit Span. Wechsler's test of Digit Span has two parts. In the first, the experimenter calls out in a regular unhurried voice a series of numbers, as 8, 7, 3, 5, 1, and asks the subjects to reproduce it exactly. Subjects who succeed go on to a longer series. If they fail they have a second attempt with a different series of the same length. In the second part, the experimenter starts with short groups of three and finishes with groups of eight, but subjects must now try to reproduce the numbers in the reverse order (the series 4, 5, 9, 1 would be reproduced as 1, 9, 5, 4). If they succeed they go on to a longer series, but if they fail they have a second attempt at the same length. The subject's score is the number of digits reproduced forwards plus the number reproduced backwards. A normal young adult should score about 13 (7 forwards and 6 backwards).

Wechsler claims that performance on this test (up to a maximum of 9 forwards and 8 backwards) reflects a person's general mental ability. Scores are correlated with scores on tests of general intelligence which do not involve short-term memory to any great extent. Many other tests are better indicators of general intelligence – some people have a special aptitude for this sort of memorizing, and an outstandingly good memory span does not imply an outstandingly high level of general intelligence.

The effects of ageing on memory span for digits are not excessive, because the test is fairly straightforward. For men and women of above average intellectual ability, the mean score forwards decreases slightly, the mean score backwards decreases more sharply. There appears to be no decline until after the age of about 45. Ageing has little effect on simple acts of short-term retention, but if the information has to be held and dealt with in some way (for example, by reversing the order of the items or by sorting the items into classes), performance declines with age.

Short-term memory or working memory sets up a temporary trace and involves a definite effort to remember – as in taking dictation or remembering a set of instructions. Long-term retention, on the other hand, provides a more durable record which usually requires little or no effort for its retrieval – as in exercising well-practised skills like driving or talking, or knowing one's personal identity. Of course, the circumstances of recall, such as prompting or association, affect retrieval from long-term memory, as do the circumstances affecting recognition. Similarly, factors like recency and rehearsal affect the kind and degree of forgetting in short-term memory. Learning involves a transfer process: information is held in short-term memory so that a permanent record can be established in long-term memory, as in learning a poem. Similarly, skilled performance requires that information be stored temporarily until an appropriate response is made, as in typing or taking down morse code.

Nowadays, Wechsler's Digit Span Test is regarded as a relatively crude measure of short-term memory and as a rather insensitive measure of the effects of ageing on intellectual capacity. For research purposes, it has been superseded by more refined techniques. In a type of test known as 'Paired Associates', the subject is presented with carefully contrived letter-groups, for example, UKJ-EDB (called 'trigrams'), and is required to learn a series of such associations. Under various conditions of initial learning, proactive and retroactive interference, time interval between items, and so on, the subject has to recall or recognize the associations. In 'Probe Recognition', the subject is required to say whether a particular digit, word or syllable was or was not present in a given series. In 'Dichotic Listening' the subject has to attend to two sources of information, such as digits or words, presented separately to each ear. Under various conditions of divided attention, length of list, time interval, similarity of stimuli, recall instructions, and so on, the subject is required to recall or recognize the stimuli previously presented, or to identify incidental stimulus characteristics, such as pitch or accent.

The study of the effects of ageing on short-term memory has constituted a technical, vigorous and complicated area of research in behavioural gerontology for many years. The results so far confirm the generally deleterious effect of ageing on short-term memory under conditions of divided attention, but the contemporary debate is concerned with the mechanisms underlying this and other deficits in learning and memory. The basic problem is how to measure the effects of ageing on registration, retention and retrieval separately when all three are closely interlocked. Careful control of experimental conditions and refined methods of statistical analysis are used to investigate this problem. Short-term retention is affected by a number of factors, including initial level of learning, inhibitory processes such as fatigue, facilitation, cognitive context and strategy, rehearsal, sensory modality, interference and 'time'. Conflicting evidence makes it difficult to summarize the main findings briefly, and the issues raised encroach on topics dealt with in other chapters, such as psychogeriatric assessment, intelligence and skill.

The decline with age in memory function is probably not attributable entirely or even mainly to failure in one particular mental function, such as registration, learning strategy or retrieval. It is more likely to result from a combination of failures in all the component processes, including a reduction in the speed of mental processing.

Further methods of measuring short-term learning and remembering include having subjects recognize or recall pictorial designs or words previously shown to them, having them learn a sequence of items by 'rote', and having them recall information which they had not intentionally tried to commit to memory. All show a decline with age but the rate varies with the nature of the task. The various methods of measuring short-term memory are used partly for practical reasons, for example, in diagnostic psychological testing, and partly for theoretical reasons, as in the investigation of theories about ageing and memory function. The recall of recent experience is thought to be particularly susceptible to deterioration with age as compared with established memories of past experience.

Disuse naturally leads to some loss in long-term memory, which is recoverable on relearning. Long-standing memories may be quite inaccurate. In studying long-term memory it is difficult to control for such aspects as initial level of learning, practice, importance and so on. Under certain conditions, there is a phenomenon of memory regression, in which an elderly patient shows impairment of short-term memory and memory for recent events, but seems to have access to some memories formed at a remote time like childhood, and confuses features of his or her present life with features from the past; for example, mistaking a daughter for a sister. Long-term memory, however, is not as resistant to the effects of ageing as it sometimes appears to be. Consider, for example, the patchiness of recall of life-events in such aspects as time, place, person or purpose. Autobiographical memory is an emerging field of inquiry – see Wagenaar (1986).

Metamemory could be defined as knowledge of how to facilitate learning and remembering; for example, by the use of mnemonics, rehearsal, control of the learning process, and mediational strategies such as imagery and associative cues. It appears, surprisingly perhaps, that older adults make less use of metamemory than younger adults. Why should this be? In so far as metamemory functions are not automatic (but require attention, speed and mental effort) they could be expected to decline somewhat with age (as does fluid intellectual ability). Failure to develop metamemory, or disuse of metamemory brought about by withdrawal from education and training, might contribute to individual differences in memory performance. However, it appears that a decline with age in metamemory is difficult to demonstrate.

(iii) NUMERICAL ABILITIES

The ability to calculate and handle numerical relationships is a useful index of general intelligence. Wechsler includes a series of problems in mental arithmetic as a sub-test.

Arithmetic. This test measures the ability to deal with simple numerical facts and relationships. 'How much change would you expect from £1.00 after buying three cakes at 28p each?' 'A man bought a car for three-quarters of its original cost. He paid £6,000 for it. How much did it cost originally?' Marks are awarded for speed as well as accuracy. The subject has to remember the question and work out a solution, so the test involves short-term memory, but not to any great extent.

The decline with age shown by the Arithmetic Test is greater than for Digit Span, but far less than for some other tests described below. Mental arithmetic is a relatively simple cognitive skill, well practised in childhood and used from time to time throughout adult life, so that it tends not to fall into disuse. The test is short and does not sample the various arithmetical operations fully or systematically, and the time allowances are wide. It requires little arithmetical reasoning or problem-solving (the problems call mainly for accuracy of computation). This sort of skill, like reading or writing, does not involve the more complex functions of intelligence – finding relationships, working out implications, and so on. If we distinguish the 'mechanical' aspects of arithmetic from the more 'thoughtful' aspects, by using tests of numerical reasoning, we find little or no decline with age in the former (except that brought about coincidentally by a deterioration in memory span and speed of mental working). But there is some decline in the capacity for 'relational thinking' which lies at the heart of intelligence, since the ability to solve relational problems decreases with age. High-level accomplishment in mathematics reaches a peak in the early thirties and declines thereafter.

(IV) ABSTRACTION AND GENERALIZATION

Similarities. Wechsler's Similarities Test uses the ability to discern abstract relationships as an index of general intelligence. 'In what way are a diary and a log-book alike?' 'In what way are winds and clouds alike?' Questions of this sort measure the ability to think in abstract and general terms. A person who sees that a diary and a log-book are similar because they are both ways of keeping a record shows a capacity for orderly categorization at a high level of abstraction. A person who says that winds and clouds are both aspects of weather is more 'conceptually' competent than a person who says that the wind blows the clouds. Subjects are given as much time as they need; older people are not penalized by their slower performance. Responses are scored according to their level of abstractness: a person who consistently finds similarities by seeing both objects as members of a more inclusive class obtains a higher score than a person who can see only trivial or practical similarities. Performance on this test falls off somewhat as age advances.

The tendency for older people to become less capable of thinking in abstract terms is difficult to explain. Tests which purport to measure abstraction ability or conceptual thought measure high-grade intelligence or relational thinking. Tests involving abstract classes and relationships (such as sorting tasks, proverb interpretation and series completion) reveal a decline in performance with increasing age, even when no time limits are set. Qualitative differences in the cognitive processes of older and younger subjects can be examined by analysing the sorts of errors they make.

Ask an old person to explain the proverb 'A burnt child dreads the fire', and the chances are that he or she will reply 'If a child is hurt by fire he will keep away from it', rather than 'Pain and disappointment make us wary', tending to be more literal, more concrete, more concerned with tangible and immediate impressions, less able to detach himself or herself from the particular example and consider the general class or principle, less able to ignore the individual fact and think in hypothetical terms. Old people may use proverbs and metaphors without grasping the abstract and general rules implied in them. They are also led astray more easily by the particular content of an analogy, and therefore perform less well on tests of analogies – which are a favoured way of measuring general intelligence.

These later-life changes in the quality of intellectual function have not yet been studied in sufficient detail to permit us to say that there is a systematic regression with age through successively more deteriorated levels of cognition. Although there is probably some similarity to juvenile stages of cognitive development, late-life changes probably represent a dissolution of the cognitive system rather than a systematic regression.

One of the better-known tests of relational thinking, Raven's Progressive Matrices Test, consists of a series of incomplete spatial patterns. The subject has to identify the missing piece by working out the logical relationships running down and across the design, only one piece fitting the pattern correctly. The score is given by the number of problems correctly solved within a limited time. The normal effects of ageing on performance on the Progressive Matrices Test are pronounced, falling from about 45 to 25 items correct for the average adult between the ages of 20 and 70. Even if subjects are allowed sufficient time to attempt all the items, the effects of age are still substantial because older subjects cannot deal with the more complex relationships in the later items. The noticeable effects of age revealed by Raven's Progressive Matrices contrast with the negligible effects of age on word-knowledge as measured by, say, the Crichton Vocabulary Scale – see Raven (1982).

(v) NON-VERBAL (PERFORMANCE) ABILITIES

Five sub-tests in Wechsler's Adult Intelligence Scale, referred to as 'non-verbal' or 'performance' measures, are thought to be little affected by educational attainments. In spite of their apparent differences they are highly correlated. They sample various intellectual functions including short-term retention, mental speed, problem-solving, attention to detail and the capacity to compare performance against appropriate standards. Most of the time involved in an older person's mental reaction is occupied by 'central' processes (perception, thought, decision), whereas only a small part of it is occupied by sensory and motor processes. This fact is relevant to understanding the effects of age on a simple coding performance – Wechsler's Digit Symbol Substitution Test.

Digit Symbol Substitution. This test measures the ability to translate one set of symbols into another set. For example, digits could be coded as follows: 1 = [, 2 = <, 3 = − and so on. Subjects are presented with several rows of random numbers, and underneath each number they write the symbol corresponding to it in the code. After a short practice period, performance is timed over ninety seconds. The score is the number of digits correctly coded. The results confirm other observations which show a marked decline with age in the speed of mental work.

Superficially there is nothing 'intellectual' about this task. It is a simple clerical operation, and part of the age decline is brought about by the older person's slower eye-movements and speed of writing. But other processes are slowed down too. Consider each step in the performance: attend to the first digit, store it in short-term memory, shift attention to the code, find the same digit, translate it into the equivalent symbol, store it in short-term memory, shift attention back to the first digit, retrieve symbol from store, write in the symbol; attend to the next digit, and so on. Obviously, to the longer actual movement times for eyes and hand we must add the longer fixation, shift and decision times. The attention of older persons is more likely to be distracted so that they have to go back to the beginning of the cycle, or they may make mistakes. In either case total output is reduced.

The fact that performance on the Digit Symbol Substitution Test is strongly associated with measures of general intelligence (in spite of its apparent lack of intellectual content) shows how important sheer mental speed is as an index of intelligence. Moreover, mental speed and short-term memory interlock, because information is spread over time and must be stored temporarily until ready for use. If a person works too slowly the backlog of information grows too large for short-term memory to store and he or she begins to omit items and make mistakes. Writing down numbers in a game of Bingo, taking down dictation or morse code, and map-reading whilst travelling in a car are all examples of what psychologists call 'paced work', and performance in paced (and timed) work shows up the older person's intellectual deficiencies.

Picture Arrangement. This measures the ability to arrange a set of pictorial facts in a logical sequence. Sets of pictures, four or five in each set, of the type found in humorous comic strips, are presented in a disorderly array. The subjects study them and work out the relationships between them to find a meaningful order.

Picture Completion. This measures the ability to detect omissions and errors. The pictures portray common objects, such as a house or a fish; a detail is missing and the subject has to say what it is. This calls for fast systematic visual search and conceptual analysis.

Block Design. This measures the ability to translate a small design (on a card) into a full-scale design (of coloured cubes). As with the Matrices Test, there is probably an element of 'spatial reasoning' (a special aptitude for dealing with shapes, spatial relationships and geometrical transformations). There is nothing unduly complicated about the designs, and given sufficient time a person of average intelligence can complete even the most difficult of them. But speed is important in the scoring, as it is for Picture Arrangement and some other sub-tests, so that few people complete all the designs quickly enough to obtain the maximum possible score.

Object Assembly. This measures the ability to compose a picture from its separate pieces. Subjects are presented with three jigsaw puzzles, and the speed and accuracy of their performance determines their score. Performance does not decline with age as rapidly as it does for the three tests just mentioned, but there is, nevertheless, a steady loss of efficiency. The test calls for intelligent guesswork, rapid rejection of inappropriate moves, sensitivity for spatial forms, and other aspects of general mental ability.

These eleven sub-tests constitute a sort of 'sample' of adult intellectual capacities and attainments. They do not measure discrete mental functions; instead, each draws in a different way on a common 'pool' of intellectual ability. Performance on these sub-tests reveals what is called a 'differential decline with age' in mental ability, since they differ markedly from each other in their relationship to chronological age. This has been one of the key findings in the study of adult intelligence – see below. Other intelligence tests tend to confirm the findings of Wechsler and others regarding the differential decline with age in mental abilities. Attempts to isolate discrete or 'primary' mental abilities have met with some limited success, but attempts to examine the effects of ageing on them have been hindered by a variety of conceptual and methodological difficulties; for example, the problem of establishing the validity of a test over a wide age-range. Different tests and sub-tests of intelligence do not correlate perfectly with each other, nor are they perfectly reliable.

The search for other 'kinds' of intelligence – the ability to deal with people or with things rather than the ability to handle ideas – has not been successful. Surprisingly, in view of the scale and importance of intelligence testing, and apart from developments in factor analysis, there has been remarkably little progress in the *theory* of intelligence. However, there have been developments in the study of information processing, continuing the line of work referred to above under 'mental skills'. The advantage of studying particular sorts of mental processes is that we are more likely to be able to establish specific brain-behaviour relationships, as, for example, in the study of neuropsychological disorders.

(c) Standardization of the WAIS

The WAIS (recently revised as the WAIS-R) is accepted and widely used as a measure of general intelligence. A similar method, the Wechsler Intelligence Scale for Children (WISC and WISC-R), is used with younger groups. The problems and methods involved in the construction and standardization of Wechsler's tests of adult intelligence are technical; it is sufficient to say that Wechsler took what he believed to be representative samples of people of different ages, and calculated the mean and the spread of scores obtained on each of the eleven sub-tests.

The original test, known as the Wechsler-Bellevue Scale Form 1, was standardized on approximately 1,000 adult men and women. The revised test, known as the WAIS, was standardized on approximately 2,000 men and women ranging in age from 16 to over 75 years. Standards of performances were established to assess the mental abilities of a subject relative to those of other people. The highest total scores in the original test were obtained by the sample aged 20–24, whereas in the revised version the highest scores were obtained by the 25–29 age group. Moreover, the subsequent decline with age in total score was lower for the revised test than for the original version. Wechsler did not attempt to explain these discrepancies or to deal in detail with the age of onset and the relative rates of decline for the functions measured by different sub-tests. The technical problems of psychometric studies on this scale are too great for anything more definite to be said; for example, in the 15 years between the two tests, the apparent improvement in average performance could have arisen because of improvements in educational and living standards, better physical health, and greater familiarity with and easier adaptation to mental tests. Different tests and different samples might have given different results, but even Wechsler's revised figures showed that peak performance for Digit Symbol Substitution, Block Design, Picture Arrangement and Object Assembly – the more exacting tests of intellectual efficiency – occurs in the 20–24 age group.

Wechsler's results and those of other workers agreed in finding the peak of intellectual capacity (not to be confused with attainment) somewhere near the age of 20. It seems reasonable to say that this peak coincides with, and is probably an expression of, biological maturity. There has, however, been a swing of opinion away from the view that intelligence (general cognitive capacity) declines substantially in adult life. This has come about because the results of most longitudinal studies show little or no decline, or even gains, and because it has been recognized that secular trends and environmental differences may have been misinterpreted as age-effects in cross-sectional studies. The study of adult intelligence is grounded in the concepts and methods used in the study of juvenile intelligence; but are such concepts and methods the best ones for dealing with cognitive processes in adult life? Perhaps an analysis in terms of 'mental skills' or the 'skills of experience', as in understanding people and events, would provide a more interesting and useful focus for research.

Several contributors in Charness (1985) offer different perspectives on the effects of ageing on cognition. Berg and Sternberg (1985) have proposed a new theory of adult intelligence. Flynn (1987), reporting massive cohort effects on standard tests of intelligence and attainment, seems to argue that the traditional tests are not measuring intelligence.

The WAIS-R (1981), a further revision of the Wechsler Adult Intelligence Scale, is based on US norms but an anglicized version is available for use in the United Kingdom. The standardization of the WAIS-R is based on results from a sample of 1,880 normal healthy adult subjects aged 16 to 75 years tested between 1976 and 1980.

Equal numbers of males and females were tested totalling between 160 and 300 in each 5-year interval. Demographic variables such as race, religion and occupation were controlled to some extent.

Some subjects took the earlier as well as the revised version of the test for comparison purposes. The theory underlying the test, its construction and the sub-tests, are essentially unchanged. Minor adjustments were made to item content and scoring and the order of administration of the sub-tests. The scaled scores for each of the eleven sub-tests were based on a sub-sample of 500 subjects aged 20–34 years. The distribution of raw scores was converted to a normally distributed standard scale with a mean of 10 and s.d. of 3. Estimates of IQ (intelligence quotient) can be obtained by assuming a normal distribution of IQs with a mean of 100 and a s.d. of 15 to match the scaled scores for the verbal sub-tests, the performance (non-verbal) sub-tests, or the full set of eleven sub-tests.

There are limits to what can be achieved in the way of test standardization even with a sample of nearly 2,000 subjects. Consequently, the results across age-groups and sub-tests are not perfectly coherent. Reliability coefficients (measures of the consistency of a sub-test) are fairly high except for Object Assembly. The WAIS-R correlates well with the WAIS, and with the version prepared for juveniles – the WISC-R. It appears to be a valid test of adult general intelligence, and in the hands of an experienced clinician it may provide hints about possible mental disorder or brain damage. Specially designed diagnostic tests, however, are needed to follow up such hints.

The study of adult intelligence is developing in a number of ways. The emphasis is not on the construction, standardization and application of tests of general intelligence, like the WAIS, since the demand for such information is not as great in adult life as in the juvenile years, for scholastic assessment and occupational selection. The emphasis, rather, is on research into the pathology of specific forms of mental processing with reference to clinical diagnostic conditions such as dementia and brain injury. There is also a tendency to study intelligence in the wider context of adaptation to the environment. This includes consideration of the 'sorts' of intelligence (fluid or crystallized) needed for everyday coping in later life, and the processes (metacomponents) we use to manage our mental processes (remembering, solving problems, for example) – see Berg and Sternberg (1985).

(d) Intelligence Quotient (IQ) and Efficiency Quotient (EQ)

The scoring of the WAIS is arranged so that for a young adult the average score on each sub-test is 10 points. Since there are eleven sub-tests, the average score is 110 points, which is equal to an IQ of 100 (average intelligence). However, for persons aged 75 and over, the average total score is 69 points, which is, by definition, equal to an IQ of 100. Although 75-year-olds may be of average intelligence relative to other people aged 75, they are obviously less efficient intellectually than the average young adult, for whereas an average old person gains a total score of 69 points, a young person gains 110. Moreover, whereas the younger person's scores are likely to be distributed fairly equally over the eleven sub-tests, the older person's scores are likely to be high on some and low on others, since some mental functions are adversely affected by ageing, whereas others are very little impaired.

There are two ways of expressing an adult person's intelligence: Intelligence Quotient (IQ) – intellectual ability relative to that of his or her age group; and Efficiency Quotient (EQ) – intellectual ability relative to young adults at the peak of their intellectual and biological efficiency. A 75-year-old who gains 130 points altogether is bright compared with other people aged 75 for on average they gain only about 69 points; the equivalent IQ would be 136. A score of 130 points obtained by a young adult is equal to an IQ of 112; so the older person's EQ is 112, since this is a measure of intellectual brightness relative to young adults who are at their best. The average 75-year-old scoring 69 points has an IQ of 100 but an EQ of 76. The overall or average effects of ageing are assumed to be as follows: in the years between young adulthood and old age, intellectual efficiency falls from 100 to about 76. In the young adult, IQ and EQ are equivalent and mean the same thing, but for the older person the IQ stays more or less constant, by definition, while the EQ diminishes steadily. The young person with an above-average IQ (and EQ) of 115 who lives to the age of 75 can expect to have an EQ of about 90 at that age. A person of average ability at the age of 20 can expect to be of average ability, relative to age peers, at the age of 70; a person in the top 5 per cent of an age-group for intelligence can expect to stay in the top 5 per cent of that cohort for the rest of his or her life, provided he or she does not suffer from mental disease or pathological brain damage. (The statistical data can be found in the *WAIS Manual* and Wechsler's book *The Measurement and Appraisal of Adult Intelligence* – see Matarazzo, 1972 and Wechsler, 1981.)

Longitudinal studies of juvenile intelligence show that measured IQ is by no means constant over the years. This affects the theory of intelligence, such as it is, and the interpretation of an individual's test performance, but not the practice of intelligence testing, which has a sort of actuarial basis. Longitudinal studies of adult intelligence also show that over a period of a few years some subjects improve with age, whereas some get worse and others stay about the same. We are not yet in a position to obtain repeated measures of intelligence at frequent intervals over long sections of adult life; so we can say little or nothing about variations within individuals, or about the causes and conditions of increases or decreases in measured intelligence in adult life. One could speculate that stress, physical or mental illness, or improvements in living conditions, might induce such fluctuations.

The Wechsler tests have sometimes been used in a short form; for example, using only the sub-tests of Comprehension, Vocabulary, Block Design and Object Assembly, or, alternatively, using a small sample of items. Short tests of intelligence are useful for screening purposes, but are clearly less reliable than full-scale tests, so they are unlikely to be of use as repeated measures.

(e) Intellectual deterioration

Wechsler classified his sub-tests into two kinds: more resistant to age-effects, and less so. The former – Vocabulary, Information, Object Assembly and Picture Completion – he calls 'Hold' tests; the latter – Digit Span, Similarities, Digit Symbol Substitution and Block Design – he calls 'Don't Hold' tests. In one respect the estimated decrease with age of 24 points of E Q for the person of average intelligence, as mentioned above, is an underestimate, since the total number of points gained on the W A I S by older and younger people alike is compounded of scores on 'Hold' and 'Don't Hold' tests. If intellectual efficiency is measured only by the tests which show a decline with age (the so-called 'Don't Hold' tests), the decline with age is far higher than when it is averaged out for all eleven sub-tests. There is some disagreement about this aspect of Wechsler's work, because it is recognized that scores on the timed non-verbal tests fall off more rapidly with age than scores on even the least resistant verbal tests (Similarities or Arithmetic). Wechsler argued that verbal and performance tests measure different intellectual functions. The eleven Wechsler sub-tests can be accounted for in terms of three basic 'factors' of intelligence: verbal ability; spatial ability; and short-term memory. The mental speed factor is absorbed by the spatial (performance) sub-tests. Note, however, that sub-tests composed of items which vary in level of difficulty may load on different factors, depending upon the sample of subjects tested. Sub-tests may tap different abilities at different ages.

It is not unusual to find that a person's verbal I Q is different from his or her performance (non-verbal) I Q. The well-educated person who reads widely is likely to get a relatively high verbal I Q, whereas the quick, dextrous, practical person is likely to get a relatively high non-verbal I Q. The mental abilities involved in the untimed verbal tests are maintained quite well as age advances whereas the mental abilities involved in the timed performance tests are not.

Wechsler estimated the extent to which a person has deteriorated intellectually by comparing scores in tests which show a decline with age with scores in tests which show little or no decline. He included both verbal and performance tests in each of the two categories 'Hold' and 'Don't Hold', so as not to over- or underestimate the extent to which the subject had deteriorated over the years. One objection is that the two performance scores in the 'Hold' category (Object Assembly and Picture Completion) do not hold up particularly well with age, and the two verbal scores in the 'Don't Hold' category (Digit Span and Similarities) are, relatively speaking, only slightly diminished by ageing. It is obviously unsatisfactory to find, for example, that the performance test (Object Assembly) which declines least, still declines more than the verbal test (Arithmetic) which declines most. The criticism could be met either by introducing time limits into the verbal tests or by finding a number of non-verbal tests of intelligence which do not show a decline with age. Alternatively, one might include verbal tests of intelligence which show a steep fall in score with increasing age, such as Analogies or Verbal Reasoning.

Investigators have used the discrepancy between verbal IQ and performance IQ, or various combinations and weightings of the WAIS sub-tests, in attempts to find the optimum deterioration quotient (DQ) for diagnosing specific psychiatric conditions, such as organic impairment, or neurosis. The usual method of demonstrating normal intellectual deterioration is to measure the difference between declining and non-declining functions, as follows:

$$\text{Deterioration Quotient (DQ)} = \frac{\text{Hold score} - \text{Don't Hold score}}{\text{Hold score}} \times 100$$

A person aged 60 who scores 45 points on the four 'Hold' sub-tests and 28 points on the four 'Don't Hold' sub-tests shows an overall loss of 17 points – approximately 38 per cent of the 'Hold' score. This amount of deterioration is far in excess of that expected for an average 60-year-old, which is approximately 18 per cent. The discrepancy suggests intellectual deterioration over and above that of normal ageing. According to Wechsler's original figures, a normal person in his or her late thirties shows a 5 per cent loss of efficiency. Remember that percentages quoted in connection with psychometric (ordinal) measurements are purely for convenience or comparison. They do not signify an absolute amount of anything.

Another method of calculating intellectual deterioration shows a zero if the person's scores have fallen normally with age, but the logic of the procedure is still the same. In practice people

sometimes do better on the 'Don't Hold' than on the 'Hold' sub-
tests, because some are verbally fluent and quick-witted, others are
practical, careful and persistent. It follows that positive as well as
negative discrepancies between the 'Hold' and 'Don't Hold' scores
can occur. A negative discrepancy has no meaning; it is an error
of measurement.

The concept of 'intellectual deterioration' as a measurable process goes back some years. As long ago as 1930 intellectual deterioration was being measured by taking the difference between a
person's estimated previous maximum mental level (as a young adult)
and his or her present level of efficiency. Previous maximum mental
level was measured by a vocabulary test which required only the
reproduction of the meanings of words (there are other ways of
measuring vocabulary). Present efficiency was measured by a variety
of tests calling for new learning and fast mental work – decoding,
immediate memory, maze-tracing and rote learning. The discrepancy
between the two sets of scores measured intellectual deterioration.
During the growth period and up to early maturity, vocabulary and
the ability to think and to learn increase together (provided the
circumstances are appropriate). During middle and late maturity,
vocabulary, which is resistant to the gradual and cumulative degenerative processes of ageing and relatively unaffected by some
sorts of mental disease and brain injury, remains more or less constant,
whereas the ability to think and to learn is gradually eroded by
normal ageing or abruptly diminished by physical and mental disorders.

Some investigators argue that the decline in adult intelligence is
a myth – the result of a misinterpretation of data from cross-sectional
studies (comparing different cohorts, i.e. people of different ages) –
and that longitudinal studies (comparing the same people at different
ages) show little or no decline at least up to about the age of 60.
Unfortunately, the methodological obstacles to research in ageing
combined with the conceptual and psychometric problems peculiar
to intelligence testing leave us in some doubt as to the exact nature
and extent of age-changes in adult intelligence, although I believe
that the broad outlines sketched in this chapter are correct. Further
problems arise because chronological age is merely a convenient
index which represents in fact a variety of age-related variables –

health, education, cohort, experience, social position and so on. The effects of 'ageing' on adult intelligence must eventually be referred to these and other age-related variables, including intrinsic psychological changes associated with normal ageing.

Wechsler distinguished between the normal decline that occurs gradually as age advances, and the abnormal deterioration that occurs in conditions of mental disease and brain damage. There are similarities between these kinds of deterioration and Wechsler saw dementia in late life as a normal long-term consequence of cumulative degenerative effects. Some people never suffer dementia because they die prematurely – of cancer, accident, pneumonia or heart failure. Dementia, however, is more usually thought of as a pathological condition. Patients showing signs of dementia, compared with normal old people, are relatively more impaired on the Information and Comprehension sub-tests of the WAIS, which suggests that the condition is not so much an exaggeration of normal old age as a disturbance of it.

After the age of about 45 an increasing proportion of normal subjects make abnormal or deficient responses on tests which are sensitive to brain damage – including tests of abstraction and generalization such as block-sorting or proverb interpretation. Hence, normal ageing seems to be accompanied by a gradual but cumulative impairment of the physical basis of intelligence, although most normal people in old age do not appear to be mentally confused, and they manage the routine affairs of everyday life without evidence of intellectual deficit. It is only when they are examined closely and tested to their intellectual limits by means of psychological tests that signs of intellectual deterioration can be detected. Primitive or abnormal forms of thought among elderly subjects are found in responses to tests of intellectual function. The detailed analysis of errors and curiosities in performance is a further aspect of diagnostic and experimental testing in neuropsychology and geriatric clinical psychology.

Diffuse damage to the brain could lead to cumulative adverse effects, since the number of working units eventually falls below the minimum required to fulfil various functions. It could also decrease the 'signal to noise' ratio, and thus hinder cognitive organization at all levels.

Experiments with animals have shown that learning capacity is directly related to the amount of cortical tissue available, but the relationship may not be as direct in human beings on account of cortical localization. Brain-damaged subjects, however, learn less well than normal subjects, and have poorer short-term memory. It has not proved possible to demonstrate conclusively that enduring cognitive structures (concepts, schemata, long-term memories, semantic knowledge) are located in particular parts of the brain, but at least some apparently specific and fixed memory traces seem to be located in the temporal lobes.

Normal intellectual degeneration with age appears to be gradual and cumulative, though this might be an artefact of the methods used to investigate the effects of ageing. Substantial deterioration may appear in an individual over a relatively short period of time.

The theory of intellectual deterioration has a number of weaknesses. First, the various tests are by no means perfectly valid or reliable. That is to say, they do not necessarily measure what they are supposed to measure and they do not always yield consistent results. Also, a score like the DQ which is derived from the difference between two or more imperfect scores is not likely to be a very reliable measure. Second, mental disease or focal brain damage can have selective effects on the various functions measured by tests of deterioration, e.g. word meanings, object recognition, whereas the term 'intellectual deterioration' implies a diffuse or general impairment. Third, the actual deterioration score depends upon the functions contrasted as being 'more' or 'less' resistant. For example, if a person's score on the Mill Hill Vocabulary Scale is contrasted with his or her score on the Progressive Matrices Test (Raven, 1982), the index of deterioration is different from that obtained by contrasting his or her scores on Wechsler's 'Hold' and 'Don't Hold' sub-tests. The indices should, however, arrange persons in approximately the same rank order of intellectual deterioration.

(f) Current issues in adult intelligence

(I) SPECIALIZED AND UNSPECIALIZED INTELLIGENCE
The many quantitative and differential effects of ageing on mental abilities can be assimilated to a theoretical frame of reference which

defines two basic aspects of intelligence. One refers to the unspecialized or fluid function of intelligence. It can be thought of as a natural endowment – innate general cognitive capacity – and is measured by tests which call for productive relational thinking and mental speed, but require no special knowledge or experience. The other refers to the specialized or crystallized function of intelligence. It can be thought of as an acquired characteristic – general knowledge and special experience – and is measured by tests which call for the reproduction of information or the exercise of a learned skill.

The exercise of fluid intelligence is relatively effortful (we have to 'think hard'); the exercise of crystallized intelligence is relatively effortless (we 'know' what to do). The problems we face vary according to the demands they make on our fluid and crystallized abilities. Our ability to solve them reflects our 'effective' intelligence.

Unspecialized or fluid intelligence is a hypothetical entity, a concept we need in order to make sense of individual differences and correlations in intellectual performance. It is estimated, as in the measurement of IQ, by reference to a person's mental performance relative to other people. Most intelligence tests, however, measure effective intelligence – cognitive competence – because the unspecialized function can only be expressed through actual performance, which entails some acquired knowledge and skills. Hence tests of 'intelligence' do not measure pure unspecialized intelligence directly. This could be done only by identifying and measuring the physiological or genetic basis of intelligence, and we appear to be a long way from such revolutionary discoveries.

If mental abilities are ranked according to their susceptibility to the normal effects of ageing, it becomes apparent that those which are more resistant (hold up with age) are relatively specialized, whereas those that are less resistant (don't hold) are relatively unspecialized. If mental abilities are then ranked according to their 'g' saturation (the extent to which they express the factor common to all intelligence tests) then the method of criterion analysis shows that the age factor and unspecialized intelligence are very highly, but negatively, correlated. The wisdom of older people is the wisdom of experience because as unspecialized mental ability declines with age, older people rely more on what they have learned. The wisdom of younger people is the wisdom of intelligence because, as specialized mental ability is lacking for want of experience, younger people must rely on problem-solving.

It is possible to think of unspecialized (fluid) intelligence as the process by means of which our experience is organized. The existence of distinctive talents in, say, chess, mathematics, music and language, strongly suggests that there are areas of specialization too. From conception onwards we are exposed to widely different environmental conditions which have cumulative effects and long-range consequences on our effective intelligence. It is not altogether surprising that we differ considerably from one another at any age and follow different pathways of growth and decline.

(II) COMPONENT MENTAL ABILITIES

The measurement of intelligence is full of conceptual and technical difficulties. General intelligence is best regarded not as one kind of human ability but as a collection or system of abilities, some of which can be measured relatively independently of one another. Under natural conditions, particularly, these abilities interact not only with each other but also with so-called 'non-intellectual factors', such as persistence or anxiety. The number and types of component abilities is a matter of debate, but they include the following: fluid intelligence, comprising inductive reasoning, relational thinking, short-term learning and remembering, and speed of reasoning; crystallized intelligence, comprising verbal and educational level, mechanical and social knowledge; acquired forms of spatial reasoning and visualization; skilled perceptual and motor performance; habits of accuracy and carefulness.

Psychometric methods cannot distinguish fluid from crystallized ability in an absolute sense, but the conceptual distinction is convenient. It is not that one is innate and the other acquired; each type of intelligence could be determined by both genetic and environmental conditions. This statement may be confusing at first glance; but the argument, admittedly speculative, is that the neurophysiological bases of the two types of intelligence are somewhat different and therefore liable to different genetic and environmental influences, even though they are closely interlocked in a functional sense.

One well-known test, Thurstone's 'Primary Mental Abilities', distinguishes five supposedly distinct mental abilities. It is based on a complex statistical procedure, too technical to be dealt with here, which purports to show that intelligence can be regarded not as one general ability, but as several component abilities (different from those listed above): Verbal Meaning, the ability to understand ideas expressed in words; Spatial Reasoning, working out relationships involving two or three dimensions; Logical Reasoning, or the ability to solve rational problems, to foresee, to plan, to deduce implications and to generalize from experience; Number Ability, or the capacity to handle figures and deal with simple quantitative relationships; Word Fluency, or the ability to produce ideas easily and quickly. The tests are all timed, but provision can be made for extra time so that a 'power' or 'accuracy' score as well as a 'speed' score can be obtained.

It is not difficult to predict the effects of age on these primary mental abilities. For subjects over the age of 50, allowed to complete the tests in their own time, the largest age decline is in Logical Reasoning, and the next largest in Spatial Reasoning. Both Number Ability and Verbal Meaning decline with age, but the decreases are small. Time limits reduce the range of scores for all subjects and obscure the differences between the tests as regards the effects of age. Nevertheless, when time limits are imposed a consistent age decline occurs for all five measures (Word Fluency is always a timed test). See Schaie and Hertzog (1983) for a longitudinal study of the effects of age on primary mental abilities.

Eight 'factorially pure' measures of mental ability – comprehension, verbal fluency, spatial relations, number, memory for names and faces, reasoning, dexterity and perception – applied to over 600 subjects aged between 16 and 89 years, yielded a score, based on all eight measures, which declined with age. The first four measures showed no decline until after the age of 40, whereas the second four showed a progressive decline throughout the age-range.

The work on component mental abilities has been made possible by the use of factor analysis as a method of accounting for the interrelations between tests. Attempts have been made to describe age-changes in the structure and organization of intellectual functions.

The attempt to identify distinct intellectual functions by means of factor analysis appears not to have contributed significantly to our understanding of the pathology of cognition, juvenile cognitive development, or adult intelligence. The so-called 'mental abilities' derived from factor analysis seem not to represent intellectual functions, in the psychological or neurological sense. Hence, factorially based Wechsler scores and profile analysis seem to have had little theoretical importance or practical use. Unfortunately, investigations of this sort are beset with methodological problems, so that it is not yet possible to say what the age-changes are. One possibility would be for the factorial structure – of, say, the WAIS Tests or Primary Mental Abilities – to become less differentiated, i.e. for the general factor loadings to increase, and for the group factor and specific factor loadings to decrease. Alternatively, the structure could become more disorganized or, more likely, distorted in the direction of verbal attainments. Factor-analytic studies of the WAIS generally identify two main factors, corresponding broadly to fluid and crystallized ability, and a minor memory factor. The effects of age on these and other factorial abilities are described above.

The distinction between convergent and divergent processes in cognition is a further aspect of the modern study of intelligence, and one also beset with conceptual and methodological complications. However, defined in terms of the rate and extent to which subjects can formulate original and rare ideas in response to relatively simple test materials, intellectual creativity declines with age even among bright subjects, men and women alike. Thus Lehman's findings regarding the decline with age in creative intellectual endeavour (referred to below) can be accounted for in part by a decline with age in fluid intelligence – because psychometric measures of intellectual creativity correlate substantially with other estimates of fluid intelligence. Furthermore, the decline with age in creativity can be observed using untimed tests; the imposition of time limits amplifies the adverse effects of age.

In open-ended situations – that is, those calling for divergent or creative thought – older subjects gradually become less capable of thinking up new possibilities for relevant action; at least this is so if the situation calls for the application of intelligence rather than experience. Not only are creative rational responses fewer, but also abnormal irrational responses, confusions and misunderstandings are more common. Similar shifts in the level of mental functioning, namely, towards a more concrete, literal, undifferentiated kind of thinking, have been demonstrated in patients suffering from certain mental diseases and brain injuries.

(III) THE MAINTENANCE OF ABILITIES

Little is known about the effects of mental or physical exercise on the maintenance of intelligence in adult life. It is reasonable to suppose that intellectual activity which is 'demanding' improves cognitive capacity by making good the adverse effects of disuse; some functions seem to be capable of growth in response to demand until relatively late in life. The evidence from animal studies has important implications. It suggests that the brain cortex – the physical basis for the organization of more complex forms of behaviour – responds to the demands of environmental stimulation by growth, not in the number of nerve cells, but presumably in size, organization and in supporting tissues and weight. The most pronounced effects are during juvenile development, but under appropriate conditions continued growth at a diminishing rate carries on into the adult phase. It is too early to evaluate this line of work and further investigations may lead to less dramatic conclusions. Even so, it would come as no surprise to many psychologists if it were found that age-changes in adult intelligence were related to early juvenile development.

The little evidence about the differences between men and women in the way intelligence is affected by ageing suggests that the changes are much the same for both sexes. The problem is complicated by sex differences in longevity, education and life-style. In any event standardized intelligence tests eliminate items which discriminate between males and females.

Psychological as well as physiological factors bring about age-changes in mental ability. The poorer performance of some older people arises, in part, from diminished interest and motivation. However, after initial reluctance, older subjects usually become interested in a task, persist and try to do well (reluctance and lack of confidence are found among younger people too). But regardless of their willingness and efforts, older people tend to perform less well than younger people. Emotional complications and self-defeating attitudes play a part in lowering the level of performance of some older people, but most systematic investigations are carried out on volunteers, so their grosser effects are screened out. The overall effects of ageing on intelligence, therefore, have probably been underestimated.

Intellectual functions can fall into disuse through lack of practice. This too will account in part for age-difference in performance on initial testing. Older people can improve their test performance substantially through training and practice; but younger people tend to improve more. It has been argued, on the basis of experimental data, that older subjects can improve their intellectual functions through mental exercise. This is undoubtedly true in the sense that training and practice in a certain kind of performance will improve that performance and transfer possibly to other related kinds of performance, namely those that share the same elements and/or principles. The main question is the nature of and the extent to which this kind of intervention improves *competence* (which would be reflected in generalized benefits) or simply improves *performance* (which would be reflected in benefits restricted to the sorts of performance used in the intervention training). Intervention research rather than psychometric surveys may provide the more fruitful and useful way of investigating adult intelligence.

Most studies of the effects on intelligence and achievement of growing up and growing old have been carried out by comparing the performances of people of different ages and using the 'cross-sectional method' (see p. 308). The effect of averaging the performances of groups of people at each of several age-levels produces a relatively smooth curve of development and decline; it tends to mask stepwise changes and fluctuations in the development and decline of performance for individual cases. This would be revealed only if the same group of people were closely followed through part of the lifespan by using the 'longitudinal method'. Abrupt falls in intellectual ability might follow severe illness or mental distress or a period of intellectual stagnation, with partial recovery later. The longitudinal method, however, has its drawbacks, and there is considerable disagreement, currently, about the nature of adult changes in intelligence. Compared with cross-sectional age-differences, longitudinal age-changes reveal substantially less overall effect of age on the WAIS sub-tests (performance on some verbal sub-tests improves), but the relative effects are much the same. Familiarity and practice almost certainly contribute to the improvements in score in follow-up studies.

The pervasive effect of speed of mental processing on intellectual abilities of all kinds has revived interest in relatively simple cognitive functions such as reaction time. Speed of mental processing can be assessed in several ways: simple reaction times, choice reaction times, encoding times, short-term memory scanning, evoked potential times. Ageing tends to slow down these reactions, and such reactions seem to be more closely correlated with general intelligence than had been supposed. These simple measures of mental speed are reliable and correlate well.

Simple tests of speed of mental processing may prove to be of value in monitoring the progress of dementia. Among the more widely used diagnostic tests have been the so-called tests of mental status which assess low-level crystallized abilities by means of questions testing for orientation and general knowledge. Other devices have tested simple forms of learning and remembering. The WAIS has proved to be of limited value as a diagnostic psychological test of brain injury and dementia, but then it was not designed on that basis. Even neuropsychological test batteries specially designed for diag-

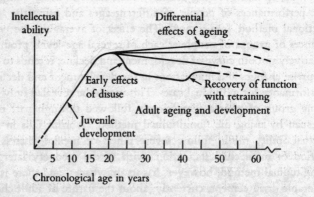

Figure 8.1 A schematic representation of some of the complex relationships between chronological age and intellectual ability

nostic purposes have not proved particularly successful and have made little impression on the study of the normal effects of ageing on cognitive processes.

There is, as yet, no adequate theory of adult intelligence. Such a theory would have to be co-ordinated with theories of intellectual development up to maturity and describe age-changes in the structure of abilities, accounting for alterations in the quantity and quality of intelligence in both normal and pathological conditions. Figure 8.1 illustrates some age-related effects.

2. Adult Intellectual Achievements

(a) Achievements in science, literature and the arts

Psychometric and laboratory methods are generally concerned with investigating people's capabilities by measuring their behaviour in clinically or experimentally controlled conditions, rather than with describing what people actually accomplish in real life. In considering the effects of ageing on real-life achievements – in the arts and sciences and in other areas of intellectual endeavour – we must distinguish between natural ability, which provides a kind of potential for achievement, and actual accomplishment, which obviously depends upon a variety of conditions, such as opportunity, circumstances and health, in addition to such potential.

Historical documentation has provided a multitude of examples of human achievements. Tennyson published poetry and a play in his seventies. Galileo's discovery of the diurnal and monthly oscillations of the moon was made when he was 73 and he published his dialogues on mechanics at 74; however, he achieved his insight into the movements of the pendulum at the early age of 17. Jane Austen wrote *Pride and Prejudice* when she was 21 and Marconi had transmitted radio signals by the time he too was 21. Obviously, intellectual achievements can occur throughout adult life, but citing examples and counter-examples is only the first step in the analysis of this problem, which requires a systematic method of compiling and analysing the relevant data.

The best work on this aspect of human ageing was begun by Lehman in 1928 and eventually published in *Age and Achievement* (1953), and in sundry other publications. Lehman's method was simple but laborious. He tabulated the ages at which people had made significant contributions to art, science, music, literature, technology or medicine (he also examined outstanding achievements by entertainers, soldiers, sportsmen, explorers or industrialists). The information was obtained from various sources: historical surveys, works of reference and encyclopedias; cross-references were used to obtain greater accuracy. Large samples of achievements enabled reliable comparisons to be made between different age-groups.

One source was Hilditch's *A Concise History of Chemistry* containing the dates on which nearly 250 noted chemists first published their accounts of contributions that later proved to be outstanding. Nearly one thousand contributions were tabulated. Lehman ascertained each chemist's date of birth and worked out the average rate of output for each 5-year interval for the lifespan (usually from the age of 15 to the age of 80). The highest average rate of output was 0.165 (approximately one-sixth) of a contribution per person per annum, found between the ages of 30 and 34 inclusive, i.e. one contribution in six years by the best men in the field. Between the ages of 40 and 44, the annual rate of output fell to 0.115 of a contribution per person per annum, i.e. about one contribution in nine years. Similar rates of output were calculated for each 5-year interval. Using 'rate of output' makes allowance for the different numbers of people left alive in each age-group. As it is convenient to make direct comparisons between rates of output in different fields, Lehman transformed the observed rates into percentages by taking the highest rate for any 5-year interval as 100 per cent and finding the proportionate percentages for each other 5-year interval. The highest rate of output for the chemists was in the 30–34 age-group, i.e. 0.165, which became 100 per cent; the 40–44 age-group, annual rate of output 0.115, became 70 per cent. The general picture is portrayed in Figure 8.2.

The general conclusions are as follows: one, between the ages of 15 and 19 the rate of achievement in chemistry is low – about 0.005 of a contribution per person per annum (3 per cent of the maximum rate); two, the rate rises steeply and steadily to a peak between 30 and 34; three, after about 34 the rate falls fairly steadily to 0.078 (47 per cent) between 45 and 49, and to nearly zero after the age of 70.

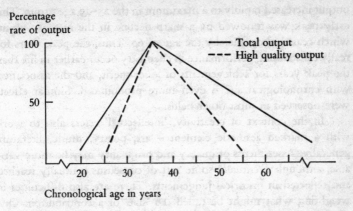

Figure 8.2 A schematic representation of the relationship between chronological age and rate of output for many kinds of intellectual achievement

Lehman also obtained age-distributions for rates of output in many fields, including mathematics, practical inventions, chess, medical discoveries, philosophy, all kinds of music, art and literature. With few exceptions, these and other kinds of intellectual achievement show a similar relationship to chronological age.

The relative importance of the quality of a contribution was judged by the amount of space allocated to it, or by the number of times it was referred to. Recent achievements, especially those of people still alive, proved difficult to evaluate and to analyse in terms of age-effects. An analysis of then contemporary American music composed between 1912 and 1932 showed an age-relation quite different from the typical one. Productivity rose up to the age of 35, levelled off, and then remained fairly steady until the age of 70. Some of these works did not stand the test of time, since they were still in manuscript in 1932. There is usually a consensus of opinion about the merits of work produced by people long dead.

Lehman asked a number of competent colleagues to select the hundred most important contributions listed in Hilditch's *A Concise History of Chemistry* and two-thirds of them agreed on 52 contributions. The age-distribution for this set of very high-quality contributions did not begin until the early twenties, but the rate of output increased rapidly to a maximum in the 25–29 age group. This early peak was followed by a sharp decline in the rate of output, which ceased altogether by the age of 60. Thus, the peak years for really outstanding performance in chemistry occur earlier in life than the peak years for achievements of lesser merit, and the association with chronological age is even more pronounced. Similar effects were observed in most other fields.

In the context of creativity, 'intellectual' refers also to work with a marked aesthetic element – art, poetry, music, literature generally. Assessments of quality and originality may be more variable, although eventually some sort of consensus is usually reached and reflected in historical judgements. There are also difficulties in weighting what might be called the 'size' of a contribution. One contribution may represent five years' work, another two years'; yet both may be judged to be of high quality in their field and given equal weight.

Studies using a large number of persons and many contributions show the effects of ageing on 'quantity' of output; studies using a small number of persons and a few very high-grade (highly original or outstanding) contributions show the effects of ageing on 'quality' of output. The total output of a sample of authors falls off with age relatively little, but when the 'one best book' (a measure of quality) is considered, the rate of output falls fairly steeply after the middle thirties. In philosophy generally, the age period 35–39 is the most productive, both in quantity and quality. In some areas, e.g. psychology, the age-trends observed by Lehman are based on relatively small numbers at each age-level and so fluctuate, but the general picture is consistent.

The peak years varied: in metaphysics, for example, they were 40–49. Psychologists started relatively late, in the period 25–29 years, and reached a peak at age 35–39, after which their output diminished gradually until it stopped at about the age of 80. The average number of contributions made by astronomers increased rather unevenly from the late teens to the early forties and then declined fairly steadily to the sixties and seventies. By contrast, a study of 45 authors producing over 600 poems showed an early peak at 25–29, followed by an abrupt decline to the ages of 35–39, then a gradual and uneven decline to the age of 90.

Lehman was unable to find sufficient data for the construction of separate age-curves for women, especially in science and technology, since so few women had contributed to these fields and many had not revealed their date of birth. One study, based on a few creative contributions made by women in science, showed an age relationship similar to that for men. Another study, of children's classics written by women, showed the usual peak years for output at 30–34.

There appear to be few or no differences between men and women in the rate at which their intellectual capacities diminish with age. Intelligence tests, unfortunately, are constructed in such a way that sex differences in performance are minimized. This does not mean that men and women are equal, on average, in native intelligence, rather it is *assumed* that they are equal. There are some measures which suggest, however, that the two sexes are in fact comparable in intelligence, at least within the normal range. On the other hand, it is possible that rather more men than women may be endowed with extremely high general intelligence and special aptitudes of the sort frequently associated with creative intellectual achievement. Adverse social factors probably play a major part in limiting the contribution that women have made to various fields of human achievement. It will be many years before women have full equality of opportunity with men, and even then child-rearing and domestic constraints will undoubtedly restrict their intellectual achievements, especially in the period in which one would expect them to do their most creative work. Such evidence as there is suggests that the age relationship will be similar to that for men.

Literary achievements follow much the same age-trend as other forms of achievement. However, bestsellers have (or used to have) a late-appearing maximum rate between the ages of 40 and 44, followed by a rapid drop. Poetry, by contrast, is typically a younger person's accomplishment, the peak years occurring between 23 and 35. The rate of output for poetry of very high merit falls off with age more rapidly than for poetry of lesser merit. Novels tend to be written later in life but, rather surprisingly, the rate of output for superior novels rises more slowly and reaches its maximum at age 40–44 (later than the rate for novels of lesser merit). The subsequent decline in performance is more pronounced for 'superior' novels.

There is a general tendency for 'great books' to be written by people under 40 years of age; but at every period of life, from the early twenties onward, one author or another has produced a masterpiece. Achievements in art and music showed broadly the same association with age as achievements in science, technology, medicine and philosophy. The age-relation for output in music was much the same for people of different nationalities.

Some important discoveries, inventions and artistic achievements have been produced by very young men. Men who start to achieve early in life usually accumulate a larger number of attainments than men who start their creative work late. The average starting age of 135 chemists who each produced only one major contribution was 36 years, as compared with 22 years for six chemists each contributing over 20 major contributions. The less prolific workers also finished their creative life earlier. Total creative output, in chemistry at least, is brought about mainly by many persons making a few contributions each, rather than by a few persons making many contributions. The relationship between early creativity, recognition by others, and total eventual output also holds for English literature, physics, German literature, oil-painting, composing grand opera and philosophy. There is, therefore, a sort of triangular relation between eminence, productivity and early achievement. Relatively little is known, however, about the effects of juvenile development and experience on adult intellectual achievement.

Ageing affects not only the *rate* of intellectual achievement, but also the *kind* likely to be pursued. The creative achievements of older people are more likely to include published work previously presented by means of the spoken word – lectures, personal memoirs and recollections. Older people write textbooks, which are often accumulations of specialized experience; they are frequently recognized for their achievements in the co-ordination of related areas of knowledge; they tend to complete work undertaken at a younger age or to revise earlier work; they excel at history; and, as one might expect, they write about old age.

A more detailed study of the kinds of achievements best suited to late life could be helpful, not only in unravelling the causes and conditions of age-changes in intellectual output, but also in helping older research-workers to plan for their declining years.

(b) Methodological issues in Lehman's research

Few people are so productive throughout their lives that their individual output shows the age relation clearly. But if the 1,086 patents taken out by Edison are arranged in chronological order, the highest number occurs at age 35 and the overall effect conforms to the general picture described above. The point on the age-scale that divides output into two equal parts (early-appearing versus late-appearing) – the 'median' age – occurs *after* the age of 35, because the distribution of output, especially of high quality, is 'skewed'. Productivity is greater in the earlier part of the working life but continues right up to death, falling off in maturity and old age. The creative years are all the years between puberty and death. The period around 35 years is merely the age at which the rate of achievement tends to be at a maximum. Lehman's findings most certainly do not imply that creative effort is worthless after 35 or any later age. Individual differences apart, older adults have a great deal to contribute throughout their active lives as teachers, administrators, critics, historians and as creative thinkers in their own right.

Lehman's method constitutes an interesting departure from the usual run of gerontological investigations because it makes use of naturally occurring records, some of which can be cross-checked for consistency; in effect, it presents a lifespan account of human achievement by averaging the results for many subjects in overlapping longitudinal sets. Lehman examined secular trends in achievement but not specifically in relation to methodology.

The relationship between age and achievement varies because one type of performance – for example, patenting electrical inventions – depends upon conditions different from those affecting another, such as painting pictures or making medical discoveries. It is difficult, therefore, to make exact comparisons for different *kinds* of achievement, and to achieve comparable levels of excellence in the different fields. Lehman's use of percentages was an attempt to overcome this difficulty but despite his wealth of evidence and his careful arguments, objections have been raised about his methods and the interpretation of his results. Variations on Lehman's method have been attempted.

(c) Factors affecting age and achievement

Lehman suggested a number of contributory causes for the decline with age, after the early thirties, of achievement in the arts and sciences, although the exact role of each cause is not known. Some also play a part in the decline of intelligence and athletic achievement. Among them are: a decline in physical vigour and energy; a decline in sensory and motor capacities; physical and mental ill health; changes in motivation and attitudes; the encroachment of administrative and other duties; the negative transfer of obsolete ideas and methods. Other factors which could be equally important are: a decline in imagination; a decline in the speed of mental processes; a reduction in the amount of time devoted to creative work; loss of contact with creative people and new ideas; changes in interpersonal rivalry and co-operation; changes in the nature of scientific achievement, say from personal research to supervision of others; diminished incentives – pay, conditions, prestige and promotion – for creative work; failure to keep up with changes in scientific activity, as in the greater use of mathematics, computers and electronic instruments, and with new research methods and concepts; a disinclination to take professional risks.

Some of the factors mentioned above, contributing to a decline with age in intellectual achievements, operate because of age-changes in the individual; others because of cultural or historical changes. Note the interlocking of social, psychological and biological influences. Case-studies and personal experience, as well as research investigations, have shown the relevance of some of these factors to the productivity of scientists, artists and writers; but we know very little about their relative importance for any class of people or any individual, or about the way they interact with each other to produce cumulative effects. There are probably counter-balancing forces – steady habits of work, the positive transfer of experience, improved opportunities and so on – which tend to maintain the quantity and quality of intellectual output after the age of 30.

Lehman was unwilling to admit to a substantial decline with age in adult intelligence, arguing that adult intelligence is inextricably tied up with the motivation to think and to learn, and with the natural tendency to work from experience, which is greater for older people. The fixed attitudes, reduced physical stamina, poorer biological efficiency and less adequate environmental opportunities of older generations made it impossible, in his opinion, to compare their intelligence with that of younger generations. These factors obscure age-differences in intelligence, but they are by no means as confusing as Lehman made out. Even highly motivated and persistent older subjects usually perform less efficiently on tests of intelligence than younger subjects. Furthermore, fixed (but now inappropriate) attitudes persisting into maturity and old age can be regarded as a sort of intellectual handicap which lowers the older person's effective intelligence. The biological, social, psychological and environmental causes of the relationship between age and intellectual achievement are not known – or rather, their relative importance, interaction and mode of operation are not known, but the general decline in intelligence and mental speed is probably an important contributory factor.

Creativity among established scientists sometimes finds indirect expression through the achievements of younger researchers working under their direction. Older scientists may get the credit for work done by younger colleagues. Delays in publication and the acceptance of new ideas means that, for younger people at least, the rates of output calculated by Lehman are two or three years behind the ages at which the actual intellectual work took place. Older people who have already made their mark professionally probably find it easier to publish, take out patents, or obtain facilities for further research.

One of the more serious effects of ageing is a fall in the rate at which a person can perform intellectual activities; so that an older person, even if capable of achieving high-grade performances, would achieve fewer of them in a given period of time. The amount of time devoted to research can be an important factor governing the annual rate and total output of older workers because of a reduction in the speed at which they accomplish intellectual tasks. It is difficult to carry out adequate surveys which would throw light on this problem.

The vagaries of the creative imagination do not alter the fact that intelligence needs the raw materials of observation and experience in order to produce new intellectual constructions, and these assimilative and productive processes require time. It is not difficult to demonstrate experimentally that quantity and quality of intellectual productivity go together. If subjects are faced with a problem which calls for a series of solutions or for a variety of possible solutions, those solutions which occur later in the series are, on average, better than those which occur earlier. It follows that subjects who are more productive will produce more of the higher-quality solutions and that subjects who are slower (including older subjects) must produce fewer responses overall, and fewer higher-quality responses in a given period of time. The increased delay in creative conceptual processes can be demonstrated experimentally by timing performance on sorting tests. If, for any reason, older subjects devote less time to creative work, they will be doubly handicapped.

Three facts help to account for the decline with age in intellectual output: older people devote less time to creative work; they assimilate (and produce) new ideas more slowly; and their creative capacity is reduced.

One possible reason for the relatively rapid decline in quality of output is that 'superior quality' often means 'original', and an original contribution in art or science generally means a breakthrough into a new set of ideas, a new method, or a new set of facts. The often surprising and unpredictable process of scientific discovery seems to depend to a large extent upon chance and imagination rather than upon the more mundane, predictable and systematic (but typical) processes of scientific research. Sensitivity to problems and relations is what counts, plus the ability to break through existing forms of thought and expression, which probably depends upon unspecialized intelligence, whereas acquired specialist knowledge can sometimes be a hindrance. The systematic inquiries of the research-follower are made largely because he or she has acquired (not discovered) some specialized techniques of inquiry in science or techniques of expression in art, namely, those that were developed by an innovator. The more familiar an idea or a method becomes, the less intellectual merit its use has; but innovators, having produced new ideas, are inclined and even encouraged to exploit them, rather than to produce more original ideas.

The effects of ageing on achievements of higher and lower merit cannot easily be explained by the factors which Lehman has chosen to emphasize. He says that the older person's waning interest and reduced efforts bring about a diminution in output, and that these factors are probably far more important than a decline in intellectual ability. But Lehman's own data clearly show that the *quantity* of work done by older scientists, philosophers, composers, writers and artists falls off more slowly than the *quality* of that work. If waning interest and reduced effort were the important factors, they should produce a decline in total output, with little or no difference between achievements of greater or lesser merit (unless the older person makes less effort to improve its standard).

The reduction with age in the quality of intellectual achievements could come about because a young innovator, having staked a claim to novel ideas and methods, spends the later years working out the implications and applications. A younger person hoping to work creatively must make new discoveries, unless he or she is merely to follow up the work of other people. This selective factor directs younger people towards fresh fields of endeavour, since 'quality' of achievement tends to be defined in terms of its originality.

Experimental studies of creative intelligence, using open-ended tests, help to explain the effects of ageing observed by Lehman. Both the quantity and the quality of the responses decline with age, but the decline is more marked for the high-quality responses. The fact that creativity, as measured by open-ended tests, correlates highly, but not perfectly, with unspecialized intelligence gives further weight to the suggestion that much of the decline with age in creative intellectual achievement is accounted for by a decline in unspecialized intelligence and a mental slowing-down.

There is no reason to suppose that the age-changes and the peak periods catalogued by Lehman are fixed and unalterable. Indeed, secular trends and the observed variations from one field of endeavour to another suggest a complex network of causes and consequences, so that there is probably much that we could do to bring about improvements, once the critical influences are understood.

(d) Secular trends (cohort effects)

It is difficult to compare the merits of achievements occurring at different periods of history because of uncertainty regarding remote dates, changes in attitude towards publishing, and so on. The secular trend, in the age at which people achieve *social* eminence (see Chapter Five, Section 5), is for later-born generations to attain status at older age-levels. This could be the effect of an increase in life expectation, plus the longer period of learning needed for leadership in modern societies. The opposite trend – in scientific achievement – might be produced by improvements in physical health and education, which lower the age of biological maturity and reduce the amount of time required to acquire the skills and knowledge needed to make original contributions to science and other fields of intellectual endeavour. Despite the fact that there is much more knowledge available, factual groupings, obsolescence and conceptual simplifications take place, so that knowledge tends to become orderly and systematic, more specialized and easier to learn and remember – for example, cell theory in molecular biology or solid-state electronics. Improvements in education and in the techniques of acquiring knowledge – brought about by television, computers, libraries, scientific instruments, and so on – may help to explain the secular trend in the age at which intellectual achievements occur most frequently. An increase in the average duration of life should make it possible to lengthen the range of the creative years, though without shifting the peak years for intellectual creativity. The age-distribution for certain kinds of output is much the same for those who die early as for those who die late (where comparisons are made over the appropriate parts of the life-span).

The historical shift in the age-distribution of scientific achievements is considerable. In physics, for example, the rate of contribution of scientists born between 1785 and 1867 rose steadily from the age of 25 to a peak at the age of 35 and then declined steadily to 65; the rate of contribution for scientists born before 1785 rose steadily from the age of 25 to a peak at the age of 45 and then declined – sharply at first, then more steadily – to 75. Lehman published similar findings for many other areas of achievement. A comparison of early-born versus later-born individuals in chemistry, astronomy and oil-painting, however, failed to reveal similar findings. In some cases, the decline in output was sharper for the later-born contributors. Lehman suggested that the delay between achievement and recognition became shorter because of improvements in publishing and patenting, and this may help to explain why later-born persons seem to make their contributions at earlier ages. Social changes, furthermore, have taken art and science out of the hands of the amateurs and the privileged leisured classes and handed them over to full-time professionals.

According to Lehman's data, the peak years for established leadership status occur between the ages of 50 and 70, whereas those for intellectual and sporting attainments occur between 20 and 40. Moreover, whereas social leaders appear on average to be older than their predecessors in similar positions, creative artists and scientists appear to be doing their best work at earlier ages. The distribution of achievements throughout the lifespan covers a wider range of years for earlier-born as compared with later-born generations. This effect could arise for a number of reasons, such as greater competitiveness, improvements in publication, financial incentives. Secular trends in health, education, and possibly intelligence further complicate the issue.

References and Suggestions for Further Reading

Berg, C. A. and Sternberg, R. J., 'A triarchic theory of intellectual development during adulthood', *Developmental Review*, 5, 1985, 334–70.

Charness, M. (ed.), *Aging and Human Performance*, Chichester: John Wiley, 1985.

Craik, F. I. M. and Trehub, S. (eds), *Aging and Cognitive Processes*, New York: Plenum, 1982.

Flynn, J. R., 'Massive IQ gains in fourteen nations: what IQ tests really measure', *Psychological Bulletin*, *101*, 1987, 171–91.

Frank, G., *The Wechsler Enterprise. An Assessment of the Development, Structure and Use of the Wechsler Tests of Intelligence*, London: Pergamon Press, 1983.

Lehman, H. C., *Age and Achievement*, London: Oxford University Press, 1953.

——'More about age and achievement', *Gerontologist*, 2, 1962, 141–8.

——'The most creative years of engineers and other technologists', *Journal of Genetic Psychology, 108,* 1966, 263–77.

Matarazzo, J. D., *Wechsler's Measurement and Appraisal of Adult*

Intelligence (5th edn), Baltimore, MD: Williams & Wilkins, 1972.

Plemons, J. K., Willis, S. L. and Baltes, P. B., 'Modifiability of fluid intelligence in aging: a short-term longitudinal approach', *Journal of Gerontology, 33,* 1978, 224–31; for subsequent correspondence and references, see *Journal of Gerontology, 36,* 1981, 634–8.

Poon, L. W., Fozard, J. L., Cermak, L. S., Arenberg, D. and Thompson, L. W. (eds), *New Directions in Memory and Aging*, Proceedings of the George Talland Memorial Conference, Hillsdale, NJ: Lawrence Erlbaum Associates, 1980.

Rabbitt, P. M. A., 'A fresh look at changes in reaction times in old age', in D. G. Stein (ed.), *The Psychobiology of Aging*, New York: Elsevier/North-Holland, 1980.

Raven, J. C., *Revised Manual for Raven's Progressive Matrices and Vocabulary Scales*, Windsor: NFER, Nelson, 1982.

Schaie, K. W. and Hertzog, C., 'Fourteen-year short-sequential analyses of adult intellectual development', *Developmental Psychology, 19,* 1983, 531–43.

Vannieuwkirk, R. R. and Galbraith, G. G., 'The relationship of age to performance on the Luria-Nebraska neuropsychological battery', *Journal of Clinical Psychology, 41,* 1985, 527–32.

Wagenaar, W. A., 'My memory: a study of autobiographical memory over six years', *Cognitive Psychology, 18,* 1986, 225–52.

Wechsler, D., *Wechsler Adult Intelligence Scale – Revised, Manual*, Cleveland, OH: The Psychological Corporation, 1981.

Nine
Psychological Disorders

1. Adult Life

It is not yet possible to specify with any accuracy the complex organic changes and processes involved in many psychiatric ailments. Some abnormal mental conditions are caused by damage to the brain or by metabolic or endocrine disorders which may or may not be inherited or related to age-changes. Psychological stresses appear to precipitate mental illness in persons who are predisposed. This has led to the practice, in psychiatry, of distinguishing two broad categories: organic disorders and functional disorders. An organic ailment can be traced, directly or indirectly, to a definite disease, injury or malfunction, particularly in the brain – for instance, a tumor, lesion or toxic state. A functional ailment is one for which no definite disease, injury or malfunction of the body can be found and might therefore arise either because of an organic condition which cannot be detected by existing methods, or through the acquisition of maladaptive patterns of behaviour such as depression, paranoid ideas or phobias. There is disagreement about the aetiology of some conditions. Although the inadequacy of the distinction between organic and functional mental illnesses is widely recognized in psychiatry, it nevertheless provides a convenient diagnostic framework at least for the main part of adult life. In later life, however, the distinction between organic and functional disorders is less clear because of the complex interactive effects of normal ageing, disease processes and life-events. So for example: there is a condition referred to as paraphrenia – schizophrenia of late onset: there are so-called 'burned-out' schizophrenics – patients who have lost their more florid symptoms; there are similarities in the symptomatology of dementia and depression; there are dementias which occur early or late; there are psychological stress reactions which lead to medical complications.

Of patients over the age of 60 admitted to psychiatric care, about half have functional disorders, and about half have organic disorders.

(a) Acute and chronic brain disorders

One broad class of mental disorders is caused by or associated with malfunction of the brain tissues. Within this broad class there are two subsidiary classes: acute and chronic.

The acute disorders (which reach a critical condition relatively quickly) include those brought about by: infections in the brain or elsewhere in the body, drugs or poisons including alcohol, head injury, cardiovascular defects, faulty metabolism, growth or nutrition, and neoplastic, e.g. cancerous, conditions. In acute brain disorders there is a temporary, fluctuating impairment of the brain and of behaviour during which patients are confused about their identity, their whereabouts and their relations with other people. Their mind wanders, and they may have hallucinations and brief mild delusions: they may be moody or aggressive, and sleeping and eating habits are often disturbed. A common acute brain disorder in old people is delirium caused by infections or toxic states; delirium can also be caused by impaired blood flow to the brain in heart or chest disease, for instance, or by cerebral embolism (obstruction of a blood vessel in the brain).

The chronic disorders are relatively long-standing and usually progressive. They include brain disorders associated with cerebral arteriosclerosis or other cardiovascular disturbances, senile and pre-senile brain disorders, and epilepsy. Other conditions causing permanent and sometimes progressive brain damage are infections such as syphilis, and toxic states such as those brought about by the prolonged use of alcohol or drugs. Head injuries can cause cerebral damage leading to psychiatric illness. In old people living alone malnutrition may be an important precipitating cause of psychiatric illness. The adverse effects on behaviour of chronic disorders are permanent and progressive, although the progress of the disease may be slow. The course of some chronic brain disorders is less progressive and more variable, more unpredictable, than others. The psychological effects appear in the gradual erosion of a patient's memory, poor retention of recent learning and experience, impaired judgement and problem-solving, and the gradual loss of normal habits of adjustment.

(b) Functional psychoses

In functional psychoses the disturbance is such that patients can no longer deal appropriately and realistically with the environment; their perceptions, thoughts and actions are often bizarre and disorganized, and their relationships with other people are grossly impaired.

(I) AFFECTIVE PSYCHOSIS. The term 'affect' is used in psychology and psychiatry to refer to feeling and mood. In affective psychosis the feelings, emotions and moods of patients are severely disturbed, provoking changes in behaviour. In mania they feel greatly elated or irritable, and become over-active, over-talkative, and carried away by a flight of fanciful ideas and extravagant action. In depression they feel hopeless and full of despair; thoughts and reactions are often painfully slow, they may become anxious without good reason or, more rarely, irrationally agitated. In manic-depressive psychosis some patients have alternate episodes of depression and mania. Patients may suffer from perceptual distortions, delusions and hallucinations. Such disorders sometimes ease for a time and then recur. Depression is a major psychiatric disorder in later life, commonly divided into two categories: psychotic or endogenous (caused by factors within the person), and reactive or exogenous (attributable to stresses imposed on the person). There is usually a history of depressive episodes in the former. It is often difficult to determine whether a depression in old age is endogenous, or a reaction to external stress, or a symptom of an organic cerebral condition; an important problem because it bears on the choice of treatment, e.g. electroconvulsive therapy (ECT). Depression in later life can give rise to symptoms which may be mistaken for those of dementia – a form of 'pseudo-dementia'.

Affective disorders are found throughout adult life. In late maturity and old age depression predominates, sometimes accompanied by severe agitation. The distinction between a psychotic depression and the depressed phase of manic-depressive psychosis is usually made because some patients have a history of manic episodes, whereas others do not.

(II) SCHIZOPHRENIA. Next to the mental disorders of senescence, schizophrenia is probably the largest, most intractable and least understood group of mental disorders. Older people may develop schizophrenia, but usually it begins as an illness of late adolescence or early adult life. The disorder is characterized by a disorganization of the personality. Patients become psychologically 'detached' from the real world, suffer from various disorders of thought or feeling and, in severe cases, appear to be incapable of more than brief occasional periods of lucidity when they can make contact with other people. Schizophrenia is often sustained for many years. Many elderly psychotic patients, originally diagnosed as schizophrenic, continue to survive in mental hospitals until late maturity and old age. In old age their symptoms change towards those characteristic of the mental disorders of senescence, and the differences between the various clinical types of schizophrenia become less marked.

At one time long-stay mental patients frequently became 'institutionalized', that is, apathetic, habit-bound and intellectually deteriorated. Patients with schizophrenia, senile psychosis or other serious mental illnesses were unlikely to improve under routine hospital conditions. Nowadays, efforts are made to keep such patients active and interested in life and to return them, whenever possible, to community care. Even so, the adverse effects of institutional routines are clearly observable in geriatric wards and homes for the elderly. These effects are compounded by physical infirmity which limits mobility, and by a decrease in activities requiring psychological effort.

(III) PARANOIA. Although paranoid symptoms sometimes dominate a schizophrenic condition, many psychiatrists distinguish a separate kind of psychiatric disorder known as paranoia. Paranoid patients are relatively rare. They have delusions of grandeur or persecution but tend not to hallucinate. Abilities are well preserved, and the more intelligent patients build up a comprehensive and detailed system of delusional ideas, often centred on one or more actual events in their life. Although the delusional system occupies an important place in their life they may be able to conduct most of their affairs normally. Paranoid delusions occur in mental illness in middle life and later, and the milder conditions may be difficult to distinguish from socially acceptable degrees of suspicion and eccentricity.

(c) Neuroses and psychosomatic disorders

Neurosis refers to prolonged and exaggerated reactions, such as anxiety, depression and bodily discomfort (which all of us experience sometimes, even in normal health). Neurotic symptoms can be psychological, somatic, social and behavioural, or a combination of these. Neuroses differ from psychoses in so far as gross personality breakdown or bizarre delusions and hallucinations are absent. The typical neurotic patient has a history of psychological maladjustment which often dates back to childhood and manifests itself in periodic states of anxiety, phobia or depression, and less frequently in dissociation and other 'hysterical' symptoms.

Conspicuous neurosis and psychosomatic illness rarely appear for the first time in old age, but minor neurotic ill health and physiological disorders of psychological origin can arise in middle age or later, and may be maintained into later life, sometimes complicating the clinical picture when symptoms based on degenerative changes begin to appear. The prevalence of neurotic maladjustment among the elderly living in the community has been estimated to be about 10 to 15 per cent. Old people who are markedly neurotic are likely to have shown severe maladjustment or neurosis in earlier life. Neurotic conditions starting only late in life are usually linked with stress such as physical illness or bereavement. Unmarried or divorced people, and those who experience neurotic breakdown in middle age, are also somewhat more inclined to neurotic disorders late in life. These vary in intensity. Mild forms of obsessional behaviour, morbid and irrational fears, and worry about personal health are more common in late life, especially among anxious introverted people; but these do not amount to an incapacitating neurotic breakdown. Other kinds of maladjustment, not usually regarded as psychological ailments, such as withdrawal, suspicion, tiredness, poor standards of conduct and bad temper, are probably also more common, if only because our physical and psychological resources are reduced as age advances. Conspicuous changes of this sort, however, may foreshadow a more serious psychiatric disorder.

The clinical description of neurosis is based on the symptoms presented by younger adults rather than on abnormal behaviour in the elderly, who are likely to show a different kind of 'neurotic' behaviour. A considerable amount of psychiatric experience may be required in order to judge the relative contributions of predisposition, environmental stress and ageing.

Psychosomatic disorders are physical illnesses precipitated or aggravated by psychological factors. One interpretation is that psychosomatic symptoms, such as asthma, some skin disorders, high blood pressure, migraine or peptic ulcers, are physiological complications brought on or made worse by stress and emotionally disturbing conflicts. Another view is that psychological strains merely aggravate an existing illness, or act as the precipitating factor for a type of illness to which the individual is constitutionally predisposed. Organic changes associated with prolonged frustration and conflict may not appear for some considerable time, or not at all if the person is not constitutionally predisposed to a psychosomatic disorder. There is considerable variation between individuals. Psychosomatic disorders are different from the various bodily symptoms which we all experience at times of strain (such as 'butterflies' in the stomach, cramps, palpitations or excessive perspiration). Such symptoms are common and can be severe in neurotic individuals. The constitutional factor is thought to be important.

Malfunction in an elderly person is likely to be treated as if the condition were an inevitable consequence of old age, but the discerning general practitioner or psychiatrist may see from the patient's medical history, and from other evidence, that some assurance and psychiatric support is called for in addition to physical treatment. The situation as regards minor physical ailments in late maturity and old age is complicated by the natural increase in the older person's concern about his or her physical condition, and this may lead to hypochondriacal preoccupations.

(d) Other kinds of abnormal behaviour

Several kinds of abnormal behaviour may occur in later life but cannot be dealt with in detail. They can occur in the absence of psychiatric illness and could be referred to just as conveniently elsewhere. They are briefly mentioned to illustrate the scope of social and behavioural gerontology.

(I) CRIME. This occurs mostly in the 15–40 age-group. Crimes such as assault or indecency committed by elderly people for the first time may follow from natural degenerative processes outside the individual's control, but can occur without demonstrable intellectual deterioration. Certain crimes, such as forgery or embezzlement, are more often committed by older persons. Crimes associated with poverty and mental disorder (vagrancy, chronic drunkenness) increase with age.

(II) SEXUAL DEVIATION. This may be symptomatic of one or other of the disorders already mentioned, as, for example, schizophrenia. Sexual potency, interests and activity normally decline gradually in late maturity and old age, but the onset of degenerative changes and the loss of normal sexual outlets can lead to a temporary loss of self-control, giving rise to sexual misdemeanours.

(III) DRUG ADDICTION AND ALCOHOLISM. These are frequently consequences of personality disorder, but as it often takes many years for the full effects to develop, the chronic and severe cases are likely to be mature adults. Drug addiction has become a more common cause of mental illness; milder forms of habituation are developed through regular medication with sedatives or sleeping tablets among adults. There are, however, cultural differences and secular changes in the use of drugs, including alcohol, nicotine and narcotics. Alcohol misuse is far greater in men than in women.

It is not unusual to find that older people have been prescribed an excess of drugs for medical purposes; this can lead to unexpected drug interactions, high dosage levels (because of slower excretion of drugs), and undesirable side-effects.

(IV) STRESS REACTIONS. Exposure to severe or prolonged stress during, for example, a painful illness, battle or civilian disaster, may elicit, in normal adults, symptoms similar to those described for the neuroses and psychoses. The symptoms – exhaustion, anxiety, phobias and hallucinations – are a consequence of the emotional shock but the precise mechanism, as in many psychiatric disturbances, is not known. If the person is rested and treated, and circumstances return to normal, the symptoms disappear at a rate commensurate with the predisposition to break down. Adult life and old age can bring painful and prolonged emotional stresses – illness, injury, bereavement, unemployment or retirement. In Britain in 1983, 60 per cent of people aged 65–74, and nearly 70 per cent of people aged 75 and over, reported having a long-standing illness. Other types of stress have yet to be catalogued and their frequencies counted. The reaction to stress in old age is likely to be both more intense and longer for individuals with a history of neurotic or psychotic breakdown.

(v) SOCIAL ISOLATION AND SUICIDE. Social isolation contributes its effect in a variety of psychiatric disturbances, as, for instance, in depression. Studies of suicide have shown that the highest rates occur in areas where family and neighbourhood ties are few. Even the relatively high rate of minor neurotic ill health among older women might be explained in part by the contributory effect of a reduction in family and social interaction. On the other hand, it is likely that the personal dispositions which lead to social down-grading and an inability to enter into new social relationships also predispose to mental ill health and suicide. Unfortunately, the extensive literature on empirical studies of suicide seems to have provided little support for many widely held theories. In Britain, in 1979, suicide accounted for less than 1 per cent of all deaths each year. In the age-group 25–44 suicide accounted for about 13 per 100,000 male deaths and about 6 per 100,000 female deaths; in the age-group 65–74, the proportions increased to about 16 per 100,000 and 12 per 100,000 respectively. Thus at all adult ages men are more likely than women to kill themselves, and suicide occurs more frequently in late maturity. According to *Social Trends* (12, 1982), in 1979 the suicide rate for men aged 75 and over was about 3 times the rate for women of the same age.

Some normal or relatively normal individuals use suicide as a way out of an intolerable social situation or medical condition; others suffer from mental illness in which severe depression plays a part. It may happen to patients who are in the early stages of an untreated psychosis or recovering from a severe neurotic depression. Depression is common in both sexes, probably more frequent among women. Suicide is more likely among individuals predisposed to affective disorder and among their relatives. Thus suicide and affective illness are associated. Physiological, social or psychological factors play a part in bringing about a suicide. Some individuals are aware of their serious physical condition; others are lonely and see no point in living. Sometimes social attitudes and personal values delay the act; at other times a crisis or an opportunity precipitates the event. Official statistics underestimate the number of suicides because coroners are likely to be biased towards a verdict of 'accidental death', thus sparing the dead person's relatives the social stigma associated with suicide. Suicides in late life may not be regarded as such simply because the person is known to have a fatal illness and is presumed to have died a 'natural' death.

Psychological research into the problem of suicide can be carried out by analysing suicide notes, reconstructing the dead person's history, studying the precipitating factors (in so far as they can be discovered) and studying evidence supplied by persons who made unsuccessful attempts to kill themselves. Some people take, say, an overdose of drugs to draw attention to their desperate plight without really wishing to end their life. But many older people who attempt suicide are suffering from severe depression, and it is more difficult in these cases to separate out those patients who attempt suicide as a threat or demonstration from those who fail because of technical incompetence or the vigilance of other people. Threatened suicide, contrary perhaps to popular belief, often precedes actual suicide. Both suicide and mental illness are found with greater frequency in the lower socio-economic classes, and especially in urban areas which are run down and socially disorganized. It is probable that at least half of the suicides in later life are committed by people who have some sort of psychiatric illness, and that proper social care and psychiatric treatment, especially if made available early, would drastically reduce the number. Physical illness is a frequent contributory factor in suicide.

2. Some Methodological Difficulties

Age-trends in mental illness are difficult to assess, for several reasons. First, mental illnesses vary from relatively severe disorders to relatively mild cases. The age-trends for similar psychiatric conditions which vary in severity are not identical, although the broad trends are not in dispute. Second, there is some lack of uniformity in the diagnosis and labelling of mental disease; doctors vary in their ability to diagnose mental illness and to keep detailed records. Some people are reluctant to admit to conditions which might categorize them as 'mental' patients. Third, age, sex and social class differences in behaviour complicate the assessment of the prevalence of mental illness. Fourth, differences in the way investigators compile and interpret their observations influence the results – for example, diagnostic criteria, source of data, duration of the study and type of community sampled. Fifth, there are secular changes associated with developments and fashions in theory and treatment, and with the effects of social attitudes, migration, demographic changes and so on.

In the course of one year approximately one adult in five sees a doctor about symptoms which are obviously emotional in origin (or, at least, with somatic symptoms lacking apparent organic pathology). In many cases the symptoms are mild, though it must be remembered that we do not have reliable standards of *normal* mental health – whether a person is regarded as abnormal depends not only on the observer's judgement but also on other factors, such as local social norms, or the tolerance of the family. The proportion of women patients with neurotic ill health rises to about 50 per cent for women in their sixties. This may have something to do with gender differences in social roles, expectations, circumstances and expressive behaviour, or possibly with the way physicians (mostly male) perceive women's ailments. Whatever the explanation, it is not likely to be a simple one. The complexity of the sex difference in the occurrence of psychiatric ill health is shown, for example, by a greater prevalence of mild neurotic ill health for women and yet a higher suicide rate for men.

Neurotic conditions often have no definite time of onset or recovery, so that little can be said about their duration. The mildest last for about two to four months. People who experience a more severe illness, like a neurotic breakdown which makes them unfit for work, have a longer expectancy of illness – 60 per cent recover within two years, 90 per cent within five years. After recovery, patients appear to have a greater risk of further breakdown. Neurotic conditions often recur over a number of years. Sometimes a moderate to severe neurosis coexists with a physical illness. The psychological consequences of ordinary illnesses have not been studied in any great detail. Neurotic patients consult their doctors about twice as often as do non-neurotic patients, partly because some neurotic patients have both neurotic and physical ailments.

3. Old Age

(a) The prevalence of psychiatric disorders

In old age the risk of mental illness reaches a peak. Much of it is associated directly or indirectly with pathological processes in brain tissues, and in the cerebral blood vessels. Psychiatric illness in old age is a serious problem in social medicine which will worsen as the proportion of elderly persons in the population increases, but no part of adult life is free from susceptibility to mental illness.

Accurate estimates of the prevalence of psychiatric illness are difficult to make for many reasons, and figures must be treated with great caution, but roughly speaking about 5 per cent of people over the age of 65 suffer some sort of psychosis. From 5 to 15 per cent suffer less serious disorder, and approximately 10 to 15 per cent suffer from neuroses or other disorders. In Britain patients over the age of 60 make up at least 25 per cent of admissions to hospitals, and, if account is taken of private facilities and home care, the percentage requiring psychiatric treatment is certainly much higher. Of these patients, at least 10 per cent, probably substantially more, appear to have some brain damage, though only about 5 per cent are seriously affected. About 5 or 10 per cent have some sort of psychotic disorder, mainly depressive; the contrasting condition – manic or hypomanic state – is much less frequent and possibly accounts for 5 or 10 per cent of affective disorders in late life. About 10 per cent have fairly conspicuous symptoms of neurosis. Almost half the patients with dementia have cerebrovascular disease, and about a third have other cerebral deterioration. In about one-fifth, both are present. Paraphrenia accounts for nearly 10 per cent of first admissions of women aged 65 and over. By some estimates, therefore, about three-quarters of the elderly are normal by psychiatric standards (see Table 9.1), but estimates vary widely.

Table 9.1 Crude Estimates of the Prevalence of Psychogeriatric Disorders in Urban Populations

Category	
A	Psychogeriatric morbidity (all conditions combined) Lower estimate: 25 per cent Upper estimate: 40 per cent
B	Organic disorder (dementia and confusion): 6 per cent of A (i) Symptomatic confusion: 36 per cent of B (ii) Chronic brain syndrome: 64 per cent of B
C	Depression: 10 per cent of A
D	Diseases of the CNS: 10 per cent of A
E	Functional psychoses: 2 per cent of A
F	Neuroses and behaviour disorders: 12 per cent of A

These estimates indicate the prevalence of psychological disorders in persons aged 60/65 or more. Note also psychological factors in: stress reactions; psychosomatic disorders; symptoms and ill-defined conditions; accidents, poisonings, violence; suicide and attempted suicide; multiple disorders; physical illness and disability.

(b) Pathological changes in the aged brain

Some aspects of age-changes in the brain were dealt with in Chapter Two. Post-mortem studies show various pathologies in the brains of old people with dementia. These include thickening and hardening of the main cerebral blood vessels, and damage and occlusion in the fine network of cerebral blood vessels. Changes in the blood vessels seem partly independent of changes in the nerve cells and glial tissues. The latter changes include: gliosis – an increase in the supporting tissue (neuroglia) of the brain and spinal cord; the loss of many nerve cells and adverse changes in the structure of others; wider and deeper fissures on the surface of the brain, and larger ventricles (fluid-filled spaces within the brain); the disruption of cortical lamination (patterned layers of brain tissue);

the appearance of senile plaques – small, irregular-shaped areas of degeneration in the brain, which show up as dark blobs when revealed by the staining techniques of microscopy; neurofibrillary changes in which the fibrils within the neuron become thickened, tangled and severed.

Vascular and primary nerve-cell changes are both common, so they may appear together. Damage to the brain may be either focal (occurring in one or more small local areas) or diffuse (spread throughout the brain tissues). Such changes, which become apparent at post-mortem, are strongly associated with the organic psychoses, but they occur quite frequently, though usually in less marked degree, in patients diagnosed as functional psychotics, and, indeed, in old people who have shown no mental abnormality during life and are assumed to have a normal brain.

The degree of overlap of symptoms between different psychiatric categories is large, and a good deal of variation exists between patients within any one category. The severity of degenerative changes in the brain is correlated with the severity of the symptoms displayed by the patient when alive, the association being more pronounced for psychoses with definite organic origins, i.e. showing the characteristic 'organic' mental symptoms associated with the term 'dementia'. As it is difficult to assess the severity of symptoms in 'normal' people and borderline psychiatric cases – since they do not come under systematic observation – we do not know to what extent severity of degeneration in the brain is associated with normal intellectual impairment and personality change in old age. Such degenerative changes can, however, be observed at post-mortem in people without a history of mental illness or brain damage. This could mean that some people can tolerate a degree of degenerative change in the brain, in much the same way, presumably, as they can tolerate other sorts of anatomical and physiological defect. On the other hand, there may be certain areas in the brain where a small amount of damage can precipitate conspicuous symptoms and signs of psychosis. Damage to the mammillary bodies and their connections, for example, seems to be associated with memory disturbance, though psychotic symptoms such as delusions and hallucinations do not appear to be regularly associated with damage to particular areas of the brain.

The brain is an extremely complex physiological system. Disturbances and damage originating in one part can be expected to have repercussions throughout the system. Given our present limited understanding of the physiology of the brain, theories about the way the brain ages, based on pathological and physiological data regarding lesions, post-mortem studies, EEG records, and so on, are at best tentative. But recent technical developments such as computerized axial tomography (CAT) and positron emission tomography (PET) promise greatly to improve our understanding of the physical basis of age-changes in behaviour.

The particular sequence and pattern of symptoms shown by a patient with brain damage depend to some extent on the kind of personality the patient had before the onset of the disease, and on the particular kinds and amounts of brain damage. Moreover, since each person has his or her own biochemical individuality, the complexity of the problem can be easily imagined. Certain clinical symptoms such as dementia, failure of memory and disorientation in time and place, however, are very characteristic of patients with definite brain damage irrespective of personality or aetiology.

(c) The classification of disorders

The classification of psychiatric disorders in later maturity and old age is by no means settled, but broadly speaking the illnesses are as follows: senile psychosis; psychosis with cerebral arteriosclerosis; affective psychosis; late paraphrenia; and in middle age, presenile dementia. The International Classification of Diseases (ICD) gives a detailed coding of diagnoses of psychiatric disorders in adult life and old age. The *Diagnostic and Statistical Manual* (DSM III) classifies diagnoses under senile psychosis and under arteriosclerotic psychosis, depending upon the other conditions with which these disorders are associated.

Psychiatric illness is presumed to arise through the interaction of predisposing factors (the product of genetic characteristics and basic life experiences) and precipitating factors (such as physical illness or emotional stress).

(1) SENILE DEMENTIA OF THE ALZHEIMER TYPE. Senile dementia usually appears from about the age of 70 onwards. It is more common

in women than in men, and its onset is gradual. Intellectual deterioration is relatively slow but progressive; patients lose interest and become less responsive; they lose the finer shades of feeling and emotion. As their physical and mental resources diminish, they are confined more and more to their own, possibly confused, mental states, and restricted to their home surroundings. Memory impairment is one of the more obvious early signs of an impending senile psychosis, and the recall of recent events seems to be more markedly affected than the recall of events in the patient's early life. Memory disorders are sometimes associated with disturbances of affect. Patients have less energy and become easily upset; they sleep fitfully and their behaviour patterns are disorganized.

The senile psychotic may wander about at all hours, and shout and scream in imaginary arguments. Loss of conscious control and coarsening of social feelings can lead to anti-social conduct. The main distinction between senile dementia and normal ageing lies in the far greater extent and rapidity of the deterioration and the higher mortality in senile dementia. The pathological changes in senile psychosis are diffuse.

In the earlier stages the prevailing mood is typically one of shallow depression sometimes involving transient paranoid ideas and morbid, misplaced fears of retribution for non-existent sins and crimes. The patient's short-lived delusions are feeble attempts to find some pattern of meaning for his or her disordered thoughts, perceptions and feelings. In the late stages patients may no longer recognize family members and acquaintances; they may accuse people of theft or interference, and become confused about the identities of people. In these respects senile dementia and cerebral arteriosclerotic psychosis are similar.

Physical stress, physiological upset or social disorganization may bring on a delirium in which the patient becomes restless, difficult to manage and suspectible to auditory and visual hallucinations. Many cases first come to the attention of the hospital authorities because of the disturbance caused by the delirium. Some patients show paranoid suspicions which lead them to issue threats or assault other people. They usually regain some conscious control of their behaviour after the delirium, but most of them are left with a more marked dementia.

Within about six months of the onset of the disease, though the rate of progress is variable, senile psychotic patients have usually become physically enfeebled, mentally slow, emotionally dull and apathetic, and easily tired. Their grasp of circumstances and events becomes worse, and they attempt to fill in the gaps in memory with guesswork and fantasy. For a time they may try to disguise their real condition by covering up and excusing mistakes, and by putting on a cheerful, friendly attitude. As the illness progresses they can recall less of their past life, and even outstanding events are forgotten (although sometimes preserved as isolated memories). As patients lose their hold on reality they become confused and deluded about their present environment, and about the people around them. Their reduced mental capacities make their thoughts vague and incomplete. They cannot cope with unfamiliar circumstances. As with normal old people, they may reveal their failing powers by trying too hard, or making excuses, or doing the wrong thing. Eventually the disease encroaches on lifelong habits, and patients cannot think properly, speak coherently or write effectively. They tend to talk around the issue, wander off the point, repeat themselves and use empty phrases. Their speech becomes incomprehensible, inappropriate, and finally meaningless. Social and emotional behaviour deteriorates with similar severity and rapidity. The mood is usually vague, flat, dull and apathetic, and emotional reactions are slow and weak.

Where elderly individuals have to fend for themselves, their senile condition may bring about a decline into filthy conditions and appalling neglect. Many are already in a fairly advanced stage of the disease when admitted to a mental hospital, and mortality is high. Death may follow an infection, or simply bring to an end an existence in which the patient is unconscious, or malnourished, incontinent, with falling blood pressure, and suffering loss of body weight and decreasing temperature.

The causes of senile psychosis are not yet fully understood, though general nursing care and medical measures can mitigate symptoms. Functional capacity is sometimes diminished by disuse and can be restored to a limited extent. Genetic factors may play a part, although the mode of inheritance has not been determined — for example, there may be a connection between Alzheimer's disease and Down's syndrome. Nor is it known to what extent neuro-physiological defects, biochemical factors or other factors are involved. It is probable that neuropathological changes – presumably biochemical in origin – are an indispensable condition of 'true' senile dementia, though there is a wide range of individual suscepti-bility.

Given adequate medical advice and family resources, a person in the early stages of senile dementia may be looked after at home, unless or until he or she becomes unmanageable. Patients do not need to be confined to bed unless they are exhausted or ill; a modicum of activity, social interaction and recreation is beneficial. Nutrition, cleanliness, toilet habits and the avoidance of accidents will be the main home-nursing problems. When psychiatric and medical prob-lems arise, professional advice should be sought, and hospitalization may become necessary.

(II) PSYCHOSIS WITH CEREBRAL ARTERIOSCLEROSIS. Senile changes, and the psychological symptoms that accompany them, can be compared with those associated with cerebral arteriosclerosis. The two conditions, however, are not independent either as regards the behaviour they produce or their physical basis. They are frequently combined, as in the condition referred to as 'chronic brain syndrome'. Arteriosclerotic psychosis was thought to develop more rapidly, to fluctuate in severity, and to clear up temporarily. In addition there are certain signs and symptoms characteristic of cerebral vascular disease.

Dementia clearly associated with cerebral arteriosclerosis usually begins in late maturity as the result of disturbances in the circulation of the blood through the brain. The degenerative sclerotic process may affect the main and the small arteries of the brain, and the smallest blood vessels and capillaries can be restricted or blocked. These changes include many widespread areas of infarction (an 'in-farct' is an area of tissue which has died from lack of adequate blood supply) or haemorrhage, areas of softening and changes in the texture and appearance of the cortex. Patients frequently have high blood pressure or a history of cardiovascular disturbances.

Like other elderly psychiatric patients, patients with cerebral arteriosclerosis often come to the attention of the psychiatrist or geriatrician only when the disease has made considerable progress or when the patient has suffered an acute delirium or 'stroke' (a sudden loss of sensation and movement resulting from brain haemorrhage or thrombosis). This is probably the best-known manifestation of cerebral arteriosclerosis, though a similar process, affecting other parts of the brain, may cause less conspicuous lesions. Both may be associated with cerebral dysfunction if the lesions are sufficiently large. The 'stroke', resulting in a localized neurological defect (such as hemiplegia – a consequence of a vascular lesion interrupting the motor pathways) and associated with mental confusion or unconsciousness, is a common occurrence and a frequent 'presenting' symptom. On examination it often turns out that a patient's memory has been failing for some time, that he or she has been restless, emotionally disturbed, and wandering in the mind for some months before the delirious episode; and may have had headaches, giddiness, black-outs and palpitations. Within a short time memory impairment becomes more marked, concentration suffers and patients become slow to grasp the meaning of a situation, especially an unfamiliar one. Gradually the deterioration encroaches upon habitual performance, making work inefficient, narrowing the range of interests and initiative, and altering emotional reactions. The general effect of the disease is to destroy the more complex and subtle features of the personality, though judgements based on experience, and the more salient personality traits, may remain relatively intact. This is supposed to contrast somewhat with senile dementia, which has an unremittingly progressive destructive effect on the central organizing dispositions of the personality.

Patients with cerebral arteriosclerosis react to their condition by becoming morose and pessimistic; their emotional control is weakened so that when tearful they are likely to weep bitterly, when amused to laugh uproariously. The symptom is thought to arise partly as a consequence of lesions in neural motor pathways controlling emotional expression. The normal effects of ageing on emotions are not well understood.

The word 'delirium' is used to refer to a transient disorganization of cognitive functions because of a disturbance of cerebral metabolism brought about, for example, by infection or reaction to medication.

A confusional state is a state of acute mental imbalance and excitement which usually occurs during the course of cerebral arteriosclerosis, though it may also occur in other physical illnesses. The delirium puts patients out of touch with reality and makes them appear seriously demented. This sometimes happens in the early stages of the disease. Patients tend to recover quickly and leave hospital for a time. This cycle of events can repeat itself several times, until the cumulative brain damage and dementia make institutional care necessary. In a number of patients the deterioration is gradual and mental confusion may not occur. In the clouded state, patients are confused and inaccessible for hours, days or even weeks, and 'clouding of consciousness' can become a frequent and seriously disabling symptom. Confusion may be apparent, or greatly accentuated, at night. Patients wander about the house or the streets, turn on the gas, switch on the lights, start fires, talk incoherently and resist attempts to get them back to bed. Each successive delirious episode, even if it occurs several months after the previous one, leaves a patient more deteriorated; but with proper encouragement patients may, for a little while at least, partially recover and appear reasonably competent.

Mental disturbances often cannot be traced to any particular cause. In old people a delirium is often brought on by a physical illness, such as pneumonia, anaemia, heart failure or severe bronchitis. It can be associated with post-operative complications or metabolic deficiencies, hospitalization, avitaminosis or a high temperature. Old people are much more likely than young people to become delirious because of a physical illness, which again illustrates the older person's greater susceptibility to pathological processes. Distinguishing between these transient confusional states on the one hand, and those associated with senile psychosis and psychosis with cerebral arteriosclerosis on the other, is a diagnostic problem for the physician, made more difficult by the patient's confused mental state. But in practice, unless there is evidence to the contrary, it is assumed that the condition is caused by the physical illness, which is treated energetically. It can often be shown that the physical illness preceded, and can account for, the onset of the delirium.

Feelings of depression occur frequently in cerebral arteriosclerosis, but not usually as severely as in affective psychosis in later life. The patient's mood is shallow and shifts easily from one extreme to the other. Suicidal tendencies may be pronounced in a delirious episode, but disappear abruptly when the patient's mood shifts. It sometimes happens, too, that a psychotic patient with cerebral arteriosclerosis is also predisposed to an affective disorder, in which case there has usually been a history of episodes of depression (or mania) earlier in life, unconnected with vascular disease.

In cerebral arteriosclerosis the onset of serious lesions in the brain is indicated by partial paralyses, tremors, speech disorders and, less often, by sensory defects (temporary or permanent), or, more rarely, by convulsions. These are caused by the clotting of blood in the arteries of the brain (cerebral thrombosis). In cerebral haemorrhage the outcome depends on the brain tissue destroyed by the bleeding; in severe brain haemorrhage the patient becomes comatose and dies. Certain neurological signs may herald the onset of the disease before the psychological abnormalities become apparent. For example, the pupils contract and dilate slowly in response to changes in illumination, the muscular contractions elicited by tapping the tendons may be unequal, and stroking the sole of the foot elicits an upward rather than a downward reflex action of the big toe. Death need not be caused directly by arteriosclerosis – common causes are pneumonia and heart failure.

Various disorders of perception and understanding may follow a 'stroke' – a hemiplegic patient, for example, may appear to be demented (mentally deteriorated) but actually be aphasic (unable to use or understand language) and so present a problem of rehabilitation. Many patients can be cared for at home or in hostels, where the general atmosphere and social amenities may be better than in hospital, and where rehabilitation includes visits by social workers, supervised nutrition, participation in small groups and recreation.

Hypertension (prolonged high blood pressure) usually appears for no apparent reason, but sometimes as a consequence of kidney disorders. Ageing brings about an increase in blood pressure, and hypertension can lead to impairment of brain functions by damaging the blood vessels. Very severe hypertension can cause serious symptoms such as fits, unconsciousness or transient muscular weaknesses. High blood pressure makes the walls of the arteries thicker and stronger, but other factors are probably involved as well. People who are overweight are more likely to suffer from hypertension and from other diseases of the heart and blood vessels. Hypertension can lead to structural alterations in the kidneys, which can, in turn, lead to a constriction of the blood vessels. A few patients, whose hypertension is caused by a diseased kidney, may be cured by its surgical removal. High blood pressure can sometimes be controlled with the aid of drugs, diet and relaxation training without, of course, reversing structural changes that may have occurred in the brain.

Prolonged or periodic emotional stress of considerable severity can lead to a rise in blood pressure. Some individuals are more prone than others to strong cardiac reactions when emotionally upset, and such people may be prone to hypertension. Patients are usually advised by their physician to take a rest, have longer periods of sleep and find a more settled environment, in the belief that this will alleviate the condition, or at least delay the onset of its more serious consequences. For those who are reasonably intelligent and co-operative, a lot can be done to improve physical health, emotional outlook and life activities. The earliest symptoms are similar to those of mild neurotic disorders – headaches, fatigue, sleeplessness.

Apparently, the distinction between 'senile dementia' and 'arteriosclerotic dementia' is not as clear as it was formerly thought to be. The pattern and course of dementia vary in relation to a variety of contributory factors – physiological as well as social.

Similarly, the distinction between senile and presenile dementia seems to depend on an arbitrary age criterion. The complexity of biomedical and psychological conditions in late life helps to account for the variety of signs and symptoms observed, and for the overlap in psychiatric diagnostic categories.

The incidence and prevalence of chronic brain failure and symptomatic mental confusion are difficult to estimate – because of diagnostic problems, problems of measuring the degree and duration of the disorder, and problems of making community surveys of this sort.

(III) AFFECTIVE PSYCHOSES. Depression is a common complaint in elderly patients for several reasons. First, the various stresses of old age such as retirement, bereavement or physical illness are likely to provoke feelings of frustration, failure, disappointment, grief or resignation. Also, more people are surviving into later life to suffer from depressive psychotic illnesses and other functional psychiatric disorders. Moreover, the degenerative processes of old age, and the organic disturbances of the brain, intensify and sustain depression. Withdrawal and depression in response to any physical illness also become more likely as age increases. 'Depressive reaction' is diagnosed if the emotional disorder is disproportionate to the stress, or fails to clear up when the patient's circumstances improve. In psychotic depressives the history need not reveal a precipitating factor, but there is often a history of previous breakdowns.

The diagnosis and clinical description of psychiatric disorders in adult life and old age are difficult because of the multiplicity of factors involved, the range of differences between individuals, and the differential effects of age, sex and general health on aetiology and symptoms.

Patients who get severe depression for the first time late in life appear to be constitutionally different from those who suffer from depressive psychosis at an earlier age. Some of the depressions of old age occur in patients who have suffered from a depressive psychosis for a large part of their adult lives, to which the symptoms of senescence are then added. Elderly depressives become anxious, guilty and restless; they can be markedly worse within a few weeks – increasingly restless, hopeless, miserable and unable to sleep or to eat properly. The risk of suicide increases with depression. Patients who are severely depressed may attempt to kill themselves not merely because they feel they have nothing to live for but also because of their delusions.

These dramatic symptoms can be contrasted with a simpler type of depressive reaction which differs only in degree from the normal reactions of older people to bereavement, illness and other kinds of stress. Some patients in this category become slower in their thoughts, words and actions, constipated, unable to sleep, greatly concerned with their physical condition and uncertain of themselves. The symptoms of depression in later life, however, are somewhat variable, and depressed patients may not have these particular symptoms.

Old age seems to bring out latent neurotic conditions or to aggravate existing ones, so that it is not unusual to find some of the commoner symptoms of neurosis, such as anxiety, aggressive selfishness, intermittent depression and morbid preoccupation with bodily functions.

Many elderly psychotics come from the lower socio-economic strata of society. They are poor, badly clothed and housed, and physically debilitated. Their unfortunate circumstances intensify the feelings of apathy and hopelessness brought about by the disease.

Functional depressions often appear abruptly without obvious earlier indications, whereas depressions secondary to brain damage usually appear gradually, with mild early symptoms such as impaired recall for recent events, intellectual deterioration, absent-mindedness and disorientation, poorer personal and social habits, and cruder emotional reactions. Depressions secondary to brain damage also fluctuate, have a more 'superficial' quality, and lessen as the effects of brain disease become more pronounced and dementia supervenes. Sometimes psychiatric illnesses are precipitated by a physical illness which patients had ignored or were unaware of – such as an infection, kidney or heart disease; this can give rise to secondary psychological symptoms which complicate the clinical picture.

Mania is usually mild in later life and much less frequent than the depressive reaction; the rate of recovery is lower. It can appear suddenly – the patient becomes over-active and has a feeling of well-being, but no insight. In the elderly and infirm mania brings an added risk of exhaustion and aggravation of physical illness. It can occur without definite signs of organic impairment or intellectual deterioration.

(iv) LATE PARAPHRENIA. Late paraphrenia has been described as a kind of schizophrenia of late onset, in which the main symptom is the delusion of persecution. It is sometimes difficult to distinguish from paranoid depression and organic brain disease. Many patients have a predisposition towards seclusiveness, suspicion and anxiety about people; they are socially isolated, eccentric and difficult to deal with. The personal characteristics of patients with late paraphrenia include quarrelsomeness, religious extremism, egocentricity and lack of affection for others. Jealousy, arrogance and lack of emotional control are also fairly common. The personal qualities and habits which have been effective in coping with problems of adjustment during adult life can become more (or less) appropriate in old age. Women patients outnumber men considerably, and many are either unmarried or living alone for other reasons, though bereavement, as such, seems not to be a precipitating factor in late paraphrenia. It is more likely to be the social upheaval, or possibly the reduction in close social interaction, which follows the loss of a husband, child or close companion.

The usual age of onset is after 60, unlike paranoia proper, which occurs at an earlier age. Partial or total deafness is thought to occur more frequently than in other psychiatric groups of the same age, but physical health is not greatly impaired. Defects of hearing (and of vision in some patients) may contribute to the development of hallucinations and confusions. Senile degeneration or cerebral arteriosclerosis in persons with a pronounced 'schizoid' disposition may result in late paraphrenia, especially when sensory impairments and social isolation are also involved. Paranoid delusions are often linked with hallucinatory experiences. Patients feel that radio transmitters are being used to control their thoughts, that people are walking through their rooms, that unseen enemies are threatening them or urging them to act, or that they are being sexually assaulted. The coincidental actions of other people and everyday sounds and events are woven into the delusions. Gradually the delusional beliefs disrupt their ordinary everyday activities. Finally their behaviour becomes socially unacceptable (because of their accusations, hostility and strangeness) and they are obliged to enter hospital for care and treatment.

When brought face to face with other people, late paraphrenics may seem alert and aware of what is going on. They show distress, anxiety and anger when their delusions are touched upon, but their emotions and attitudes are sometimes out of keeping with their professed beliefs. They may, for instance, refer to an alleged sexual assault in a flat matter-of-fact tone of voice, or smile vaguely when talking about the way their neighbours spy upon them.

(v) DEMENTIA IN MIDDLE AGE. Dementia in middle age can be a *secondary consequence* of a number of disorders including cerebral vascular disease (with cerebral hypoxia), brain injury, toxic states (such as alcoholism), infection (such as meningitis or syphilis), brain tumour and other conditions. Patients with dementia, therefore, must be examined by a physician since the cause of the dementia may be amenable to treatment. The examination consists of an evaluation of the history of the condition, a physical examination, and investigation by means of biomedical tests. Psychological tests are used to assess brain damage and intellectual deterioration.

As mentioned above, an interesting speculation is that patients with Down's syndrome exhibit the symptoms of dementia earlier than normal adults. They have a shorter expectation of life anyway, but the genetic factors involved in normal ageing, Alzheimer's disease and Down's syndrome may be related.

4. The Care of Psychogeriatric Patients

There are psychological and behavioural aspects to *any* physical illness. But, more particularly in old age, respiratory inadequacy, heart failure, malnutrition and stroke have definite psychological effects, such as confusion and anxiety. About one-third of the elderly sick develop psychiatric problems, though only a small percentage need prolonged in-patient treatment. In fact, most people live their lives in reasonable health and vigour and die without having experienced serious psychiatric disorders in later life. More is being done to improve the conditions in which geriatric patients spend their last years, though much still remains to be done. The problem is likely to be a growing one, unless we are able to find preventive measures to stave off senescence.

Increases in the number of geriatric patients create serious problems; financial and human resources on a large scale are needed because elderly sick people need a great deal of medical and social care. Different kinds of patients need different kinds of accommodation: some are better off at home or in sheltered housing, others in mental hospitals, in the geriatric units of general hospitals, or in adequately equipped and serviced homes or hostels for old people. The treatment of psychiatric patients and the elderly infirm has been improved in recent years by the development of 'day hospitals' which selected patients can attend for medical or social reasons or as part of their rehabilitation. Such hospitals have a number of advantages –

they are flexible, economical in the use of medical resources, 'community orientated' and well suited to the needs of individual patients.

The 'demand' for geriatric and psychiatric treatment and care is considerably in excess of the available health and welfare services. The resources for coping with these problems are *relatively* much less than for other kinds of social and medical service. The attitudes of many medical students and practitioners (and the rest of us) tend to lag behind modern developments. Individuals living in the community (rather than the health and welfare services) carry the main burden of ageing. At present the health services deal with the tip of the 'iceberg' of psychogeriatric illness, since only a small proportion of old people with psychiatric disorders are cared for as hospital inpatients or as residents of homes. Perhaps the most effective ways of dealing with the problem would be to improve the facilities for domiciliary care by, for example, payments to kin and for fostercare, maintaining registers of all old people at risk, making greater health and welfare provision for the elderly and, perhaps no less important, raising the standard of health education in the community and changing social attitudes through health promotion.

Hospital treatment has a number of advantages: the risk of suicide is reduced; patients can be observed continuously, examined and treated more conveniently and effectively; family and friends can obtain some relief from the heavy burden of care. A frequent cause of referral (of an elderly person to a physician) is the difficulty experienced by the family, which has led to emotional stress, loss of sleep, loss of earnings, interpersonal conflicts and other frustrations. Hospital treatment, which brings rest, a change of surroundings and proper food, can lead to recovery and discharge. Some patients recover, but then relapse and are readmitted to hospital; this sequence of events may be repeated.

The effectiveness of out-patient treatment and community care depends to a large extent on such obvious factors as the patient's material resources, his or her domestic circumstances, local psychiatric facilities, co-operation from family, friends and neighbours, and local voluntary services. Not the least important consideration is the effect that the patient living outside an institution has on the people who have to look after him or her.

Patients may become confused and disorientated if they are transferred abruptly, and without explanation or support, from familiar domestic circumstances to the unfamiliar circumstances of a nursing home or hospital. Full explanations and repeated assurances are needed to allay their fears. A considerable amount of subsequent support and guidance may be necessary to get them settled in and actively participating in social activities. Left to themselves, they may just sit and remain withdrawn and apathetic. Some old people need a lot of convincing that they are too ill to live at home. Men, especially, resist the suggestion that they are sick and in need of care and treatment, and women need to be assured that they are not being rejected by the family.

How can one decide that the benefits derived from transfer to improved physical and social surroundings are not offset by the costs incurred in making the readjustment – especially for vulnerable aged people? They may not survive for as long or as well as they would have if treatment had been limited to the elimination of serious defects in their original environment. The effects of treatment are hard to evaluate. Treatment often cannot be allocated on an experimental basis; nor can one rely simply on clinical impressions of individual cases or even on a comparison of patients before and after treatment. Some recent research into the effects of various sorts of treatment and rehabilitation seems not to have demonstrated substantial or lasting improvements for geriatric patients in general, presumably because the comparisons have been between existing and new treatments rather than between treatment and no treatment. This is an indication of the severity and extent of the degenerative effects of ageing and of the difficulty in achieving substantial and lasting improvements in functional capacity and well-being.

There is a growing awareness of the needs of the elderly, and efforts are being made by hospital staffs and those in residential homes to create optimum physical and social surroundings. The built environment is important, since many patients are unable to climb stairs or walk without support. Many need guidance about wearing glasses and using hearing aids if they are to make the most of their opportunities for entertainment and recreation. Mobility can be improved by treatment of the feet and by physiotherapy; ergonomic considerations and 'environmental geriatrics' can make useful contributions to the design and layout of 'behaviour settings' and to the effectiveness of 'prosthetic' aids and domestic utensils. Accidents and infections must be guarded against. Efficient and imaginative nursing care can do much to ease the discomforts of chronic physical illness. The environment and the daily routines should be uncomplicated and satisfying. The more competent patients should be able to leave from time to time to stay with relatives or friends.

The rehabilitation of elderly psychiatric patients who recover from a mental illness requires supervision and subsequent follow-up, since patients cannot cope with the normal problems of adjustment. At present this is inadequate because of the shortage of money and trained personnel. However, more small residential homes are being established where old people with manageable psychiatric disorders can be helped to make a readjustment. People are becoming more aware of the severity and extent of the disorders of old age, and this is leading to earlier and more effective forms of care and treatment. Wherever possible, elderly psychiatric patients are encouraged to stay active and participate in social activities.

The treatment of mental illness in old age is not a once-and-for-all affair. Psychiatric disorders require treatment maintained after discharge from hospital. After improvement some patients relapse and need renewed examination and treatment. Follow-up often includes hospital out-patient attendances for the supervision of maintenance treatment. Sometimes special treatments are required, such as physiotherapy and occupational therapy, and it is desirable to have home visits by a social worker or health visitor.

Preventive psychiatric techniques lie in the future. Present treatment methods for psychogeriatric conditions are largely supportive and palliative. Even so, economies could be secured if it were possible to predict the benefit that any particular patient would get from treatment. For example, certain drugs are effective in reducing the severity and duration of exhausting mental disturbance and may therefore help to prevent patients from hurting themselves and other people. There has not been nearly as much research on the effects of drugs on psychiatric illness in old age as in early adult life. The use of drugs in the treatment of elderly psychiatric patients (and preventively) constitutes an important area of research. These drugs are intended to help re-establish physiological and psychological equilibrium, but their use in the treatment of elderly people presents difficulties. Their effects are not necessarily the same over a wide age-range, and the behavioural and physiological measures used to assess them must be validated independently for each age-group and diagnostic group. Some drugs administered to older patients may elicit unusual reactions – even reversals of effect are not discounted; the side-effects may be different from those seen in younger patients, and the dosage levels may have to be adjusted – as with barbiturates or appetite inhibitors. Individual differences in reaction to drugs are not likely to diminish as age increases, and this makes it difficult to establish reliable norms and base-lines for the assessment of the effects of age in response to drugs. The older person's greater physiological inadequacy adds to the difficulty of assessing the effect of a particular drug. The growing demand for treatment to prevent, retard or ameliorate the adverse effects of ageing is stimulating drug research and sales pressure. But it would be unfortunate, to say the least, if commercial interests were to override scientific and ethical considerations.

5. Geriatric Clinical Psychology

(a) Assessment

Changes in the brain in old age have been thought of in terms of diffuse brain damage – hence the term 'chronic brain syndrome' (CBS). But these changes can also be thought of as the accumulation of a number of specific neurological defects. From this point of view, senile dementia can be characterized as a collection of focal deficits set in a context of more general impairment. Memory impairments may be a consequence of damage or dysfunction in certain parts of the temporal lobes, hippocampus and mammillary bodies. Neurological changes in senile dementia and normal old age may have adverse effects on memory and emotional expression through their involvement in the limbic system. Loss of short-term learning and memory capacity is conspicuous in senile dementia. It is an amnesic syndrome – greatly in excess of normal memory impairment in later life. It involves the loss of recent memories, an inability to profit from new experience, disorientation – for time, place, person and circumstance. Confabulation and guesswork may substitute for a rational account of one's actions. Elderly patients suffering from CBS have poor orientation for time and place even if their sense of personal identity is still intact. They are easily distracted and confused, and likely to misunderstand what they see and hear. Their emotional reactions are exaggerated and tied to momentary circumstances, rather than modulated and kept in perspective. Language impairment affects meaning rather than grammar and vocabulary. Psychomotor impairment and other signs of brain damage, like perseveration and aphasia, can be demonstrated by neurological tests.

Diagnostic psychological assessment of the elderly consists largely of the assessment of mental status and behavioural competence by means of simple questionnaires or by more systematic psychometric investigation in a medical context (though possibly in a domestic setting). The assessment of feelings and desires is less formal, and is normally done through intuitive appraisal of expressive behaviour during clinical interviews. More formal methods of assessment, however, are available; for example, in relation to the measurement of anxiety and depression. Rating scales, symptom check-lists, biographical inventories and other clinical instruments are employed. The WAIS was described and discussed in Chapter Eight.

There seems to be some need for a critical reappraisal of the aims and methods of psychological assessment in relation to adult ageing, and especially in relation to psychological disorders in late life. Methods of assessment validated on young adults are not necessarily equally valid or appropriate for the old. Furthermore, if adult ageing is the accumulation of various interrelated pathological conditions, then it may not be profitable to think in terms of distinguishable diseases, and more emphasis would have to be given to the assessment of individual cases. Rather than attaching diagnostic labels and prescribing blanket treatments, more emphasis should be given to individualized assessment and treatment programmes, taking into account the milieu as well as the person.

Normal ageing, mental disease and brain damage all impair cognitive capacity in both general and specific ways – hence differential diagnosis is frequently difficult and inaccurate. The problem of base rates and the risks of misclassification in diagnostic assessment are too well known to need elaboration. The frequency of misclassification depends upon a variety of factors; there is no fixed rate for a particular test or index.

A mental status questionnaire examines a patient's orientation for time, place and person, and the ability to follow simple instructions, and so on. Patients with dementia are deficient in this kind of general functional competence relative to normal old people. A patient's mental status is usually established at an initial assessment for screening purposes, but may prove useful in connection with diagnosis and prediction. Systematic rating scales are used to assess physical disability, drug effects, motivation (apathy), communication and social behaviour, and so on. The assessment of behavioural competence, however, has to be more narrowly focused, so that specific functions can be assessed directly; for example, the patient's ability to manage the activities of daily living or to understand and carry out instructions. Global measures of biological function or intellectual capacity appear not to be particularly useful. Indeed, mental status questionnaires are needed partly because senile patients cannot cope with the ordinary sorts of intelligence test.

Tests of residual cognitive capacity, capable of yielding comparable measures at frequent intervals, might have particular value as sensitive indices of treatment, showing, for example, the effect of a drug or a retraining programme. So far, however, little progress has been made, although the advent of automated psychological testing has provided some useful hardware for research of this sort. The idea behind such tests is that a simple non-verbal task, like matching to sample, can be administered repeatedly at intervals with different but equivalent samples of items. The patient's errors and performance times are recorded and, if the measure is sensitive, they should vary with physical and mental health and in response to treatment.

Tests of residual cognitive capacity, however, should prove useful to clinical psychologists working with elderly patients by providing baseline measures – with patients acting as their own controls. They avoid some of the difficulties associated with item content, norms and undue reliance on verbal comprehension. They are intended to be sensitive to small variations in pathology and treatment effects. Their chief asset would be the opportunity to repeat virtually the same measure on successive occasions.

What is also needed is a bridge between neuropathology and

psychological assessment. Whether this will be achieved by identifying the neurological deficits underlying performance inadequacies on psychological tests, or by constructing psychometric or other instruments to define the behavioural counterparts of neurological deficits, remains to be seen. It seems likely that serial variations and trends in performance as well as 'snapshot' assessments will have diagnostic utility. This implies a need for the construction of tests giving repeated measures which will provide norms for, and record the course of, intellectual deterioration in normal and pathological ageing. At present, we are largely restricted to single assessments which reveal abnormal discrepancies within a patient's cognitive abilities or between that performance and some standard of comparison, or reveal relative differences between diagnostic groups, but do not reveal the trend in his or her performance over time or under different treatment conditions. One difficulty is to design tests which can be validated against concurrent or post-mortem neuropathological findings regarding focal damage. Another problem is to construct psychological theories which explain any differential effects of normal ageing, brain damage and mental disease on cognition.

The disadvantage of intellectual performance as a single behavioural index of the state of the brain is that it is globally impaired by *various* organic and functional conditions. What is required is a set of behavioural indices which are differentially sensitive to focal (specific) neuropathological or psychopathological conditions. Sometimes focal impairment can be treated by surgery whereas diffuse brain damage cannot – this is one aspect of diagnostic psychological assessment.

The psychological assessment of dementia and pseudodementia has been a problem for many years. There are, of course, various psychometric measures of cognitive function – for example, mental status questionnaires, memory tests, neuropsychological tests, the Wechsler Adult Intelligence Scale and the Kendrick test battery. What has been lacking is agreement on a standardized procedure, i.e. a routine cognitive measure (suitably scaled), with an appropriate item content, based on reliable norms, and capable of repeated use with one and the same subject. In addition to psychometric measures of dementia, an investigator can make use of direct observation, self-reports, and ratings from care-givers (the difficulty of interviewing patients should be obvious). It is possible, by these means, to grade degrees of dementia. There is a considerable overlap between patients living at home and those in institutional care in the degree of mental impairment.

Changes in cognitive performance are only one aspect of the effect of psychopathology in later life. There are also changes in personality, feelings, motivation, social behaviour, moods, attitudes, and the activities of daily living. Some of these can be assessed psychometrically, i.e. by means of self-reports, observers' ratings, and behaviour check-lists. They may be used diagnostically, or to monitor the effects of treatment, or to ascertain the kinds and amounts of services to be provided, or to measure the 'burden of care' carried by care-givers.

(b) Treatment

Minor psychiatric disorders are sometimes not referred to the general practitioner or not recognized for what they are. As with physical ailments, people learn to live with their condition and do not think of themselves as needing treatment. Many elderly people especially are at risk because they are relatively isolated and do not have friends or relatives to encourage them to seek help. Thus preventive or early treatment is not given, and disturbances respond less well to late treatment. Suicide and attempted suicide, for example, are often associated with neurotic depression and depression provoked by physical illness. Physical illness – to which middle-aged and older people become increasingly liable – creates stress and may provoke a variety of psychological reactions to aggravate the overall situation; surgical disfigurement too may lead to depression, anxiety, loss of self-esteem and social withdrawal.

Counselling procedures suitable for younger people are not necessarily suitable for the elderly. Elderly patients' increased dependence upon others is real, not imaginary, and their environment is genuinely difficult. Their intellectual and emotional resources are reduced and they can no longer organize their behaviour adequately. Thus therapeutic procedures need to be adapted to suit the special conditions of neurosis and maladjustment in later life. Treatment is limited to handling specific problems over short periods of time, providing guidance and support. The psychotherapist can expect only marginal improvements and frequent relapses, and may have to establish a relationship with elderly patients which is more natural (less formal) and more superficial (in the sense of dealing with immediate practical issues) than with younger patients. The aim is to alleviate present symptoms rather than to produce lasting changes in the personality. Deep psychotherapy is regarded as difficult, inappropriate and ineffective for elderly neurotic patients. Psychological counselling, on the other hand, can help an older person to solve current interpersonal problems and perhaps to handle disturbing emotions.

Group psychotherapy has beneficial results with some elderly patients; social interaction and discussion obviously differ from that found among groups of younger patients, but the social psychology of group dynamics in relation to ageing has received relatively little attention from experimenters. The apparent increase with age in social conformity may be partly a function of older people's diminished confidence in their performance.

Reminiscence – often thought of as more prominent in late life – does not necessarily signify lack of concern with the present or future, since it is found at all ages. It can be used as a source of biographical data. In late life it serves a communicative and an expressive function: that is, it makes explicit – so that others may understand and learn – the ideas and beliefs that form the contents of the old person's experience; it expresses feelings, attitudes and values. Through the process of life-review, it provides the elderly person with opportunities to re-examine his or her past life and to reorganize present activities and attitudes. Psychotherapeutic intervention can use reminiscence to improve the process of self-analysis: elderly people are, as it were, predisposed to free-associate. By helping them to explore the ramifications of the life-review, to resolve the conflicts and contradictions in it, to reassess and reinterpret what has happened, the psychotherapist may improve the older person's self-image and promote more effective strategies of adjustment. Documents and audio-visual aids can be used to stimulate recall, and in group settings.

This method seems particularly appropriate if there is a risk that a patient will lose a sense of personal identity because of relocation or institutionalization. It also seems appropriate in counselling maladjusted people suffering from a mid-life crisis of identity. The institutional environment – physical as well as social – can help improve and maintain a patient's sense of personal identity. The patient's life-review may be shaped by techniques of behaviour modification; that is to say, he or she can be led by means of suitable rewards to express opinions about personal matters, past life and present circumstances which are conducive to good adjustment and realistic self-appraisal. There seems to be no reason why behaviour modification and related techniques should not prove useful in the treatment of psychogeriatric patients, if only to supplement pharmacological and psycho-therapeutic methods, and to help counteract the effects of disuse.

Behaviour therapy or 'contingency management' has been attempted in institutional settings with the elderly. Beneficial effects can be obtained, at least temporarily and under favourable conditions. Are the time, effort and resources needed cost-effective? A treatment known as 'reality orientation' seems to be more effective in improving the quality of patient care than in improving patients' sense of time, place and person. Cognitive behaviour therapy – a treatment which combines procedures for modifying overt behaviour with procedures for achieving understanding and self-control – appears to have beneficial effects in the treatment of depression in later life.

Following careful diagnosis the first response to psychiatric illness in late life is usually the prescription of drugs or other physical forms of treatment. In the longer term, however, counselling and behavioural management may be more appropriate, especially if the patient has to adjust to a changed life-style or to community living. Some institutional settings can be designed as 'therapeutic environments', in the sense that the physical layout, facilities and services, selection and training of staff, and management style, are all directed towards improving the patients' health and welfare.

The inability of demented patients to communicate and co-operate with care-givers, and learn and remember, means that psychological intervention is severely curtailed, although by no means excluded. The main emphasis is on management, once the medical condition has been optimized. This means training care-staff to understand and handle demented patients, and arranging the physical and social environment to minimize hazards and social disruptions, and to give ample opportunity for activities which seem satisfying and beneficial to patients. The 'contingencies of reinforcement' in a 'therapeutic environment' should be such as to shape the behaviour of all concerned (not just that of the patients!) in socially desirable ways. Consider, for example, what might be done to minimize incontinence, interpersonal hostility and wandering on the part of patients, to maximize job satisfaction on the part of staff, and to reduce stress on visitors (and on family care-givers whenever a patient returns home).

References and Suggestions for Further Reading

American Psychiatric Association, *Diagnostic and Statistical Manual of Mental Disorders* (3rd edn), Washington, DC: American Psychiatric Association, 1980.

Bulbena, A. and Berrios, G. E., 'Pseudodementia facts and figures', *British Journal of Psychiatry*, *148*, 1986, 87–94.

Central Statistical Office, *Social Trends*, no. 12, London: HMSO, 1982.

Chaisson-Stewart, G. M. (ed.), *Depression in the Elderly. An Interdisciplinary Approach*, New York: John Wiley, 1985.

Coleman, P. G., *Ageing and Reminiscence Processes: Social and Clinical Implications*, Chichester: John Wiley, 1986.

Corbin, S. L. and Eastwood, M. R., 'Editorial: Sensory deficits and mental disorders in old age: causal or coincidental associations?', *Psychological Medicine*, *16*, 1986, 251–6.

Corkin, S., Davis, K. L., Growdon, J. H., Usdin, E. and Wurtman, R. J. (eds), *Alzheimer's Disease – A Report of Progress in Research*, New York: Raven Press, 1982.

Gibson, A. J. and Kendrick, D. C., *The Kendrick Battery for the Detection of Dementia in the Elderly*, Windsor: NFER, Nelson, 1979.

Gurland, B., Copeland, J., Kuriansky, J., Kelleher, M., Sharpe, L. and Dean, L. L., *The Mind and Mood of Aging. Mental Health Problems of the Community Elderly in New York and London*, New York: Haworth Press, 1983.

Haynes, S. G. and Feinleib, M. (eds), *Second Conference on the Epidemiology of Aging*, Bethesda, MD: National Institute on Aging, National Institutes of Health, 1980.

Jorm, A. F., 'Subtypes of Alzheimer's dementia: a conceptual analysis and critical review', *Psychological Medicine*, 15, 1985, 543–53.

Leuchter, A. F. and Spar, J. E., 'The late-onset psychoses. Clinical and diagnostic features', *Journal of Nervous and Mental Diseases*, 173, 1985, 488–94.

Norman, A., *Mental Illness in Old Age: Meeting the Challenge*, London: Centre for Policy on Ageing, 1982.

Oliver, C. and Holland, A. J., 'Down's syndrome and Alzheimer's disease: a review', *Psychological Medicine*, 16, 1986, 307–22.

Schatzberg, A. F., Liptzin, B., Satlin, A. and Cole, J. O., 'Diagnosis of affective disorders in the elderly', *Psychosomatics*, 25, 1984, 126–31.

Thienhaus, O. J., Hartford, J. T., Skelly, M. F. and Bosmann, H. B., 'Biological markers in Alzheimer's disease', *Journal of the American Geriatrics Society*, 33, 1985, 715–26.

Woods, R. T. and Britton, P. G., *Clinical Psychology with the Elderly*, London: Croom Helm, 1985.

Ten
The Terminal Stage: Dying and Death

1. Introduction

The relatively recent growth of interest in adult development and ageing and in the health and welfare of the aged is breaking the taboo on open discussion of and enquiry into dying and death which, to put it paradoxically, are facts of life, with a special relevance to ageing. Although death can occur prematurely – through disease or accident – for many people death occurs late in life from one or other of the common and expected causes. Our attitude to our own death (and to the death of others close to us) depends in part on whether it is early, on time, or late (this affects the extent to which we can prepare for death and adapt well to the process of dying) and also, naturally, on the manner of dying. People want to avoid the prolonged pain and misery of progressive chronic fatal disorders. Considerable advances have been made in the treatment and management of dying patients – often in hospices. Such special facilities and services provide models for types of care that might be appropriate in other settings, including home care of the dying.

This chapter's concern is with death from 'natural' causes in late life and with the forms of behaviour and experience leading up to that event. The force of mortality (the probability of dying) increases with age. According to the Gompertz equation, our chances of dying double every seven years. In late life, therefore, the force of mortality is rising very steeply.

We shall refer to the period leading to death in late life as the 'terminal stage'. Thus we are not concerned with dying and death in children, or through violence, or even with premature and unanticipated death in adult life. It is convenient to regard dying as a distinct stage in the human life-path, ending in biological death. In some instances this stage begins with the onset of an illness known to be fatal; the illness continues its course with or without the person realizing or responding to the prospect of death. In other instances, the terminal stage emerges gradually as the person becomes aware of and behaves in response to his or her greatly foreshortened, residual expectation of life.

At least three facets of dying can be distinguished: biomedical, social and psychological (or behavioural). The biomedical facet reveals the physiological and medical processes, i.e. normal physical degradation and disease. The psychological (or behavioural) facet reveals the thoughts, feelings, needs and actions of the dying person. The social facet reveals the social, institutional and cultural processes associated with dying, death and bereavement.

The biological moment of death can be defined by a number of medical criteria such as the cessation of breathing, loss of heartbeat, or disappearance of electrical activity in the brain. The different parts of the body do not all die at the same time; some organs can be recovered shortly after death and used in transplant operations. Individuals who were thought dead according to normal criteria have recovered or been resuscitated, and others have been kept alive by massive medical and technological support, without any apparent psychological life or voluntary action on their part.

The social moment of death has a number of effects, the most explicit of which are probably those having legal significance, such as the redistribution of power and wealth. The death of an adult requires some reorganization of the social fabric and tends to be the occasion of social rituals designed to acknowledge the event, hence the associated funeral rites, mourning and commemorations.

Some of the anxiety and confusion felt in response to a person's dying arises from contradictions and omissions in our system of values and attitudes. The socialization process does not deal adequately with the business of dying, although young children are very matter-of-fact about death if given opportunities to talk about it. Anxiety about death, probably first an adolescent experience, reappears in modified forms in middle age, in later life, and finally in the terminal stage. The inadequacy of religious frames of reference for dealing with personal death is a relatively recent consequence of the secularization of society; there are also shortcomings in the various non-religious alternatives. In a sense, what matters to the individual is not the fact of death but the meaning of death.

The idea of death can be symbolized in a variety of ways and used to form potent figures of speech remote from its literal meaning. Our present-day aversion to the topic appears to stand in marked contrast to the almost obsessive preoccupation with it in the Middle Ages. Psychoanalytic theory gave a prominent place to Thanatos, the death instinct, but this concept appears to have little or no relevance to modern psychology, although the term 'thanatology' refers to the scientific study of death and dying, especially of its social and behavioural aspects.

By definition, the further expectation of life of an old person is short, i.e. the 'chances of death' are high, even if the actual cause and the time left to live are uncertain. As old people, we reach the terminal stage when we realize that there is a high probability that we could die 'at any time' from natural causes, and when our behaviour is influenced by that realization. There are ample conventions for disposing of the body and the estate of the deceased, but few norms for conduct in the terminal stage itself. Moreover, cultural changes have taken place so rapidly that nowadays few people are able to derive benefit from the limited comfort and guidance offered by traditional beliefs and practices. A wide range of differences between individuals is tolerated: we feel no particular surprise if one person suffers severe and prolonged emotional upset at the prospect of dying whereas another person exhibits a calm, even humorous, acceptance of it. Similarly, responses to bereavement encompass stoical acceptance, nervous collapse, or other, less extreme reactions. The absence of social prescriptions makes it difficult to anticipate how other people will react, and this uncertainty adds to the difficulty of reacting appropriately to dying and death.

In some primitive communities, the elderly infirm are put to death or abandoned, and expected to accept their fate. In other communities, however, especially those which emphasize filial piety and the continuity of personal identity after death, the elderly are cared for lovingly during the terminal stage, are regarded as active but invisible agents or spirits after they die, and are appealed to for help or placated by gifts.

In Britain, historical changes in the social customs associated with bereavement have resulted in substantial differences in behaviour since the First World War. There have been changes in the distribution of age at death, especially infant mortality. There is also less emphasis on religion, and the stigma of dying a pauper has been removed. Improvements in, and the greater availability of, hospital care, drugs and other medical services have further reduced unexpected deaths in the 'prime' of life. This, together with increased use of life insurance and social welfare benefits, has reduced the need for financial support of those bereaved.

Part of the difficulty of coping with the terminal stage arises from failure to understand and accept death – a process which depends upon the individual's beliefs, values and attitudes, as well as upon personal qualities and circumstances. Most religions enable believers to come to terms with death, through beliefs and ritual practices, and a well-thought-out humanistic attitude will also give 'meaning' to death, but people with no firm beliefs either way may not be able to make sense of what is happening or to reconcile themselves to the idea of death. The secular society has yet to evolve a role and status for people in the terminal stage. This is not likely to be achieved in the near future, since even the retirement period has not yet been properly incorporated into the socio-economic systems of modern cultures. In the absence of a positive philosophy which finds value in terminal behaviour, we can expect to see the evolution of voluntary and obligatory euthanasia to prevent the prolongation of lives no longer worth living. This would be one alternative to present-day segregation and negative social evaluation. Advances in medicine, however, may provide a more attractive alternative through the rectangularization of the survival curve: preventing or delaying the onset of late-life disorders, so that more people will live longer and the distribution of age at death will be compressed within a narrow range closer to the upper limit of human longevity. Yet another scenario, following advances in the fundamental biology of ageing, would be an extension of the upper limit of human life expectancy (presently about 120 years). This possibility can no longer be rejected out of hand. Biological research is moving to the point where genetic mechanisms controlling specific processes of ageing can be identified and brought under control. The main priority in these biomedical approaches is to reduce or eliminate the physical and mental infirmities associated with old age and to shorten the terminal stage.

Further consideration of the historical and anthropological issues associated with dying would take us too far afield, but there are undoubtedly systematic differences associated with sex, socio-economic class and cultural background. The ritual aspects of death have diminished steadily over recent generations, but social prescriptions for the conduct of old people who are dying from natural causes seem never to have been well formulated. There are diverse views about the nature of death – and not simply because of religious differences. For example, relatively few adults believe in heaven or hell in a literal or biblical sense, but a large number believe in some kind of personal existence after death. Some even suppose there will be continuity of personal relationships with others. Belief in the existence of the spirits of departed people is common, even in modern societies. Euphemisms have been coined to refer to this taboo topic: passed away, last sleep, gone to rest. The terminal stage is regarded with considerable aversion and thought to have little or no intrinsic worth. Death itself is regarded as so abhorrent that the psychological and social processes which make life human may be lost in the technicalities of medical care. The problem is how to reconcile length and quality of life.

2. Socio-Medical Aspects

In modern societies dying is dealt with almost exclusively within a medical framework, because of our preoccupation with the 'causes' of death. The terminal stage, however, can be studied in a wider context which includes the social and behavioural sciences, and even literature and the arts.

The terminal stage begins with the onset of a progressively worsening physical condition which runs a fatal course within a relatively short time. In many instances, the course of the illness, its duration, severity and eventual outcome are uncertain. The elderly person is usually suffering from a multiplicity of biological defects and diseases, and it is not always possible to predict the particular terminal 'path' to be taken. A physician usually carries the burden of telling a terminal patient and the family that he or she is dying. Otherwise the patient is likely to engage in self-diagnosis, or be unduly defensive or optimistic, and never reach a realistic assessment of the 'chances' of dying.

The physician's problem is not merely that of stating an opinion, but rather of 'communicating with patients' so that they can fully appreciate their circumstances and take appropriate action. If, for any reason, the physician thinks it wise to withhold the opinion that a patient is dying, he or she must still help that patient make sense of a puzzling environment – the medical treatment, family concern, bodily changes, and so on. The physician, therefore, is largely responsible for deciding what information and opinions are appropriate to a particular case, and how and when these are transmitted to the patient, family and friends.

Physicians and nurses are trained to sustain life and health, and are inclined to resist the idea that the patient cannot survive longer. They may be over-optimistic about the effects of medical treatment, especially in response to enquiries from the patient and family. They may neglect the psychological and social aspects of dying – especially if the patient is allowed to return home. They may even feel defeated and angry if patients die in spite of their efforts to keep them alive. Doctors and nurses have relatively little training in the social and psychological aspects of physical illness. They have more than average concern for human welfare, but this is insufficient in a situation which calls for interpersonal sensitivity and awareness of the wider psychological and social framework of the patient's condition: for example, emotional reactions to surgical disfigurement or disability, disrupted domestic circumstances, the depressing effect of the hospital environment, and failure to understand what is going on.

One of the less satisfactory aspects of hospital care is the tendency to treat patients as objects rather than as persons. They feel intimidated, or worse – the victims of events over which they have no control. Hence there are strong grounds for the argument that the terminal environment should be 'humanized' – as it is in a modern hospice for the dying – even if that means less emphasis on the prolongation of life. The psychological care of elderly patients who are expected to die shortly is obviously a difficult task, and there is some evidence that nursing staff, who often constitute the patient's only constant source of emotional support and information, find themselves unwilling or unable to cope with this aspect – in contrast with their efficient management of the technical aspects of life-support. Selection and training of staff, however, can be expected to lead gradually to improvements. The hospital care of terminal patients is an exacting task requiring rare personal qualities and proper training. Talks and discussions alone are insufficient; practical experience in the management of actual deaths, management of the effects of a death on other patients, attendance at autopsies, and even role-playing are the sorts of training required in order to overcome the initial aversion to work of this sort. The 'psychological autopsy' (see below) provides an ideal method – a way of studying dying in the context of the total situation.

The medical and hospital management of the dying person is obviously a central issue in the study of terminal behaviour but it is not the only issue. We need people with aptitude and training in psychological and social skills who can develop ways of helping people through the terminal stage and helping relatives and friends to prepare for their bereavement: for example, psychological counselling for the patient and for family and friends. Improvements in the socio-technical environment, especially as regards communication, relocation and the side-effects of treatment, also affect adjustment. A rational and comprehensive cost-benefit analysis of terminal care based on humanistic values would probably give increased weight to non-medical intervention in fatal illnesses. The duty of medical and nursing staff is to prolong life, but not under any conditions or at all costs. These costs include: resources withheld from other patients, the prolongation of financial and emotional stress for the family, and the prolongation of the patient's distress.

At present, then, decisions about medical treatment affect the social and psychological aspects of terminal illness. But the responsibility for decisions can be shared not only with patients but also with their close relatives and friends. Such decisions might include, for example, those relating to the diverse costs and benefits of treatment and to the social arrangements for personal care and attention, and those affecting the understanding and the emotional reactions of all concerned. Decisions about non-medical management

cannot be avoided by doing nothing, since decisions and their consequences go by default. For example, failure to communicate with
patients fully and in good time means that they suffer prolonged
uncertainty and anxiety; in the absence of proper information they
may misconstrue the situation, pick up scraps of medical information
and misinformation, mistrust people and be unable to co-operate
fully, be puzzled and distressed by the behaviour of others and by the
treatment or clinical environment that they are required to endure.

In practice there is often a great deal of uncertainty about the
patient's prospects. Among elderly people, the course of an illness can
affect and be affected by a number of concurrent physical ailments.
Possibly for this reason, physicians and nurses are reluctant to tell an
elderly patient that he or she is dying or that there is a high risk of
death. It is commonly believed that people who lose hope no longer
try as hard to cope, and that this subjective factor – giving up – reduces
their ability to fight disease and disability. It is obviously difficult to
test the validity of this belief. In some cases, possibly, the depressing
and stressful effects of bad news might worsen a poor medical condition. When asked if they themselves would want to know if there
was a strong likelihood that they would die, most physicians and
nurses say that they would, and so do most ordinary people. Nevertheless, there appears to be some reluctance to discuss this possibility
with the person most concerned, at least until it has become a largely
foregone conclusion; dying and death are still taboo topics.

3. Post-Mortem Psychology

One of the more interesting psychological approaches to the study of
dying and bereavement has been the attempt to develop a method of
'psychological autopsy' which makes a post-mortem examination of
the psychological and social factors surrounding the death of an
individual. The aim is to uncover the circumstances and events relevant to the occasion and manner of a person's death. Rational and
systematic inquiries reveal that the psychological and social factors in
terminal adjustment are sometimes different from what one expected,
and less simple than one supposed. The method, pioneered in research
into suicidal behaviour, can be used for research and training purposes
in medicine, nursing and social work. Ideally, it reveals faults and

inadequacies in the life-circumstances of the deceased person; these then provide leads for the improved management of subsequent terminal cases. In addition, it sensitizes medical, nursing and social personnel to some of the less obvious aspects of terminal care; it reasserts the importance of the community in caring for its dying members; it makes explicit some of the assumptions, prejudices and norms underlying attitudes and practices in relation to dying and bereavement.

Psychological autopsies reveal a number of interesting findings. Even among geriatric patients, a high proportion have some degree of awareness of the terminal situation. Useful psychological and social information may not be entered into the patient's records. The technicalities of physical medicine may dehumanize the patient's terminal environment. Patients are frequently discouraged from talking about their impending death; this leads to some confusion about the state of mind of the terminal patient. Some have premonitions of death, but these are not always borne out; dying and death may feature in a patient's hallucinations and delusions. Attitudes towards death vary from glad acceptance through apathetic indifference to severe anxiety. Calm acceptance appears to be the characteristic response of patients with good adjustment. Even among geriatric patients, the terminal stage provides opportunities for the expression of socially meritorious conduct and even for psychological 'growth'. Psychological autopsies have shown that behavioural and psychological changes can appear *in advance* of the final deterioration in medical condition; typically, changes are in the direction of withdrawal, inactivity, decreased interest and responsiveness, and mental depletion. Psychological and social intervention at this stage might not help much in reviving flagging biological processes, but they could improve the quality of life in the final stage. Many elderly people and people in terminal care accept the negative evaluation placed upon them by society. They regard the terminal situation as nothing more than an antechamber to death. A more positive philosophy would regard it as the last opportunity we have to express our best qualities, make amends for errors, fulfil obligations, assert rights and respond with all our resources to the challenges presented by that situation.

4. Adjustment to the Prospect of Death

Old people who are not mentally impaired cannot help becoming aware that their lifetime is almost at an end. Many of their friends and kin have died, and they realize that they are much more liable to fatal illness or accident. Thus the idea of death is not unfamiliar, and for some at least not as forbidding as in their earlier years – they have run out of important reasons for living. Others, however, become anxious, depressed and maladjusted; for example, they feel angry at the injustice or waste of their life, they fear the unknown, or they become frantic, apathetic or confused in the face of a painful situation outside their control or understanding.

It is not unusual for old people to accept their impending death in a fairly unemotional, matter-of-fact way. The normal reaction of friends and kin is to oppose this attitude and to persuade the old person, perhaps quite wrongly, that he or she has many more years of life still left to enjoy. We have a strong drive and an ingrained habit of fighting and avoiding the risk of death, and of encouraging others to be like ourselves. In opposing the old person's acceptance of the prospect of death, however, we reveal a misunderstanding of the change that has taken place in the *meaning* of death for a person who has become adapted to the terminal stage. Death and dying are difficult to come to terms with, at least in so far as they affect us personally; they may provoke strong emotional reactions – depression, anxiety, anger, guilt – but leave us powerless to intervene. There are strong social prohibitions against suicide, and against killing others whether by neglect or deliberately – witness the sanctions against euthanasia, and until recently, against abortion. But the question is whether it is right to resist changes in the old person's attitude.

A rational and empirical examination of the terminal stage obliges us to question conventional wisdom. The topic of death elicits embarrassment and defensive attitudes; the conventional response is to deny or avoid the issue, and to rationalize rejection of it as giving comfort and support to the old person. Our inability to discuss the prospect of death with an old person reinforces the idea that the terminal stage has no value and must be rejected. The reason is quite natural – dying and death are often associated with pain, fear, ugliness and hopelessness, but we do old people a disservice by blocking their attempts to come to terms with death through discussion and preparation.

People differ considerably in their reaction to the prospect of dying. Moreover, circumstances alter cases, and a person's terminal behaviour depends partly upon residual capacities and psychological dispositions, and partly upon circumstances. Interpretation of the situation plays an important part in the effort to cope with life's last challenge. Again, we are referring only to natural death in old age. Given that there is little objective information on normal behaviour in the terminal stage, we must assume that adjustment to the prospect of dying is 'characteristic' of the person, in the sense that we can recognize the operation of long-standing personal qualities – depression and apathy, stubborn independence, optimism, self-denial – which have been the central organizing factors underlying the person's adjustment to a wide variety of other situations earlier in life.

Although social prescriptions for the conduct of the dying or the bereaved are not very well defined in modern society, yet they are not entirely absent. Hence dying and bereaved persons frequently behave as they are 'expected' to behave, and this depends upon the norms governing their particular social position. Reactions to bereavement naturally vary with the particular circumstances and qualities of an individual. The usual reaction to the loss of a loved relative or friend is a sense of grief. The intensity and quality of the grief, however, depend upon the nature of the loss – momentary sadness for a distant friend, spasmodic surges of grief for an aged parent, prolonged and deep desolation upon the death of a loved one.

The grief associated with bereavement is not necessarily a clearly delineated feeling. There may be a good deal of ambivalence and variation over time; for example, sorrow and disappointment may be mixed with anger, guilt and anxiety. Bereavement constitutes a stress situation and can precipitate psychiatric disorder, psychosomatic illness or suicide. Many widows, for example (and widowers too, presumably), experience feelings of guilt about their role in the events leading up to the death of their spouse; widow(er)hood reduces life expectancy. Reorganization following the death of a spouse introduces an added source of stress, with regard to emotional deprivation and living arrangements, and this increases the risk of death of the bereaved person. There are good reasons for supposing that preparation and psychological support help to alleviate such distress and intra-personal conflict.

In old people the awareness of dying has developed slowly. There has been time to adapt to the prevailing circumstances, and time to learn appropriate strategies of adjustment. Without such adaptation, the awareness of dying is likely to evoke feelings of dread associated with a sense of isolation, loss or rejection. Stress reactions and maladjustment arising from such feelings can be ameliorated by the administration of drugs, by psychological interventions and by support from the dying person's relatives and friends.

5. Preparation for the Terminal Stage

Making an adequate adjustment to the terminal stage includes handing over responsibilities, making arrangements for dependants, effecting reconciliations, and either attending to unfinished business or enjoying residual opportunities for work, companionship, or leisure activities. The main problems of terminal adjustment, however, are likely to be psychologically demanding: coping with pain, anxiety, frustration, discomfort and depression; establishing a tolerable level of sedation; and managing the activities of daily living.

How are we to prepare ourselves for this eventuality? Most people survive into late life and die a natural death, so the question is relevant for most of us. To ignore or reject it is to deny any value to the terminal stage, and by implication, to the dying *person*.

Most of us have few or no opportunities to observe the behaviour of people who are dying or to appreciate at first hand their thoughts, feelings and wishes. Even in late life, a person who is dying, in the medical sense, is generally segregated from others, partly out of respect for the patient's privacy, partly because dying is disturbing to others. Usually, only a few people – physicians, nurses, close kin or friends – are allowed to share the occasion, which has probably been regarded as avoidable for as long as possible. Thus the actual duration of the terminal stage varies, depending upon whether one adopts a narrow short-term medical definition of dying or a broad long-term psychological definition, i.e. it depends on how one defines 'dying' and on the *meaning* of dying.

The prospect of death is itself sufficient to provoke anxiety, but anxiety-provoking situations not infrequently contain stimulus elements which elicit other emotional reactions, such as anger, depression, guilt. Such reactions have their origins in the life-history of the individual; hence the individual's response in the terminal situation is conditioned by these prior experiences. In the case of attitudes towards their own death, elderly people have had adequate time and opportunity to become adapted to the certainty of their demise, although some will avoid facing up to this eventuality for as long as possible. Where the surrounding social conditions provide opportunities for close emotional support and clarification of one's ideas and feelings through, for example, a confidant, a therapist, a social worker or a religious guide, and where these influences have been sustained over a long period, the individual can become adapted to the situation and may acquire effective strategies for adjustment which will help in coping with the more stressful conditions later in the terminal stage.

There are at least four reasons for the apparent decline with age in anxiety about death. First, through a gradual process of learning older people have reorganized their thoughts, feelings and motives to bring them into line with the now familiar fact of personal mortality. Second, they may be out of touch or out of sympathy with the modern world; hence their personal involvement and future time perspective are much reduced. Third, the ratio of the costs to the benefits of staying alive becomes increasingly adverse and the net value of their personal existence diminishes. Fourth, the process of disengagement diminishes the external pressures or incentives to stay alive. Other people, however, are often unwilling to accept the aged person's estimate of the terminal condition and in so doing may diminish the value of the terminal stage itself.

Western societies have been so preoccupied with growth and change that personal development and achievement have been highly valued, with a corresponding neglect of old age and terminal behaviour. There are some social philosophies, however, which try to give a more balanced view. Although it may seem paradoxical, what is needed is a more constructive attitude towards – or philosophy of – dying and death.

Looked at in terms of social learning, the fact that we are largely shielded from dying and death means that we are rarely exposed to relevant learning situations or 'behavioural models'. Even literature and the arts generally make little reference to terminal behaviour as we have defined it, i.e. to the behaviour of normal people dying from natural causes in late life. Perhaps the only aspect of human behaviour in response to the prospect of death which has been dealt with adequately in fiction, biography and journalism is that which concerns relatively young, vigorous people fighting in defence of legitimate rights during war or other social upheaval. Soldiers, revolutionaries and martyrs should know how to die. Their behaviour – whether in fiction or real life – exemplifies the prevailing social ethos and provides a variety of 'behavioural models' for young people to emulate, becoming legendary and heroic as it is assimilated into the history and cultural framework of a community. But natural death in old age in modern life lacks the dramatic and heroic qualities found in works of fiction and history. It is not surprising, therefore, that most of us – lacking either first-hand or second-hand experience of the normal terminal stage – do not have the concepts and skills necessary for dealing effectively with the social and psychological problems of dying and bereavement. We find ourselves at a loss: we do not know how best to console the person who is dying; we are unable to understand or manage our own reactions; we find the behaviour of other people unpredictable and disturbing. The dying person, particularly if awareness of dying has come abruptly or prematurely, may have little idea of what to do in the circumstances. With little or no background experience, we have no behavioural models to emulate. There may be no one to turn to for advice and guidance. If it were not for the process of adaptation, referred to above, the normal terminal stage would be a painful no-solution situation instigating frustration reactions such as panic, anger or apathetic resignation.

A more constructive attitude towards the terminal stage requires some reassessment of its value. One might regard it as analogous to the ending of a story – surely not the least important part. Moreover, the normal terminal stage is not devoid of opportunities for the manifestation of meritorious conduct, even if the circumstances and the responses are a far cry from those usually portrayed in fiction and biography. The terminal stage has its own values and rewards, its own peculiar merits, styles and forms of experience. Although the average old person's death is not linked with important ethical issues like that of the soldier, revolutionary or adventurer, it nevertheless offers opportunities for the expression of courage, audacity, determination, humour and so on. It is the behavioural expression of these and other relevant qualities that provides the appropriate 'models' for vicarious social learning.

The problem is that socially desirable reactions to the stress of the terminal condition are not likely to appear without some preparation. And such preparation is not systematically provided in the normal course of events. It is not surprising that the absence of opportunities to observe and critically examine the process leads us to adopt some curious attitudes and practices which have caught the interest of anthropologists, sociologists and psychologists.

The unique circumstances and psychological make-up of each individual make it difficult to prescribe exactly what a dying person would have to say or do in order to exhibit socially meritorious conduct. It is unlikely that a person who is not already strongly predisposed to behave sensibly, calmly and bravely will do so in his or her last weeks or months. One solution is to deal with the issue as and when it arises by means of short-term support and counselling. Another is to make long-term preparations by cultivating throughout life the kinds of attitudes and values that can deal effectively with bereavement and personal death. Psychological help for people in the final phase is relatively rare, and more could be done to encourage adaptive and socially desirable behaviour, to discourage maladaptive and regressive forms, and to help discover what options are still open to the terminal case. For example, the media, especially television, could incorporate dying and bereavement in late life into programmes – plays, serials, documentaries and discussions – as is done for love, hate, child care, crime, work. This would bring dying, death and bereavement more into the open, as it were, and make them easier for people to understand and deal with – through familiarization, vicarious learning and appreciation of the behavioural options. Another possibility would be to make 'death education' more widely available, not only for those professionals who work with the dying and the bereaved, but also for children and adults generally as part of their general knowledge of nature and society.

We need to familiarize ourselves with the psychological and behavioural aspects of dying while we are still alive and well. Through first-hand observation, through literature and the arts, through open discussion and scientific inquiry, we can become acquainted with the facts and values of dying. This includes consideration of the more desirable (as well as the less desirable) forms of conduct that are possible. Unfortunately, little firm evidence exists about the typical behavioural capacities, attitudes and emotional resources of terminal cases.

A certain amount of sociological research has been carried out in connection with bereavement in general and widowhood in particular. The situation faced by women widowed in late life is eased somewhat by their realistic anticipation of this eventuality and by the companionship of other widows of comparable age – this provides opportunities for mutual support and consolation, the sharing of advice and help, and so on. Widowers are usually in a less favourable situation.

Terminal behaviour is adaptive in so far as it is directed towards mastering the terminal situation. Clearly, religious and magical practices associated with dying have been designed in anticipation of the special circumstances that would follow death, in particular an after-life. Unfortunately, we can hinder the dying person's attempts to come to terms with death by denying that he or she is dying. During the terminal stage people naturally become greatly dependent upon others, and there is obviously a great deal that the community can do to support and guide them. The most obvious help is adequate medical and nursing care; but such help loses much of its worth if it is not firmly embedded in a coherent cultural system in which relevant ethical considerations operate. Ideally, such a system would enable people in the terminal stage to engage in satisfying social relationships, to maintain or enlarge their behavioural competence, to effect emotional readjustments, and to achieve mastery of the terminal situation in a manner which is personally and socially acceptable.

It would be absurd if our natural concern with the psychological and social aspects of the terminal stage led us to disregard the physical process of dying. It is obvious that medical care and treatment are salient aspects of the terminal stage. In addition to specific diseases and physical disabilities, the terminal case is likely to suffer from such ailments as aches and pains, digestive disorders and disturbed sleep. Medication, including pain-killing drugs and nursing care, is regarded as the first line of support; but these efforts may be wasted if they are not backed up by psychological and social care. The goal is not the maximum prolongation of biological life, but the maximum prolongation of human life.

Most of us cannot expect to die as we would have wished, and in any event the 'preferred form of death' varies throughout life. The problem of determining the extent to which individuals should be allowed to control their own fate during the terminal stage probably does not arise in most cases; but when it does, it raises some awkward ethical, medical and social issues. The way the individual prefers to end his or her days may conflict with the interests of others. The problem with psychological support – professional or otherwise – for the dying person is that the form it takes depends upon debatable ethical considerations, apart from uncertainty regarding its supposed beneficial effects. The kinds of psychological support proposed are fairly common-sense measures intended to provide patients with a confidant, and with opportunities to enjoy an attractive milieu, to understand what is going on, to retain some measure of personal control, to cope with feelings, and to make the most of residual resources and opportunities. In this way, it is possible to ameliorate some of the defects of present-day methods of dealing with terminal cases.

The psychological and social study of terminal behaviour is not simply a matter of easing the stresses on this or that individual but also of changing society itself – its norms, its values, its laws – and of finding a positive value for terminal behaviour especially in a secular society. The study of dying presents us with a paradox: 'Dying is a kind of living.' The practical question is, 'How can we help the dying person to live by helping him or her to die?' Some of the side-effects of dying – pain, ugliness, incontinence, insomnia – may be more disturbing and depressing than the prospect of dying. Hence the need for good medical and nursing care, and for a realistic, humane appraisal of the total situation.

The stresses experienced in the terminal stage can hardly be coped with effectively in the absence of preparation and psychological support. Preparation consists on the one hand of developing the sorts of attitudes, beliefs and values that will make sense of the terminal situation, and on the other of society's readjusting its norms and institutions so that the dying person has a recognized and valued place in the system. Nowadays more people are living longer, and we can all expect to spend a rather longer time dying. This is one good reason for attempting to incorporate the terminal stage as a *natural* final stage in the normal life-path. If it is to be lived at all, it should be lived because it has some intrinsic worth. Defensive attitudes of aversion and denial lead to segregation and avoidance of the dying. Such attitudes are likely to persist until we have a better understanding of the process of dying in late life and attach some positive value to the terminal stage.

To be educated for dying naturally in late life does not mean that we need be morbidly preoccupied with death. On the contrary, the realization that each of us will die provides many of us with a sombre reminder of the shortness of active life and of the need to use our time to the best advantage. As we have seen, the *meaning* of death is determined by both personal and social factors, and this affects our behaviour in and experience of the *process* of dying.

References and Suggestions for Further Reading

Lammerton, R., *Care of the Dying*, Harmondsworth: Penguin Books, 1980.

Parkes, C. M., *Bereavement. Studies of Grief in Adult Life* (2nd edn), Harmondsworth: Penguin Books, 1986.

Rachels, J., *The End of Life. Euthanasia and Morality*, London: Oxford University Press, 1986.

Taylor, H., *The Hospice Movement in Britain: Its Role and its Future*, London: Centre for Policy on Ageing, 1983.

Weissman, A. D. and Kastenbaum, R., *The Psychological Autopsy: A Study of the Terminal Phase of Life*, New York: Behavioral Publications, 1968.

Eleven
Gerontology:
Concluding Comments

1. Present-Day Gerontology

Progress in gerontology has been fairly rapid since 1930 for a number of reasons. Advances in biology and medicine have identified a variety of normal and pathological processes of ageing underlying the physical and mental disabilities of later life. Studies in the effects of ageing on psychological processes and social relationships have raised questions about normal ageing; for example, how to maintain functional capacities and the general quality of life in old age.

The development of journals devoted to the study of ageing began comparatively recently after some false starts at the turn of the century (Freeman, 1979, pp. 123–52), together with the establishment of scientific societies, professional organizations, and other interest groups in various countries. Scientific periodicals carry an increasing number of research reports on ageing: the US *Journal of Gerontology*, established in 1945 by the Gerontological Society, publishes reports from biological sciences and clinical medicine, psychological and social sciences, and social welfare; it carries articles on gerontological organizations in other countries, and for many years it published a valuable index to current periodical literature. In addition the society publishes a house journal, *The Gerontologist*. In Europe the scientific periodical *Gerontologia* was established in 1956. In the United Kingdom the first volume of the journal *Ageing and Society* was produced in 1981 by the Centre for Policy on Ageing and the British Society of Gerontology. Articles in a wide variety of other scientific journals continue to add to the literature of gerontology and geriatrics; a list is given at the end of this chapter.

The growing recognition of gerontology as a distinct discipline led to its appearance as a separate category in journals publishing abstracts of scientific reports and reviews of recent literature. The Forest Park Foundation of the USA financed *A Classified Bibliography of Gerontology and Geriatrics*, published in 1951; large supplements appeared in 1957 and 1963. Nowadays, such bibliographies are less important because of the availability of computer-assisted information retrieval. Many textbooks dealing with the social and psychological aspects of ageing, too numerous to list individually, have appeared in recent years.

The International Association of Gerontology was founded in 1950 on the occasion of the First International Congress of Gerontology in Liège, Belgium. Regular congresses have since been held in different countries and selected conference proceedings have been published. Several countries now have one or more research organizations dealing with the scientific problems of human ageing – as distinct from the numerous voluntary and welfare organizations which look after elderly infirm people. In Britain are: the British Society of Research on Ageing (BSRA); the British Geriatric Society (BGS); the British Society of Gerontology (BSG). The British Association for Service to the Elderly (BASE) is concerned with service delivery and social support. The voluntary organizations include: Age Concern, Help the Aged, the Alzheimer Disease Society, the National Association of Old Age Pensioners Associations, the Pre-Retirement Association. The Centre for Policy on Ageing publishes reports on the social and economic aspects of ageing. The British Foundation for Research on Ageing raises funds for research. The Medical Research Council (MRC) and the Economic and Social Research Council (ESRC) provide limited financial support.

Current developments in the United Kingdom include the establishment of institutes for teaching and research in gerontology. They include the Wolfson Institute, the Institute of Human Ageing at Liverpool, and the Institute of Ageing linking Age Concern and King's College, London.

Gerontology's modern scientific period dates from the 1930s when interest in the physiological and psychological aspects of ageing began to develop more rapidly. Cowdry's book *Problems of Ageing*, published in 1939 and reissued in 1942, is regarded as a landmark in so far as it drew together many of the strands in gerontology's multidisciplinary fabric. Since that time, the bulk of the research has been carried out in the United States, although other countries, including the United Kingdom, have made significant contributions. Nowadays, many western industrialized nations have gerontological societies and publish books and journals on ageing.

In the United Kingdom, following the initiatives of Korenchevsky, the Nuffield Foundation provided financial support for research into the effects of ageing on skilled performance, on connective tissues, on comparative physiology, and on endocrinology. Korenchevsky was also a key figure in the establishment of the International Association of Gerontology.

Biomedical research in ageing is particularly concerned with identifying the basic mechanisms underlying age-related normal and pathological changes – for example, errors at the cellular level. Social research in ageing is directed mainly towards understanding the way institutional structures affect people in later life, in terms of economic and political arrangements, housing, dependency, etc. Psychological research provides a sort of bridge between biomedical and social research; it can help to show how biological and social factors interact, for example, in relation to stress, illness and dependency. In addition, of course, virtually all psychological functions have some relationship with chronological age. The problem is to identify those that are of theoretical interest or practical importance.

Advances in scientific technology and theory have been more spectacular in biology and medicine than in the social and behavioural sciences. Consider, for example, the ways in which radioactive isotopes can be used in the measurement of hormone levels, cerebral circulation and molecular structures; and how biological theories about errors in protein synthesis, about the effects of heat and radiation, about cell-division, are guiding current research.

The advent of computers, television and telemetry, together with long-overdue improvements in the psychometrics of ageing, may help to advance the psychology of ageing; but more important, perhaps, are innovations in the way we conceptualize psychological issues in ageing and in the research methods we use to investigate them.

2. Scientific Method

There are limits to what can be sensibly contained within the covers of an introductory book such as this; consequently, no attempt is made to deal in detail with research methods in gerontology. Readers interested in such methods may refer to Bromley (1974a). What is offered instead is a very elementary explanation of what it means to adopt a scientific attitude towards the study of ageing. I have also emphasized the benefits of small-scale, short-term studies of specific issues in adult life and old age rather than large-scale, long-term investigations.

Many, perhaps most, readers of this book will not be concerned with carrying out scientific investigations. Therefore, it is argued, they can safely leave the intricacies and technicalities of scientific research to professional investigators. Would that this were so. Even professional scientific investigations not infrequently fall short of ideal standards as far as research methodology is concerned. Consequently, false information finds its way into the public domain. If people are not sufficiently sceptical, inquisitive and knowledgeable, they are liable to believe all sorts of things which do not stand up to close critical scrutiny. These erroneous beliefs and assumptions then affect the way people behave – as when a physician prescribes an ineffective drug, or a social worker misconstrues a family situation, or a psychologist makes an invalid assessment. Such mistakes can happen even to those with a high level of scientific and professional training, because empirical knowledge is only ever an approximation to the truth. That is to say, when one looks at an item of information – such as a medical symptom, a social relationship, or an individual action – its meaning may change depending upon which of the other items of information that are associated with it one chooses to take account of – various assumptions, possibilities, contextual factors, and so on. Put another way – circumstances alter cases.

Scientific and professional training is supposed to sensitize people to the complexities of the problems they are paid to deal with and to help them deal with such problems in the most effective way. Unfortunately, the nature of scientific method is not widely understood. It is not some sort of narrow technical expertise exercised by a privileged few working in laboratories, not a method which is applicable only in physics and chemistry. It is rather an attitude of mind that many people can cultivate. The experimental and mathematical aspects of scientific method are important but not all-important. What is required is penetrating and accurate observation under specified conditions, together with explicit and rational arguments which combine descriptive analysis with explanatory theory. Put this way, scientific procedure seems difficult and demanding; so it is. It is easy to fall short of its standards, easy to 'make do' with general impressions, anecdotal evidence, analogies and metaphors, and popular clichés. Scientific method consists in a willingness to deal with an issue rationally and empirically, i.e. being prepared to look closely at the inferences one is making about the available evidence, to consider alternative interpretations and, in addition, to test one's theories and expectations against the observations made by other competent investigators.

We need to cultivate a scientific attitude because ageing is an extremely complicated process and because beliefs about it have important social and personal consequences. It is not the sort of knowledge that comes to us instinctively; it has to be acquired through systematic observation and reason. The complexities of ageing are so difficult to grasp, however, that we are inclined to simplify our understanding to such an extent that it becomes distorted and fragmented – as when we try to understand the effects of age in relation to stressful life-events, or its effects on the relationship between intelligence and experience. Furthermore, ageing is so important to us that our understanding of it and our reactions to it are strongly influenced by our emotional make-up and social values, so much so that we may develop self-serving attitudes which find expression in oversimplified ways of thinking and behaving – stigmatizing the elderly, resorting to simple stereotyped judgements, discriminating against them, or neglecting them, overgeneralizing (failing to recognize individual and group differences), being overly pessimistic, or conversely, underestimating the effects of ageing, advocating inappropriate policies, making exaggerated claims, or engaging in fruitless (unproductive or counterproductive) efforts to help.

Cultivating a scientific attitude towards ageing means avoiding these irrational reactions. It means becoming more inquisitive and sceptical about the concepts, methods and findings one encounters in books, articles, lectures and conversations. It means being prepared to challenge 'authoritative' pronouncements, and learning how knowledge is produced and revised. It means evaluating the validity and usefulness of professional practices, and improving them where possible. It means being creative, in the sense of finding more effective ways of dealing with the problems of ageing. Knowledge changes and evolves; so that what passes for a fact today may be shown to be false, or less well-established, tomorrow. Becoming more knowledgeable about ageing means not just knowing more facts but knowing how these facts are established and subsequently revised.

Sympathy with and concern for the health and welfare problems of the elderly are not sufficient in themselves to solve these problems. They need to be understood and dealt with in a realistic way and, for this, scientific understanding, based on a rational appraisal of empirical observations made under controlled conditions, is necessary. Sympathy and concern, together with scientific curiosity and method, provide the motivation for investigations into the processes of ageing, and also the motivation to *apply* the knowledge gained from scientific investigations for the benefit of society and the individual. Even when it comes to applying knowledge to solve real-life problems, however, scientific standards must still be maintained; otherwise there is a risk that our actions will be governed too much by unfounded preferences and prejudices and too little by thoughtful and informed awareness of the possible consequences of our actions.

One of the safeguards against ignorance and stupidity is the sharing of information and ability between well-intentioned people. This is particularly important in gerontology, which is a multi-disciplinary area *par excellence*. Scientists, professionals, voluntary workers, elderly people themselves, and their care-givers are engaged in a common enterprise. They need to be able to communicate with and to influence each other in spite of disciplinary boundaries and status differences. Even within a single area of interest, competence shared means competence raised.

Each scientific discipline that contributes to our knowledge of ageing has its own special techniques of investigation, its own special technologies, concepts and jargon. Obviously, we cannot deal with all these aspects of scientific method. But we *can* deal with the underlying scientific attitude that these disciplines have in common, and with some aspects of scientific method that are peculiar to the study of ageing.

Experimental and laboratory methods are by no means the only methods that can be labelled 'scientific'. On the contrary, some experimental and laboratory investigations are grossly unscientific, in the sense that the results are unreliable, invalid, theoretically uninteresting or useless. On the other hand, surveys, field-work, clinical observations, case-studies and archival inquiries can be highly scientific, in the sense that they advance knowledge by means of systematic empirical observation and careful rational analysis. Of course, surveys, and other methods of investigation, like experiments, may sometimes fail to measure up to scientific standards.

What readers must ask themselves is: 'How valid is the knowledge that I lay claim to?' and 'How could I demonstrate the effectiveness of the professional skills I exercise or the services I help provide?' The attempt to answer will force them to examine the various assumptions, methods and forms of knowledge on which their discipline rests. By 'forms of knowledge' I mean the different sorts of informational backing we use to justify our arguments and professional practices – experimental results, survey data, personal experience, expert opinion, common knowledge, clinical judgement, and so on.

Scientific method in general rests upon certain assumptions. These are dealt with in 'philosophy of science', a large subject in its own right. Scientific method also operates within social value-systems which help to determine the historical development of all sciences – natural, biological and social. This leads us to believe that all knowledge is, in a sense, 'socially constructed'. The process of 'social construction' is particularly important in the social and behavioural sciences, as compared with the natural sciences. In the study of the physical world, the objective 'real world' facts to which our knowledge is supposed to correspond are in some ways clearly distinguishable from the subjective ideas (beliefs, expectations) we have about the 'real world'. In the study of human individual and social behaviour, however, in psychology, sociology, economics, history, anthropology and so on, it is often more difficult to identify the objective 'real world' facts which validate our beliefs and expectations.

Where does gerontology stand in relation to this rather abstruse philosophy of science issue? Gerontology is a multidisciplinary area – in particular, it interrelates biology, medicine, sociology, political economy and psychology. Consequently, the extent to which our knowledge of ageing can be said to be valid, i.e. to correspond with the facts of the 'real world', varies from one disciplinary area to another, and within any one discipline, from one issue to another, depending upon the extent to which scientific method is applied. Scientific method (in its general sense) is a socially shared procedure for constructing our knowledge of physical nature, the living world and human nature. The fact that it is not as widely shared as one would like is the reason for this section.

What we believe about ageing today is simply the latest stage in the evolution of gerontology as a branch of scientific knowledge. At various stages in its history gerontology has been influenced in various ways – by attempts at rejuvenation, by discoveries in pathology, by changes in the age-structure of populations, by social reforms, by technological changes, and so on (Bromley, 1974b). It is important, therefore, to be aware of the wider context of factors influencing our beliefs and actions.

It remains to mention a few methodological issues particularly relevant to the study of ageing.

Chronological age. Chronological age itself is not the cause of anything. It is simply a time-marker. The biological, psychological and social processes of ageing take place *in* time. In particular, their effects accumulate *over* time. Attempts to measure the 'biological age' or the 'functional age' of people independently of chronological age have not so far been very successful.

Cross-sectional method. Comparisons between *different* people at different ages are called 'age-differences', although the differences may be attributable to factors other than chronological age – for example, to cohort (generation) effects, sampling differences, or differential survival.

Longitudinal method. Comparisons made on the *same* people at different ages are follow-up comparisons called 'age-changes', although again the changes may be attributable to factors that are not strictly age-related, such as changes in diet, circumstances or daily routine.

Cross-sequential method. If the cross-sectional and longitudinal methods are combined, i.e. if comparable people at different ages are followed up for a period of years, interesting comparisons can be made which may clarify the relationships between chronological age, cohort (or generation), and period (time of measurement, or the period over which comparisons are made), factors which may otherwise be confused.

Much of the debate about research methodology in gerontology has been concerned with how to organize very large-scale investigations, so that the effects of age, cohort and time of measurement can be distinguished more clearly. The debate has tended to become somewhat academic, in the sense that well-organized, long-term, large-scale studies are few and far between, and inconclusive because they cannot take account of all the criticisms levelled at them.

The basic problem is how to separate out all the factors which give rise to age-differences and age-changes, so that we can identify the important intrinsic and extrinsic causes of age-related impairment, and, possibly, distinguish those causes which are 'natural' and at present unavoidable from those which are 'abnormal' or 'pathological' which we can hope to remedy.

Comparative method. Many of the methodological problems which hinder the study of human ageing do not arise, or do not present the same obstacles, in the study of ageing in other animals. Animal models of ageing provide useful indications, but are not a complete substitute for the study of human ageing. They are used, obviously, in biomedical research, as, for example, in the study of the relationship between ageing and genetic factors, physical exercise, diseases, and environmental conditions. They are also used in behavioural research because the sorts of biomedical factors just referred to help to explain age-related changes in performance – sensory functions, learning, problem-solving, emotionality, and so on. At present animal studies have little to contribute to the social aspects of ageing, although sociobiological studies of altruism may eventually throw some light on the mechanisms underlying human social reactions to the elderly.

Ageing. We are using the word 'ageing' somewhat arbitrarily to refer to what happens after completion of the juvenile period of development, i.e. to the whole of adult life, not just to the period of infirmity and dependency in old age. It is possible therefore that some of the more effective ways of combating the adverse effects of ageing may be through the study of long-term preventive measures. The current lack of emphasis on prevention together with the somewhat nihilistic attitude towards old age infirmity is an example of the way scientific and professional work is influenced by traditional viewpoints and implicit social values.

Disaggregation. One possible, and not altogether unrealistic, approach to the study of human ageing would be to de-emphasize chronological age as a research variable. Instead, one could develop an approach which dealt with adult life and old age in a much more piecemeal way, by studying small, homogeneous groups, over a short period of time, in relation to a particular issue, each study serving as one small piece of a large mosaic or jigsaw puzzle. Given enough pieces of information one could construct an account of what adult life and old age are like both generally (in terms of average and overall effects) and specifically (in terms of what happens to individuals or groups in various circumstances).

One possible advantage of such a piecemeal approach is that it should minimize the problems of sampling subjects and generalizing one's results. In small-scale experimental studies, the methodological difficulties are eased somewhat if investigators are dealing with a narrowly defined population of interest over a short period of time, and if variations of the same inquiry can test the extent to which any observed effect is robust. Thus small-scale experiments (studies in which one or more conditions are varied to test their effects) are feasible, and techniques of statistical analysis like multiple regression can be used to calculate the relative importance of the variables at work. Nowadays, it is not sufficient just to show that an age-effect is statistically significant; one must also show how large the effect is, and argue its practical importance or its theoretical relevance.

Survey method. Surveys are basically systematic observations made under controlled conditions but without any attempt to vary the conditions experimentally. Surveys differ in scale; one can of course survey relatively small homogeneous populations. The value of a survey depends on the extent to which the sample of subjects surveyed represents the population of interest. Of course, if the items in the survey questionnaire (or other instrument) are badly chosen, the results will be worthless. Survey instruments used with elderly people need to be constructed and administered with considerable care. Similarly, psychological tests – for measuring intelligence, personality, interests, or whatever – need to be valid for the age-group to which they are applied, otherwise any results will be inconclusive.

Clinical method. Clinical observations on elderly people are useful in so far as they can be seen as relevant to some kind of assessment – for the purposes of psychiatric diagnosis or social management. Such observations should ideally be direct and behavioural: first-hand reports of what a person actually said or did in the circumstances at the time, not hearsay reports or mere impressions. Direct observations can sometimes be assisted by check-lists or rating-scales, and of course by electronic recordings. Behavioural observation is less easy than one might suppose, especially if the observations are to be carried out intermittently, by several observers, over long periods of time, on different people, in different settings. Procedures for dealing with these difficulties are described in the literature on research methods in the behavioural sciences.

Case method. The intensive study of individual cases (whether of persons or organizations or events) – involving detailed description and careful analysis and interpretation – can provide interesting and useful scientific data, especially if the cases can be shown to be prototypical instances of a more general class or family of cases. In addition, case-studies and life-histories often illuminate the interactive effects of several factors – physical health, mental health, social conditions – and so illustrate the multidisciplinary nature of gerontology.

Field method. Field-studies carried out in geriatric wards, residential homes, sheltered housing or the community at large may rely on a combination of methods, of the sort used in social surveys, case-studies and anthropology, including direct observation and the use of archival material. The aim is to provide a scientific (rational, empirical) account of how a community or organization functions. Some studies may be 'naturalistic' in the sense that they attempt to study the phenomenon without interfering with it in any way (Webb, Campbell, Schwartz and Sechrest, 1966). Field-studies can now be based on rigorous 'quasi-experimental' methods (Cook and Campbell, 1979).

We have been considering small-scale scientific investigations – the sorts of investigations that can be carried out relatively quickly by individuals or small teams without the benefit of massive resources. There is no lack of problems worth investigating, although there may be problems in gaining access to the data one wishes to collect. The advantages of small-scale research of these sorts are twofold. First, they encourage a more scientific and professional attitude among those who work in the field of ageing. Second, they contribute to the 'disaggregation' of the adult population, that is, to the breaking up of the concept of ageing into a multitude of specific issues affecting narrowly defined groups in relation to narrowly defined issues over short periods of time. The areas of investigation are too numerous to list, but they include all those commonly found in the study of ageing – various sorts of physical and mental impairment, psychological reactions to different sorts of situations, organizational matters affecting the delivery of services, and so on. The choice of a specific problem as one worth investigating should be based on the likelihood that it will result in the advancement of scientific knowledge or improvements in health and welfare during adult life.

References and Suggestions for Further Reading

Bromley, D. B., 'Methodological issues in the study of human ageing', in Bromley, D. B., *The Psychology of Human Ageing* (2nd edn), Harmondsworth: Penguin Books, 1974(a).

——'The history of human ageing', in Bromley, D. B., *The Psychology of Human Ageing* (2nd edn), Harmondsworth: Penguin Books, 1974(b).

Cook, T. D. and Campbell, D. T., *Quasi-Experimentation. Design and Analysis Issues for Field Settings*, Boston, MA: Houghton Mifflin, 1979.

Cowdry, E. V. (ed.), *Problems of Ageing*, Baltimore, MD: Williams & Wilkins, 1939 (2nd edn, 1942).

Freeman, J. T., *Aging. Its History and Literature*, New York: Human Sciences Press, 1979.

Hersen, M. and Barlow, D. H., *Single Case Experimental Designs. Strategies for Studying Behavior Change*, New York: Pergamon Press, 1976.

Kane, R. A. and Kane, R. L., *Assessing the Elderly – A Practical Guide to Measurement*, Lexington, KY: D. C. Heath, 1981.

Kerlinger, F. N., *Foundations of Behavioral Research* (3rd edn), New York: Holt, Rinehart & Winston, 1986.

Korenchevsky, V., *Physiological and Pathological Ageing* (ed. G. H. Bourne), New York and Basel: S. Karger, 1961.

Palmore, E., 'When can age, period and cohort be separated?', *Social Forces*, 57, 1978, 282–95.

Pressey, S. L., 'The new division of maturity and old age. Its history and potential services', *American Psychologist*, 3, 1948, 107–9.

Webb, E. D., Campbell, D. T., Schwartz, R. D. and Sechrest, L., *Unobtrusive Measures. Nonreactive Research in the Social Sciences*, Chicago: Rand, McNally, 1966.

Periodicals

English-language periodicals on ageing in 1987 included:

Age and Ageing
Ageing and Society
Ageing International
Aging and Work (*Industrial Gerontology*)
American Journal of Geriatrics
Annual Review of Gerontology and Geriatrics
Archives of Gerontology and Geriatrics
Canadian Journal on Aging
Clinical Gerontologist
Clinics in Geriatric Medicine
Comprehensive Gerontology (new Munksgaard journal)
Death Studies (formerly *Death Education*; not confined to ageing)
Dementia
Developmental Psychology (juvenile development and adult ageing)

Educational Gerontology
Experimental Gerontology
Generations (Bulletin of the British Society of Gerontology)
Geriatric Nursing and Home Care
The Gerontologist
Gerontology
Human Development
International Journal of Aging and Human Development
International Journal of Behavioral Development
International Journal of Geriatric Psychiatry
International Journal of Technology and Aging (new Human
　　Sciences Press journal)
Journal of Aging Studies (new JAI Press journal)
Journal of the American Geriatrics Society
Journal of Applied Gerontology
Journal of Clinical and Experimental Gerontology
Journal of Cross-Cultural Gerontology
Journal of Gerontology
Journal of Geriatric Psychiatry
Journal of Gerontological Social Work
Mechanisms of Aging and Development
Omega: Journal of Death and Dying
Psychology and Aging (new APA journa()
Research on Aging

Index of Names

Index of Subjects

FOR THE BEST IN PAPERBACKS, LOOK FOR THE

In every corner of the world, on every subject under the sun, Penguin represents quality and variety – the very best in publishing today.

For complete information about books available from Penguin – including Pelicans, Puffins, Peregrines and Penguin Classics – and how to order them, write to us at the appropriate address below. Please note that for copyright reasons the selection of books varies from country to country.

In the United Kingdom: Please write to *Dept E.P., Penguin Books Ltd, Harmondsworth, Middlesex, UB7 0DA*

If you have any difficulty in obtaining a title, please send your order with the correct money, plus ten per cent for postage and packaging, to *PO Box No 11, West Drayton, Middlesex*

In the United States: Please write to *Dept BA, Penguin, 299 Murray Hill Parkway, East Rutherford, New Jersey 07073*

In Canada: Please write to *Penguin Books Canada Ltd, 2801 John Street, Markham, Ontario L3R 1B4*

In Australia: Please write to the *Marketing Department, Penguin Books Australia Ltd, P.O. Box 257, Ringwood, Victoria 3134*

In New Zealand: Please write to the *Marketing Department, Penguin Books (NZ) Ltd, Private Bag, Takapuna, Auckland 9*

In India: Please write to *Penguin Overseas Ltd, 706 Eros Apartments, 56 Nehru Place, New Delhi, 110019*

In Holland: Please write to *Penguin Books Nederland B.V., Postbus 195, NL–1380AD Weesp, Netherlands*

In Germany: Please write to *Penguin Books Ltd, Friedrichstrasse 10–12, D–6000 Frankfurt Main 1, Federal Republic of Germany*

In Spain: Please write to *Longman Penguin España, Calle San Nicolas 15, E–28013 Madrid, Spain*

In France: Please write to *Penguin Books Ltd, 39 Rue de Montmorency, F-75003, Paris, France*

In Japan: Please write to *Longman Penguin Japan Co Ltd, Yamaguchi Building, 2–12–9 Kanda Jimbocho, Chiyoda-Ku, Tokyo 101, Japan*

Adieux   Simone de Beauvoir

This 'farewell to Sartre' by his life-long companion is a 'true labour of love' (the *Listener*) and 'an extraordinary achievement' (*New Statesman*).

British Society 1914–45   John Stevenson

A major contribution to the Pelican Social History of Britain, which 'will undoubtedly be the standard work for students of modern Britain for many years to come' – *The Times Educational Supplement*

The Pelican History of Greek Literature   Peter Levi

A remarkable survey covering all the major writers from Homer to Plutarch, with brilliant translations by the author, one of the leading poets of today.

Art and Literature   Sigmund Freud

Volume 14 of the Pelican Freud Library contains Freud's major essays on Leonardo, Michelangelo and Dostoyevsky, plus shorter pieces on Shakespeare, the nature of creativity and much more.

A History of the Crusades   Sir Steven Runciman

This three-volume history of the events which transferred world power to Western Europe – and founded Modern History – has been universally acclaimed as a masterpiece.

A Night to Remember   Walter Lord

The classic account of the sinking of the *Titanic*. 'A stunning book, incomparably the best on its subject and one of the most exciting books of this or any year' – *The New York Times*

FOR THE BEST IN PAPERBACKS, LOOK FOR THE 🐧

A CHOICE OF PENGUINS AND PELICANS

The Informed Heart   Bruno Bettelheim

Bettelheim draws on his experience in concentration camps to illuminate the dangers inherent in all mass societies in this profound and moving masterpiece.

God and the New Physics   Paul Davies

Can science, now come of age, offer a surer path to God than religion? This 'very interesting' (*New Scientist*) book suggests it can.

Modernism   Malcolm Bradbury and James McFarlane (eds.)

A brilliant collection of essays dealing with all aspects of literature and culture for the period 1890–1930 – from Apollinaire and Brecht to Yeats and Zola.

Rise to Globalism   Stephen E. Ambrose

A clear, up-to-date and well-researched history of American foreign policy since 1938, Volume 8 of the Pelican History of the United States.

The Waning of the Middle Ages   Johan Huizinga

A magnificent study of life, thought and art in 14th and 15th century France and the Netherlands, long established as a classic.

The Penguin Dictionary of Psychology   Arthur S. Reber

Over 17,000 terms from psychology, psychiatry and related fields are given clear, concise and modern definitions.

FOR THE BEST IN PAPERBACKS, LOOK FOR THE

A CHOICE OF PENGUINS AND PELICANS

The Literature of the United States Marcus Cunliffe

The fourth edition of a masterly one-volume survey, described by D. W. Brogan in the *Guardian* as 'a very good book indeed'.

The Sceptical Feminist Janet Radcliffe Richards

A rigorously argued but sympathetic consideration of feminist claims. 'A triumph' – *Sunday Times*

The Enlightenment Norman Hampson

A classic survey of the age of Diderot and Voltaire, Goethe and Hume, which forms part of the Pelican History of European Thought.

Defoe to the Victorians David Skilton

'Learned and stimulating' (*The Times Educational Supplement*). A fascinating survey of two centuries of the English novel.

Reformation to Industrial Revolution Christopher Hill

This 'formidable little book' (Peter Laslett in the *Guardian*) by one of our leading historians is Volume 2 of the Pelican Economic History of Britain.

The New Pelican Guide to English Literature Boris Ford (ed.)
Volume 8: The Present

This book brings a major series up to date with important essays on Ted Hughes and Nadine Gordimer, Philip Larkin and V. S. Naipaul, and all the other leading writers of today.

FOR THE BEST IN PAPERBACKS, LOOK FOR THE 🐧

A CHOICE OF PENGUINS AND PELICANS

The Second World War (6 volumes)   Winston S. Churchill

The definitive history of the cataclysm which swept the world for the second time in thirty years.

1917: The Russian Revolutions and the Origins of Present-Day Communism
Leonard Schapiro

A superb narrative history of one of the greatest episodes in modern history by one of our greatest historians.

Imperial Spain 1496–1716   J. H. Elliot

A brilliant modern study of the sudden rise of a barren and isolated country to be the greatest power on earth, and of its equally sudden decline. 'Outstandingly good' – *Daily Telegraph*

Joan of Arc: The Image of Female Heroism   Marina Warner

'A profound book, about human history in general and the place of women in it' – Christopher Hill

Man and the Natural World: Changing Attitudes in England 1500–1800
Keith Thomas

'A delight to read and a pleasure to own' – Auberon Waugh in the *Sunday Telegraph*

The Making of the English Working Class   E. P. Thompson

Probably the most imaginative – and the most famous – post-war work of English social history.

FOR THE BEST IN PAPERBACKS, LOOK FOR THE

A CHOICE OF PENGUINS AND PELICANS

The French Revolution Christopher Hibbert

'One of the best accounts of the Revolution that I know . . . Mr Hibbert is outstanding' – J. H. Plumb in the *Sunday Telegraph*

The Germans Gordon A. Craig

An intimate study of a complex and fascinating nation by 'one of the ablest and most distinguished American historians of modern Germany' – Hugh Trevor-Roper

Ireland: A Positive Proposal Kevin Boyle and Tom Hadden

A timely and realistic book on Northern Ireland which explains the historical context – and offers a practical and coherent set of proposals which could actually work.

A History of Venice John Julius Norwich

'Lord Norwich has loved and understood Venice as well as any other Englishman has ever done' – Peter Levi in the *Sunday Times*

Montaillou: Cathars and Catholics in a French Village 1294–1324
Emmanuel Le Roy Ladurie

'A classic adventure in eavesdropping across time' – Michael Ratcliffe in *The Times*

The Defeat of the Spanish Armada Garrett Mattingly

Published to coincide with the 400th anniversary of the Armada. 'A faultless book; and one which most historians would have given half their working lives to have written' – J. H. Plumb

FOR THE BEST IN PAPERBACKS, LOOK FOR THE

A CHOICE OF PENGUINS AND PELICANS

Metamagical Themas   Douglas R. Hofstadter

A new mind-bending bestseller by the author of *Gödel, Escher, Bach*.

The Body   Anthony Smith

A completely updated edition of the well-known book by the author of *The Mind*. The clear and comprehensive text deals with everything from sex to the skeleton, sleep to the senses.

How to Lie with Statistics   Darrell Huff

A classic introduction to the ways statistics can be used to prove *anything*, the book is both informative and 'wildly funny' – *Evening News*

The Penguin Dictionary of Computers   Anthony Chandor and others

An invaluable glossary of over 300 words, from 'aberration' to 'zoom' by way of 'crippled lead-frog tests' and 'output bus drivers'.

The Cosmic Code   Heinz R. Pagels

Tracing the historical development of quantum physics, the author describes the baffling and seemingly lawless world of leptons, hadrons, gluons and quarks and provides a lucid and exciting guide for the layman to the world of infinitesimal particles.

The Blind Watchmaker   Richard Dawkins

'Richard Dawkins has updated evolution' – *The Times* 'An enchantingly witty and persuasive neo-Darwinist attack on the anti-evolutionists, pleasurably intelligible to the scientifically illiterate' – Hermione Lee in Books of the Year, *Observer*

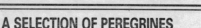
A SELECTION OF PEREGRINES

The Uses of Enchantment Bruno Bettelheim

Dr Bettelheim has written this book to help adults become aware of the irreplaceable importance of fairy tales. Taking the best-known stories in turn, he demonstrates how they work, consciously or unconsciously, to support and free the child.

The City in History Lewis Mumford

Often prophetic in tone and containing a wealth of photographs, *The City in History* is among the most deeply learned and warmly human studies of man as a social creature.

Orientalism Edward W. Said

In *Orientalism*, his acclaimed and now famous challenge to established Western attitudes towards the East, Edward Said has given us one of the most brilliant cultural studies of the decade. 'A stimulating, elegant yet pugnacious essay which is going to set the cat among the pigeons' – *Observer*

The Selected Melanie Klein

This major collection of Melanie Klein's writings, brilliantly edited by Juliet Mitchell, shows how much Melanie Klein has to offer in understanding and treating psychotics, in revising Freud's ideas about female sexuality, and in showing how phantasy operates in everyday life.

The Raw and the Cooked Claude Lévi-Strauss

Deliberately, brilliantly and inimitably challenging, *The Raw and the Cooked* is a seminal work of structural anthropology that cuts wide and deep into the mind of mankind. Examining the myths of the South American Indians it demonstrates, with dazzling insight, how these can be reduced to a comprehensible psychological pattern.